THE QUEST

THE NOTEBOOKS OF PAUL BRUNTON
(VOLUME 2)

THE QUEST

PAUL BRUNTON
(1898–1981)

An in-depth study of
category number one
from the notebooks

A Larson Publication
for the
PAUL BRUNTON PHILOSOPHIC FOUNDATION

International Standard Book Number (cloth) 0-943914-13-2
International Standard Book Number (paper) 0-943914-14-0
International Standard Book Number (series) 0-943914-17-5
Library of Congress Catalog Card Number: 85-81507

Manufactured in the United States of America

Published for the
Paul Brunton Philosophic Foundation
by
Larson Publications
4936 Route 414
Burdett, New York 14818

Distributed to the trade by
Kampmann and Company
9 East 40 Street
New York, New York 10016

87   89   90   88   86
2   4   6   8   10   9   7   5   3   1

Photograph of Dr. Brunton reproduced
by courtesy of Arthur Broekhuysen

THIS BOOK IS DEDICATED
to Anthony J. Damiani

(1922–1984)

"unknown" American philosopher, ardent friend and devoted student of Dr. Brunton, and founder of Wisdom's Goldenrod Center for Philosophic Studies: a vigorous man who came to know himself . . . through life, art, music, philosophy, and unconditionally sharing with others his fertile vision of life's manifold reality. The memory of his lifelong devotion to discovering, synthesizing, and communicating the deepest issues of the human heart is an unfailing source of inspiration to all who knew him well and to all whom he involved in the publication of these notebooks.

The works of Dr. Brunton
in order of publication

A Search in Secret India
The Secret Path
A Search in Secret Egypt
A Message from Arunachala
A Hermit in the Himalayas
The Quest of the Overself
The Inner Reality
(*also titled* Discover Yourself)
Indian Philosophy and Modern Culture
The Hidden Teaching Beyond Yoga
The Wisdom of the Overself
The Spiritual Crisis of Man

Published posthumously

The Notebooks of Paul Brunton
volume 1: Perspectives

Essays on the Quest

CONTENTS

EDITORS' INTRODUCTION

Widely recognized as one of the most influential pioneers of East-West culture in this century, Dr. Paul Brunton kept detailed personal notebooks concerning the deepening and development of one's inner life in modern circumstances. Throughout his successful literary career, these notebooks were the major resource from which he drew and developed material for publication. He authored eleven well-received books, from *A Search in Secret India* in 1934 to *The Spiritual Crisis of Man* in 1952.

The late Dr. Brunton is esteemed not only for the expertise and simple prose with which he introduced formerly esoteric ideas to the general public of the West, but also for his uncommon personal warmth, gentility, and graciousness. His was a mind in which highly developed faculties of critical observation joined an innate reverence for the sacred to explore the fundamental issues of the human heart: knowledge of its present state, of its higher potentials, of the nature of the universe in which it appears, and of its proper relation to that universe.

The success of his books brought P.B., as Dr. Brunton came to be addressed, numerous offers to take on the role of personal *guru* (teacher) for thousands of readers, to found *ashrams* and edit journals in which he would be cast as a central figure in organized movements intending to midwife the "spiritual rebirth" of the West. But such was not his own idea, and he graciously but firmly maintained a personal independence while warmly supporting many of those individuals who did take on such roles. He felt that his best service was to write for people who are not essentially "joiners" but who have sincere inner aspirations for deeper knowledge and experience of the inviolable spirit within their own hearts. In light of that disposition, he preferred to serve as simply one human being exploring ever more profound truths with increasing depth and concentration. He presented himself formally as only "a researcher, with some experience in these matters . . . and that is all." His leadership consisted primarily in personal example and in sharing ideas that had proven useful to him— rather than through directing organized groups or making concessions to the conventional teacher-student posture.

From 1952 until his death in 1981, P.B. chose to reserve his daily writings for posthumous publication. *Perspectives*, the first volume in this series titled *The Notebooks of Paul Brunton*, was published in July of 1984 as an introductory survey of the twenty-eight major topics addressed in the notebooks. This volume, *The Quest*, begins an in-depth presentation of the individual topics as roughly outlined by P.B. himself to the present editorial staff during 1980 and 1981. It deals extensively and exclusively with category number one of P.B.'s twenty-eightfold general schema.

As was the case with *Perspectives*, selection and placement of the material has been done by the editorial staff and not by P.B. himself. The editors acknowledge that much of the placement is arbitrary. Only the broad general divisions indicated by capital letters as titles of "chapters" two through six in the table of contents were given by P.B. for this category. Beyond the further grouping of related themes into secondary and some-times tertiary clusters, little attempt has been made to sequence the mate-rial. This volume and the remainder of the forthcoming series is meant as a rich resource drawn from notebooks rather than as a finished, polished work.

The table of contents and the index together provide an abridged outline of the working model established by the editors for selecting and generally structuring the material. A study guide/index volume giving the complete working model will be published as the last volume in this "Ideas" series.

A few additional remarks should be made concerning editorial policy.

Like most writers of his generation, P.B. employed the literary conven-tion of using masculine gender (for example, *he, his, man, mankind*) to refer to men and women alike. Since it is clear from his life and teachings that P.B. never viewed gender as a determinant of superiority or in-feriority—and since there are often cases in which P.B. uses "he" and "his" as third-person references to himself—we decided to leave this literary convention in place rather than to institute major editorial revisions.

It should also be noted that P.B. had a working knowledge of several languages and maintained correspondence with numerous private individ-uals throughout the world. Translations in *The Notebooks* that are at variance with other published versions of writings from non-English sources may be credited either to P.B. himself or to P.B.'s collaboration with correspondents.

Finally, the reader is encouraged to look more closely into what may appear on the surface to be unnecessary repetition of certain themes in some of the sections of this volume. Closer examination of the individual paras will bring to light important nuances of P.B.'s thinking, nuances that would have been omitted if all repetitiveness were removed. A complete presentation of the major ideas in category one has been our goal in this volume. To serve this end, even a few paras from *Perspectives* have been included here and are indicated by a (P).

Other editorial conventions are the same as those mentioned in the introduction to *Perspectives*.

We are deeply grateful to many friends at Wisdom's Goldenrod Center for Philosophic Studies for the extensive assistance and moral support that moves this project ever more steadily toward completion, and to the many enthusiastic P.B. readers throughout the world whose warm reception of these notebooks makes this work a genuine celebration of shared interest and mutual appreciation.

THE QUEST

A *letter from P.B. to P.B.:*

(1) It is not the tyranny of the ego which is to be removed most of all—although that is a necessary part of the Great Work—nor is it that the ego must be uprooted and killed forever—although its old self must surrender to the new person it has to become. No—let it live and attend to its daily work but only as a purified being, an ennobled character or quietened mind, an enlightened man—in short, *a new ego* representing what is best in the human creature. He will still be an "I" but one that is in harmony with the Overself—a descriptive name that ought to be kept and not discarded. So do not in your writings attack the ego as so many do, but lift it up to the highest possibility.

(2) The teachers increase daily and ask others to follow them. The teachings multiply and the books about them too. They are not your concern. Let them do their very much needed work. But you are to enter a new and different rhythm and tell such as will listen that they need not be forlorn, lost, or without hope because they find none to appeal to their heart or mind. They are asked only to follow *the God within themselves*, for "The Kingdom of Heaven is within you." P.B.—give this message while giving all proper respect and honour to the teachers of today and yesterday. Those who feel alone in this matter or who can only walk outside the groups on an independent path should be reminded that there *is* a God within them who can guide and help them if they turn to him.

1

WHAT THE QUEST IS

The Quest not only begins in the heart but also ends there too.

2

It is an endeavour to lift to a higher plane, and expand to a larger measure, the whole of his identity. It brings in the most important part of himself—being, essence, Consciousness.

3

"Man Know Thyself!" There is a whole philosophy distilled into this single and simple statement.

4

Between the ordinary man who takes himself as he is, and the philosopher who does exactly the same, there stands the Quester. In the first case, outlook is narrow, being limited by attending to the inescapable necessities and demands of day-to-day living. In the other case, peace of mind has been established, the thirst for knowledge fulfilled, the discipline of self realized. In between these two, the Quester is not satisfied with himself, has a strong wish to become a better and more enlightened man. He tries to exercise his will in the struggle for realization of his ideal.

5

It lifts human consciousness vertically and enlarges human experience spiritually.

6

If the Infinite Being is trying to express its own nature within the limitations of this earth—and therefore trying to express itself through us, too—it is our highest duty to search for and cultivate our diviner attributes. Only in this way do we really fulfil ourselves. This search and this cultivation constitute the Quest.

7

It offers a conception of life which originates on a higher level.

8

The Quest is both a search for truth and a dedication to the Overself.

9

By "Quest" I mean the deliberate and conscious dedication to the search for spiritual truth, freedom, or awareness.

10

The inner meaning of life does not readily reveal itself; it must be searched for. Such a search is the Quest.

11

When a man begins to seek out his real nature, to find the truth of his real being, he begins to follow the Quest.

12

It is a call to those who want inner nourishment from real sources, not from fanciful or speculative ones. It calls them away from things, appearances, shows, and externals to their inward being, toward reality.

13

After such considerations, we are led to wonder what constitutes the reality behind the universe. This is a quest which takes us into religion, mysticism, and philosophy and the great mysteries of life, a quest which eventually confirms those celebrated words of Francis Bacon: "A little thinking may incline the mind toward atheism, but greatness of study bringeth the mind back again to God."

14

The quest we teach is no less than a quest for knowledge in completeness and a search for awareness of this Universal Self, a vast undertaking to which all men are committed whether they are aware of it or not.

15

The great central questions of life for the thinking man are: What am I? What is my true relation to, and how shall I deal with, my surroundings? What is God, and can I form any connection with God?

16

Every puzzle which fascinates innumerable persons and induces them to attempt its solution—be it mathematical and profound or ordinary and simple—is an echo on a lower level of the Supreme Enigma that is forever accompanying man and demanding an answer: What is he, whence and whither? The quester puts the problem into his conscious mind and keeps it there.

17

It is a quest to make a life of better quality, both inside and outside the self, in the thoughts moving in the brain, in the body holding that brain, and in the environment where that body moves.

18

It is a clarion call to man to seek his true self, a voice that asks him, "Have you found your soul?"

19

The quest is simply the attempt of a few pioneer men to become aware of their spiritual selves as all men are already aware of their physical selves.

20

It is a quest to become conscious of Consciousness, to explore the "I" and penetrate the mystery of its knowing power.

21

The secret path is an attempt to establish a perfect and conscious relation between the human mind and that divinity which is its source.

22

When a man passes from the self-seeking motives of the multitude to the Overself-seeking aspirations of the Quest, he passes to conscious co-operation with the Divine World-Idea.

23

It is, from another standpoint, a quest for his own centre.

24

It is the opening up of one's inner being.

25

The very idea of a quest involves a passage, a definite movement from one place to another. Here, of course, the passage is really from one state to another. It is a holy journey, so he who is engaged on it is truly a pilgrim. And as on many journeys, difficulties, fatigues, obstacles, delays, and allurements may be encountered on the way, yes! And here there will certainly be dangers, pitfalls, oppositions, and enmities too. His intuition and reason, his books and friends, his experience and earnestness will constitute themselves as his guide upon it. There is another special feature to be noted about it. It is a homeward journey. The Father is waiting for his child. The Father will receive, feed, and bless him.

26

It is a movement from the outward to the inward but it is effected only with much labour, through much despondency, and after much time.

27

The aspirant enters on the Quest of the heavenly kingdom from the first moment that he becomes willing to try to give up his ego. It does not matter that it will engage his whole lifetime, that success may only be found in some future incarnation. From that first moment he becomes a disciple of the Overself, and a candidate for the kingdom of heaven.

28

It is a brave struggle for freedom, a noble refusal to be the ego's puppet or the animal-self's victim, a fine resolve to win strength from weakness.

29

How shall he deliver himself from his weaknesses? How can he get free from his pseudo-self and let his true being reveal itself? How cease to negate and begin to affirm his own best values? The quest, with its practical disciplines and mystical exercises, is part of the answer.

30

It is a way of life which calls him to deny his closest pleasures and oldest habits. So it is and must be a hard way. But a time comes when he values it out of his own clearer perception, and follows it out of his own glad choice.

31

Many aspirants wrongly believe the quest to be a movement from one psychic experience to another or from one mystical ecstasy to another. But in fact it is a movement *in character* from animality to purity, from egoism to impersonality.

32

The Quest teaches a man the art of dying to the animalistic and egoistic elements in himself. But it does not stop with these negative results. It trains him also in the art of re-creating himself by the light of the ideal.

33

Coming to this Quest in the philosophic sense simply means coming to human maturity.

34

Who does not prefer joy to grief? The instinct is universal. There is a metaphysical basis for it. Individual beings derive their existence from a universal Being, whose nature is continuously blissful. This is dimly, briefly echoed in the satisfactions of earthly desires. The quest of spiritual fulfilment is really the search for a fuller and more lasting share in the Divine Peace, the true heaven which awaits us in the end, whether in the freedom of so-called death or in the confines of physical flesh.

35

The worldling seeks to enjoy himself. Do not think that the truly spiritual man does not seek to enjoy himself too. The difference is that he does it in a better way, a wiser way.

36

Here is a goal for men and women which can bring them the fulfilment of their best purposes, the happiness of being set free from their inward bondages, and the calmness of knowing their own soul.

37

The Quest is a veritable re-education of the self, leading in its turn to a noble transcendence of the self.

38

What is the quest but a process of moral re-education and mental self-conquest, a probing for and overcoming of those faults which keep the Light out of the mind?

39

What is the hidden metaphysical meaning of the Quest? It is that the infinite self in man finds that it cannot achieve adequate self-expression in the finite and imperfect life of the world. The ego may try as it will, do what it may, but the bliss, wisdom, serenity, and perfection that are the natural attributes of the Overself, in the end elude its every move. There is ultimately no alternative except to let go of searching and grasping the outer world, and retreat within. There, deep inside its own being the journey to enduring satisfaction will thenceforth be. This is the Quest leading to discovery of Overself.

40

We ought perhaps to have particularized the significance of this word, for many men and women are engaged on the food-quest, the pleasure-quest, and so on; only a few, however, are on the Philosophical Quest.

41

Some come to the truth in a roundabout way. The Quest is direct.

42

The quest is governed by its own inherent laws, some easily ascertainable but others darkly obscure.

43

It is a search for meaning in the meaningless flow of events. It is response to the impulsion to look beyond the ever-passing show of earthly life for some sign, value, or state of mind that shall confer hope, supply justification, gain insight.

44

This quest of the soul is ageless. Never has the human race been without it, never could it be without it.

45

It is not a new thing in human experience, but rather one of the oldest. Its long history in many lands makes impressive reading.

46

It is a method, a teaching, and an ideal combined for those who seek a genuine inner life of the spirit.

47

The quest means disciplined emotions and disciplined living, sustained aspiration and nurtured intuition.

48

It is not an ideal so far off that those who have realized it have no human links left with us. On the contrary, because it is truly philosophic, it skilfully blends life in the kingdoms of this world with life in the kingdom of heaven.

49

The quest is an adventure as well as a journey: a work to be done and a study to be made, a blessing which gives hope and a burden of discipline which cannot be shirked.

50

There is another kind of exploration than that which traverses deserts, penetrates jungles, climbs mountains, and crosses continents. It seeks out the mysterious hinterlands of the human mind, scales the highest reaches of human consciousness, and then returns to report routes and discoveries, describe the goals to others so that they also may find their way thereto if they wish.

51

The spiritual quest is not a romantic or dramatic adventure, but a stern self-discipline. Nevertheless there is an element of mystery in it which at times can be quite thrilling.

52

The quest is spiritual mountaineering.

53

It is not a path of anaemic joylessness for lean cadaverous votaries, as some think. It is a path of radiant happiness for keen positive individuals.

54

Its ideals offer an invitation to nobility and refinement. "Become better than you are!" is its preachment. "Live more beautifully than you do!" is its commandment.

55

It is an uncontentious teaching, knowing that it is, in practice, only palatable to those who come readily equipped for it.

56

It is not a doctrine of life only for ageing hermits, but quite as much for keen young men who wish to do something in the world. It is a practical goal which could also be a practicable one for millions who now think it beyond their reach, if only they would accept and act on the psychological truth that "thinking makes it so." It is a strengthening reassurance to minds awakening from the slavish dreams of lust that they need not stay slaves forever. It is not an asceticism that is happy only in making itself miserable, but a comprehension that weighs values and abides by the result.

57

The quest is a continual effort of self-release from inward oppressions and self-deliverance from emotional obstructions.

58

This quest is really a system of therapeutic training devised to cure evil feelings, ignorant attitudes, and wrong thinking.

59

The high teachers of the human race have given us goals and taught us ways to approach them.

60

It is not a subject for academic students of technical metaphysics or for professional followers of institutional religion—although they are welcome to all that it has to give them, to the richer form and the inspired understanding of their own doctrine. No—it is primarily for the ordinary person who is willing to heed his intuitive feeling or who is willing to use his independent thinking power.

61

It escapes pushing into recognizable and separate divisions, definitions, or groups.

62

Let it be stated clearly that mysticism is an a-rational type of experience, and in some degree common to all men.

It is an intuitive, self-evident, self-recognized knowledge which comes fitfully to man. It should not be confounded with the instinctive and immediate knowledge possessed by animals and used by them in their adaptations to environment.

The average man seldom pays enough attention to his slight mystical experiences to profit or learn from them. Yet his need for them is evidenced by his incessant seeking for the thrills, sensations, uplifts, and so on, which he organizes for himself in so many ways—the religious way being only one of them. In fact, the failure of religion—in the West, at any rate—to teach true mysticism, and its overlaying of the deeply mystic nature of its teachings with a pseudo-rationalism and an unsound historicity may be the root cause for driving people to seek for things greater than they feel their individual selves to be in the many sensation-giving activities in the world today.

Mysticism is not a by-product of imagination or uncontrolled emotion; it is a range of knowledge and experience natural to man but not yet encompassed by his rational mind. The function of philosophy is to bring these experiences under control and to offer ways of arriving at interpretations and explanations.

Mysticism not so controlled and interpreted is full of pitfalls, one of which is the acceptance of confusion, sentimentality, cloudiness, illusion, and aimlessness as integral qualities of the mystical life—states of mind which go far to justify opponents of mysticism in their estimate of it as foolish and superstitious.

The mystic should recognize his own limitations. He should not refuse the proffered hand of philosophy which will help his understanding and train his intuition. He should recognize that it is essential to know how to interpret the material which reaches him from his higher self, and how to receive it in all its purity.

The belief that the neglect of actual life is the beginning of spiritual life, and that the failure to use clear thought is the beginning of guidance from God, belongs to mysticism in its most rudimentary stages—and has no truth in it.

The world will come to believe in mysticism because there is no alternative, and it will do so in spite of mysticism's historical weaknesses and intellectual defects. But how much better it would be for everyone if those weaknesses and defects were self-eliminated.

He has so learned the art of living that the experiences of everyday life yield up their meaning to him, and the reflections of daily meditation endow him with wisdom.

If it be asked, "What is the nature of mystical experience?" the answer given very tersely is, "It is experience which gives to the individual a slant on the universal, like the heart's delight in the brightness of a May morning in England, or the joy of a mother in her newborn child, in the sweetness of deep friendship, in the lilt of great poetry. It is the language of the arts, which if approached only by intellectual ways yields only half its content. Whoever comes eventually to mystical experience of the reality of his own Higher Self will recognize the infinite number of ways in which nature throughout life is beckoning him. The higher mystical experience is not a sport of nature, a freak phenomenon. It is the continuation of a sequence the beginning and end of which are as vast as the beginning and end of the great cycle of life in all the worlds. No man can measure it."

The *Yoga Vasistha* states, "There are two kinds of paths leading to liberation. Now hearken to them. If one should, without the least fail, follow the path laid down by a Teacher, delusion will wear away from him little by little and emancipation will result, either in the very birth of his initiation by his Guru or in some succeeding birth. The other path is where the mind, being slightly fortified with a stainless spontaneous knowledge, ceaselessly meditates upon it, and there alights true gnana in it, like fruit falling from above unexpectedly."

There are primary and secondary levels of mind and consequently primary and secondary products. The former are insights, the latter are intuitions.

Sages speak from the highest level; mystics contemplate, while genius speaks, writes, paints, and composes from the secondary levels.

Primary consciousness is exalted but calm; secondary consciousness is exalted but excited. The first does not change its settled mood, but the second falls into rapture, ecstasy, and absent-minded reverie.

63
Is the inner life irreconcilable with the world's life? Religio-mystical disciplines and practices are usually based on such a fundamental irreconcilability. Traditional teaching usually asserts it too. Yet if that be true, "Then," as Ramana Maharshi once sceptically said to me, "there is no hope for humanity."(P)

64
It is a teaching which prepares him to find a deep inner life without necessarily deserting the active outer one.

65
It is a teaching which can guide us through this world without itself becoming worldly.

66
The lower mysticism may cause a man to lose all interest in his external life, whereas the higher mysticism imparts a new because diviner interest. If the first may enervate him, the second will enliven him.

67

The term "spiritual" is very loosely used nowadays. It includes in its domain, but is not limited to, certain states of mystical consciousness, certain religious mental experiences, high moral attitudes, and non-worldly emotional reactions. Thus, one man may be called "highly spiritual" although he may not have had any mystical experience, when what is meant is that he is "highly moral."

68

Nobody, not even its bitter critics, may question the purity and nobility of its ethics, however much they may question the accuracy of its metaphysics.

69

This is not a quest which tries to tempt prospective candidates with the offer of prosperity or to bribe them with the satisfaction of their desires.

70

This quest is not in the private jurisdiction of any particular group, sect, school, or religious following. That is a narrow concept which must be firmly repudiated. It is the quest of life itself, the need of self to comprehend its own being.

71

The Quest is not to be looked upon as something *added* to his life. Rather it is to be his life itself.

72

This tormenting feeling of the lack of a spiritual state in his own experience, will drive him to continual search for it. But his whole life must constitute the search and his whole being must engage in it.

73

If you take the widest possible view, all the different sections of his action and thought are inseparable from the amount of spirituality there is in a man.

74

The truth must pass from his lips to his life. And this passage will only become possible when life itself without the quest will be meaningless.

75

It is only the beginner who needs to think of the quest as separate from the common life, something special, aloof, apart. The more proficient knows that it must become the very channel for that life.

76

The Quest is not anything apart from Life itself. We cannot dispense with common sense and balance in relation to it. No single element in life can be taken too solemnly, as if it constituted the whole of life itself, without upsetting balance.

Its importance and practicality

77

The quest is the most important adventure in human experience.

78

He who stands on the threshold of this Path is about to commence the last and greatest journey of all, one which he will continue to the end of his days. Once begun, there is no turning back or deserting it, except temporarily. And since it is the most important and most glorious activity ever undertaken, its rewards are commensurate.

79

He cannot stake too much on the outcome of such exalted strivings. Even all that the world can offer falls far below what the quest can offer. If outer sacrifices and inner renunciations are called for, the compensation will be more than just. In the end he gains immensely more than he loses. So why not let go freely if the quest bids him do so?

80

The meaning and end of all such work is to arouse men to see certain truths: that the intuitive element is tremendously more important than the intellectual yet just as cultivable if pursued through meditation, that the mystical experience is the most valuable of all experience, and that the quest of the Overself is the most worthwhile endeavour open to human exertions.

81

If there is anything worth studying by a human being, after the necessary preliminary studies of how to exist and survive in this world healthily and wisely, it is the study of man's own consciousness—not a cataloguing of the numerous thoughts that play within it, but a deep investigation of its nature in itself, its own unadulterated pure self.

82

This is the higher cause that is really worth working for, the spiritual purpose that makes life worth living.

83

In first, the discovery of the Overself, and second, the surrender to it, man fulfils the highest purpose of his life on this earth.

84

Each man has only a limited fund of life-force, time, and ability. He may squander it on worldly pleasures or spend it on worldly ambitions. But if, without neglecting the duties of his particular situation, he realizes that these are changing and transient satisfactions and turns instead to the quest of the Overself, he begins to justify his incarnation.

85

The businessman who does not know that the true business for which he was put on earth is to find the Overself, may make a fortune but will also squander away a lifetime. His work and mind have been left separate from his Overself's when they might have been kept in satisfying harmony with them.

86

Every man has another and veiled identity. Until he finds out this mystical self of his, he has failed to fulfil the higher mission of his existence.

87

If you want to know the purpose of life, read Acts 17:2: "God made man to the end that he should seek the Lord."

88

It comes to this: Are we to worship man or God?

89

Life offers man a variety of meanings, but in the end one meaning comes to the top of all the others and that is the meaning which shall reveal the truth about his relation to God.

90

When he sees life whole and therefore sees it right, he will understand why Jesus said, "Seek ye first the kingdom of heaven and all these things shall be added unto you," and why, if he is to insist upon any single renovation in human life, it must be its own self-spiritualization. If he is to put emphasis anywhere, it must be upon the rediscovery of the divine purpose of his earthly life.

91

The old Sanskrit texts tell us of the "little purpose" of human life and of the "great purpose." All know the one but few know the other; fewer still seek to realize it.

92

If men only knew how glorious, how rich, how satisfying this inner life really is, they would not hesitate for a moment to forsake all those things which bar their way to it.

93

We do not understand the depths of our own being, the mystery in which it is grounded. I speak for mankind in general, not for those few great ones who have banished illusion and ignorance.

94

What amid all the noise of the world is the hidden purpose of life, what kind of men are we ultimately meant to be? It is the business of great prophets to answer these questions.

95

Socrates: "I spend all my time going about trying to persuade you, young and old, to make your first and chief concern . . . for the highest welfare of your inner selves."

96

What grander ideal could a man have than to live continuously in the higher part of his being?

97

That which really is, as opposed to that which appears to be, behind all the countless objects of this varied universe, is one alone, beginningless, endless, the source of all, the parent of the "I"-consciousness. This truth provides the final hope for man. Somewhere along his way he will discover it, act upon it, and be redeemed. This will be his last conversion, his final salvation, his best quest. Then only will the horrors he has contributed to the race's history begin to fade out. All else is utopian chimera based upon wishful thoughts and fanciful imaginations.

98

When men acquire proper values, whether by reflecting over their experience or by listening to their prophets, they will recognize this truth—that nothing really matters except the search for the Overself. If this calls for the giving up of earthly obstacles, then they are worth giving up for it.

99

When he has become ripened by experience and reflection, he will accept this truth with the spontaneity of a biological reaction.

100

If some are to be aroused to its importance they must first be given something of its meaning.

101

"Having a human body one must think with one's heart on life's end." —Chinese text *Fachi-yao Sung Ching*.

102

This enterprise of the quest is the most serious in which a man can engage. We must treat it as such. But let this not cause anyone to lose the sense of humour.

103

In pursuing this integral quest, they have the satisfaction of knowing that they are pursuing the only quest which can bring them to a truth which is all-embracing and all-explaining.

104

The fact that so few have ventured on this quest offers no indication of what will happen in the future. If mankind could take any other way to its own self-fulfilment, this situation might remain. But there is no other way.

105

For him there must exist something more than merely being a member of the herd; there must be a higher direction leading to truth to satisfy the mind, to a nobler character to satisfy the conscience, to refined beautiful and gentler moods inspired by the arts, music, literature, and reverence. For him there must be a Quest.

106

This is the only way whereby man can impregnably demonstrate to himself the illustrious dignity of his true being. This is the only way he can obtain the power of living in and by himself, that is, of living in the only real freedom possible on this earth.

107

If consciousness is to be enlarged, if the mind's dark places are to be lit up, if a blessed inspiration for living, work, or virtue is to be discovered, then this self-quest must be started.

108

The Ideal is in these critical days no longer a mere wish: it has become the necessary.

109

It is not enough to know with the intellect that God is everywhere and everywhen. It is also necessary to establish a practical working connection with God, if we are to obtain the actual benefit of this knowledge. Moreover this, and this alone, will give absolute assurance.

110

He needs to recover his conscious relationship to the Overself: the subconscious one is never lost.

111

The vision of the world and the understanding of life which he receives from the lips or books of others will never be so true nor so real as that which he makes his own. What shall it profit a man if he hear a thousand lectures or read a thousand books but hath not found his Overself? The student must advance to the next step and seek to realize within his own experience that which is portrayed to him by his intellect. And this is possible only by his entry upon the Quest.

112

With every day that passes, a man makes his silent declaration of faith in the way he spends it. It is a poor declaration that modern man makes when he brushes aside all thought of prayer and meditation as something he has no time for.

113

To become so lost in this world of appearances, as so many have become lost, is to shut the door to the world of reality. This is why the lost art of contemplation is a necessity and must be regained if we are to open that door and let truth in.

114

What comes with the years and which is ascribed to the older people is the wisdom of practical living. This is merely information, knowledge from experience in practical affairs; it is not the wisdom which comes from the deeper being, the deeper self. That will arise only when one looks for it, aspires to it.

115

The profound meaning of life is not put before our eyes. We have to dig for it with much patience and much perseverance.

116

We must put a spiritual purpose into our lives.

117

The first duty of man, which takes precedence over all other duties, is to become conscious of his Overself. This is the highest duty and every other duty must bow before it. Even domestic happiness must not stand in the way of spiritual salvation when, and if, the two collide. The training which makes this possible may be largely unpracticable in his particular circumstances but it is never entirely so. The difficulty of performing this duty is not enough excuse to relieve him of it.

118

What a man sees and thinks is only an awareness gleaned by the shallower part of himself. There is his deeper being—indeed, the term "part" is quite inapplicable here—his real essence, the greater Consciousness from which thoughts and emotions emerge for their limited lives. To find and know this is a duty to which he *must* one day come.

119

The search for truth becomes, for such a man, neither a spare-time hobby nor an intellectual curiosity, but a driving moral compulsion.

120

The more deeply we understand the nature of man, the more reliably shall we understand the duty of man.

121

The risks of entering such a spiritual adventure may be quite formidable, but the risks of not entering it are unquestionably frightful. For the probabilities of wrong action and mistaken choice will still remain, with the painful karmic aftermath.

122

The man who fails to touch the Overself's beauty in this life and under this pressure can hardly be blameworthy, but the man who fails to *try* to touch it, is blameworthy.

123

Nobody really knows how to live correctly unless he knows the higher laws governing life itself.

124

Whether on college campus or life's school, the higher laws have to be learnt at some time, in some birth—whether by instruction when young or by experience when older. The fact of their existence may be disregarded at our own peril.

125

Man can come into the personal knowledge that there is this unseen power out of which the whole universe is being derived, including himself. But neither the animal nor the plant can come into this knowledge. Here we see what evolution means and why it is necessary.

126

The most important questions which a man can ask himself—What he is and What he is here for—must be answered before his life finds its proper course. Otherwise, in the higher sense, he remains a mere animal.

127

Both Hindu and Buddhist teachers concur in regarding the human creature as being the most fortunate of all living creatures, because he alone has the potential capacity and opportunity to become spiritually "aware."

128

Every life in the fleshly body represents an opportunity to obtain spiritual realization because man can only discover his divinity to the fullest whilst in the waking state.

129

The refusal to reach up towards the higher truth and power leaves problems basically unsolved and questions really unanswered, for the cosmic urge within must assert and reassert itself.

130

When a man comes to his real senses, he will recognize that he has only one problem: "How can I come into awareness of, and oneness with, my true being?" For it is to lead him to this final question that other questions and problems have staged the road of his whole life. This answered, the way to answer all the other ones which beset him, be they physical or financial, intellectual or familiar, will open up. Hence Jesus' statements: "Seek ye first the kingdom of heaven *and all these things shall be added unto you*," and "To him that hath [enlightenment] shall be given [what he personally needs]."

131

Because we have lost our way, these truths are once again as fresh and significant and important as if they had never before been known to humanity.

132

The earlier the age at which a man begins these studies and practices the better for him. To be born into a family where they already prevail, is to have an exceedingly good destiny. But however late in life anyone comes to them, it is never too late. He will have to contend with set ways and fixed habits that will need changing, it is true.

133

The middle-aged and the elderly should take to spiritual studies as a duty. They have come to a period of life when they can evaluate its experiences better than the youthful.

134

It is not too late at any period of life, even in old age, to obtain a firm footing upon the spiritual path and gain its satisfying rewards.

135

In the end we all must turn to the inner Source of all our best human sources, to the Guru of all the gurus, to the Overself. Then why not now?

136

NOW is the right moment to practise philosophy, to crush the ego, and to think positively.

137

The quest, with its ideas and goals, is essential to the awakened man. He could not live without it without feeling half-dead, empty and futile.

138

He who lacks the capacity to worship something higher than himself, to revere something better than himself, is already inwardly dead before his body is outwardly dead.

139

Suffering men resort to travel in order to forget their burdens, but ruefully find that memory paces the steamer deck beside them, the ego travels in their train, and mind lays its throbbing head upon the same hotel pillow. They may escape from the whole world but, unless and until thought is conquered, they cannot escape from themselves.

140

So long as man does not know the most important part of himself and the best part of his possessions, so long will he remain the blind creator of his own miseries and the duped plaything of his own trivialities.

141

If we choose to be endlessly preoccupied with external matters, business, and pleasure, if we will not turn lovingly in the only direction to which we must turn if we are to behold our divine self, then it is useless to blame life, God, or luck for our unhappy blindness.

142

Those who prefer their own ego's opinion to the Overself's impersonal intuitions, remain in the ego's darkness.

143

No man who denies the Real and rejects the True can attain happiness or peace of mind or have enough reason to be quite good.

144

The quest may seem a long and difficult affair: it is. But since even a little effort in travelling it brings a noticeable reward, while saving some avoidable suffering, and since the questless life is in comparison a useless effort to hold on to many illusions, it still offers enough inducement to make a start and exert oneself to enter on the first stage.

145

There is no other way to true happiness, as distinct from the false kind, than to follow the path which the higher power has set for him. This is to preach a hard doctrine but it is a true one.

146

So long as a man does not experience his real self, so long will he be unhappy. The possession of material things and the indulgence in material pleasures only alleviate and palliate this unhappiness, and then temporarily, and do not remove it.

147

What is the greatest need of man? I reply quite simply, Truth! For no other satisfaction will end his discontents.

148

The true mystic is always pleased to learn that an individual has started upon the spiritual quest in earnest. He knows that nothing else in life will yield such satisfaction, especially in these times of world crisis when the need for inner support is greater than ever before. There cannot be any true or lasting outward form of security today.

149

Most of his resources may carry a man through many situations because they are purely material. But they cannot carry him through all situations. There are others to meet for which he needs spiritual resources, and if he lacks them he will be in a sorry state.

150

It is true that property, money, and possessions give most men a sense of security. But it depends on them and they bring anxieties, cares, even fears, along with their comfort and support. They still need to find or to add a personal security which is independent of these externals, which is *personal*. This can come only from within. But it must be from a deeper level than their ordinary thoughts and emotions. They are too unstable, too subject to moods.

151

So long as a man is a stranger to his own divine soul, so long has he not even begun to live. All that he does is to exist. In this matter most men deceive themselves. For they take comfort in the thought that this attitude of indifference, being a common one, must also be a true one. They feel that they cannot go far wrong if they think and behave as so many other men think and behave. Such ideas are the grossest self-deceptions. When the hour of calamity comes, they find out how empty is this comfort, how isolated they really are in their spiritual helplessness.

152

Millions of other humans came into the world and after a relatively short existence disappeared. He will be no exception: his turn to vanish will also come. Thought, confronted with this terrible fact, must either despair, take refuge in the hopes of religion, or resolve to find out the truth behind the tremendous cosmic drama.

153

It is better to accept the loneliness of the quester than the complacency of the worldling who lives without any understanding of life's inner purpose.

154

Men and women try various ways to overcome their innate loneliness and with various results in the end. So long as the expedient used is something or someone outside themselves, their victories turn out to be illusions. There is no final way other than the Way which everyone has had to tread at last who ever succeeded in this objective, and which leads inwards to the Overself.

155

In their search for satisfactions outside of and apart from the Overself, men and women are really fugitives from it.

156

The response provoked in you by the entry of these ideas will determine your future.

157

We suffer from stagnation and imagine that existence in the intellect and body is enough; it is not. The primary emphasis must be laid on the living principle of our being, the central self which creates both body and intellect.

158

Here it is, the human creature put upon this round planet and left to make nothing from life, merely survive, or to make something out of it, and hold the great vision of the World-Idea, in company with the gods.

159

The making of money, the earning of a livelihood, and the attainment of professional or business success have their proper place in life and should be accorded it but—in comparison with the fulfilment of spiritual aspiration—ought to be regarded as having quite a secondary place.

160

No scientific technological advance, no political gain, no economic improvement will ever be enough in and of itself to provide a proper goal for human endeavour. It is easy to forget this in certain favourable periods, and if we do we come close to disaster in the end.

161

We use every possible moment to cultivate the uncertain fields of commerce or to grow the perishing flowers of pleasure, but we are unable to spare one moment to cultivate the certain fields of the spirit within ourselves or to grow the enduring asphodels of divine devotion.

162

The goals of progress are but imagined ones. There is only one goal which is undeniably real, completely certain, and authentically true—and that is an unchanging one, an eternal one. Yet it is also the one that has escaped mankind!

163

Here in this country, men are more eager to better their manufactures than themselves. They will accept their own imperfections quite smugly and contentedly, but the imperfections of their automobiles—never! Yet what is the use of their running from point to point on this earth if they do not even know why they are standing upon it at all?

164

Man as scientist has put under observation countless objects on earth, in sea and sky. He has thoroughly examined them. But man as man has put himself under a shallower observation. He has limited his scrutiny first to the body, second to what thinking can find. Yet a deeper level exists, where a deeper hidden self can be found.

165

He will discover that it is not enough to regard as good only that which is favourable to his physical life. He must complete the definition and sometimes even contradict it by adding that which is favourable to his spiritual life.

166

There is nothing more important in life than the Quest, and the time will come when the student discovers that there is nothing more enjoyable as well. This is inevitable in a Quest whose essential nature is one of infinite harmony and unbroken peace. No worldly object, person, or pleasure can ever bestow the satisfaction experienced in uniting with the Overself.

167

It is not the animal needs and their gratification but the realization of our divine possibilities which is the hidden justification of our presence in this world.

168

The ceaseless longing for personal happiness which exists in every human being is a right one, but is generally mistaken in the direction along which satisfaction is sought. For all outward objects and beings can yield only a transient and imperfect delight that can never be equivalent to the uninterrupted happiness of life in the Overself.

169

An existence which has no higher aims than purely physical ones, no nobler activities than merely personal ones, no inner reference to a spiritual purpose, has to depend only on its own small resources. It has failed to benefit by its connection with the power behind the universe.

170

That the truth of life must be deeper than what we see and hear and touch, is suspected by intuitive persons, believed or felt by pious persons, and directly known by wise persons. What the surface story tells us is not the whole of it, they say.

171

No one who ever gives the philosophic life a proper trial for a sufficient time is likely to desert it. Only the one who has never given it a fair trial, or who has failed to understand philosophy's real meaning, is ever likely to join the herd again and remain an unaspiring, insensitive, and prosaic creature.

172

Humans demean themselves by not caring for the dignity of their status, the ideals they ought to honour.

173

Our daily lives become mechanical, obedient to the world's demands, and our daily activities a constantly turning treadmill; but this only happens if there are no spiritual aims, spiritual aspirations, and spiritual practices to provide a resistance to this course.

174

We are regarded as odd people because we trouble our heads with the search for an intangible reality. But it never occurs to our critics that it is much more odd that they should go on living without pausing to inquire if there be any purpose in life at all.

175

A time comes in the intellectual growth of a man when he knows that he must put aside the trivialities of life and come to terms with the demands made upon him by his higher nature.

176

Those who wish to do something more than merely glide over the surface of mystical life, who wish to be fully at peace with themselves, must take to the quest.

177

To put one's own purposes in harmony with the universe's purpose is the most sensible thing he can do. Therefore there is nothing unpractical, irrational, or eccentric in the Quest. Only the unthinking crowd, who suffer blindly and drift tragically, may believe so. No one who has felt the inner peace, received the deep wisdom, and touched the rocklike strength which mark the more advanced stages, could ever believe so.

178

The moment we become convinced that the universal life has a higher purpose than the mere reproduction of the species, that moment our own individual life takes on a higher meaning, a glorious significance.

179

It is this that gives our poor personal lives their meaning and rescues them from their foamlike character.

180

Here is a concept on which the mind can linger, braced by its reminder of our human possibilities.

181

Those who move through life hopeless and dreamless, who see none of its beauty and hear none of its music, who have lost most of its battles and won none of its prizes, these can console themselves only by adopting a new set of values or by applying one if they merely theorized before. If they do this, the end can be a new beginning.

182

The discovery that there are higher concepts of human existence, that these have a validity not less than the meaner ones which are all that so‛ many people know, may prove a turning point at any age. For the young it gives some guidance, for the old getting closer and closer to death it offers some hope.

183

So short a time, so small a gain, so high a quest. For what is best, serves better in the end.

184

The importance of this work is ignored by most people and unknown to many people. They believe it to be the preoccupation of time-wasting dreamers or ill-adjusted neurotics. If they do not treat it with such indifference they treat it either with open abuse or with contemptuous indulgence. But if they could understand that it penetrates to the foundations of human living and affects the settlement of human problems, they might be less arrogant in their attitude towards it. It is not less important to the individual than to society at all times but immeasurably more so in these grave, critical times.

185

It may be asked of what social use are those who make this quest their primary occupation, and therefore make their worldly occupation and way of life conform to it? First of all, they embody, and therefore carry on and keep alive, the very idea of the quest. Secondly, their very presence, by telepathic and auric existence, *does* touch the inner beings of those who come into contact with them and *does* leaven the mental atmosphere of those who do not—however minute the effect on any particular day. Thirdly, although each has to live and express the quest in the way referable to his temperament and circumstances, he *does* offer a model—in general terms—for others to see, an example from which to draw stimulation.

186

In choosing this Path, the aspirant has taken the first step toward a Divine Power whose possession, or rather whose possession of him, will, ultimately, enable him to become a real healer of suffering mankind.

187

The view that such an existence is selfish and unproductive, is a shallow one. It takes no account of the value of higher forces. For whoever, by this quest and practice, realizes the divine presence, does so not only for himself but for all others in that little part of the world confided to his care.

188

Who are the most important human beings in the world? Those who try to bring sanity to an insane world or those who try to perpetuate its condition?

189

Our artists can find new sources of inspiration in it. Our dying religious hopes can receive an influx of unexpected new life from it. The phoenix of Divine Truth can rise again out of the ashes of materialism strewn around us if we turn our faces to that direction where the sun rises in red dawn. Yet since the spiritual is the deepest part of our nature, the process of our absorption of spiritual truths is a slow and not obvious one.

190

He may be told contemptuously that that kind of truth and reality have no practical value for us living in the world as it is, active in the world and dealing with the facts as they are, not getting lost in dreams. That in several ways this is not so can be demonstrated without too much difficulty. But let it be said that such a supreme knowledge or experience may possibly serve higher purposes which our small minds cannot yet glimpse.

191

All that really matters is how one lives one's life. But relative-plane activities do not constitute all there is to living. Consciousness rises from the plane behind the mind, and this region, like the outer world, needs to be explored with competent guides—its possibilities and benefits fully revealed by each individual for himself. Living will begin to achieve its own purpose when one's outer life becomes motivated, guided, and balanced by the fruits of one's inner findings.

192

You do not demolish the case for mystics when you show up and censure the oddities and charlatanries, the unreasons and fanaticisms of a few mystical cults.

193

If the mystical life were nothing more than a way of forgetting the dark sorrows of earthly life, a means of escaping the hard problems of earthly life, it would still be worthwhile. If its emotional raptures were nothing more than make-believe, it would still be worthwhile. We do not disdain theatres and books, films and music merely because the world into which they lead us is only one of glorious unreality. But the fact is that mysticism does seek reality, albeit an inner one.

194

He is not only an actor giving a performance on the world-stage. He is also someone who must learn to live in the still centre of his being.

195

The history of mysticism is marred by imposture and fraud, superstition and credulity. Yet with all these defects it is still the history of a tremendous discovery.

196

This is the higher purpose of life; to this men must in the end dedicate themselves: for this they must work, study, and meditate.

197

Our whole life on earth is in the end nothing else than a kind of preparation for this quest.

198

As he advances on this quest his scheme of values may change. This is partly because he learns by experience what every man has to learn, quester or not, that all is passing and nothing is stable, that the fruits of desire may turn to ashes, and that every day brings him nearer to death and farther from life. But it is partly also what the non-questers too often fail to perceive, that existence is like a dream, ultimately hollow, and that without some sort of link, connection, communion, or glimpse bringing him nearer to the inner reality his life remains unfulfilled.

199

Men of the world are not supposed to dabble in mysticism, much less exalt it to the status of religion. Yet this is precisely what they need, and need urgently.

2

ITS CHOICE

General notes

Soul-finding as Life's Higher Purpose

But curb the beast would cast thee in the mire,
And leave the hot swamp of voluptuousness,
A cloud between the Nameless and thyself,
And lay thine uphill shoulder to the wheel,
And climb the Mount of Blessing, whence, if thou
Look higher, then—perchance—thou mayest—beyond
A hundred ever-rising lines,
And past the range of Night and Shadow—see
The high-heaven dawn of more than mortal day
Strike on the Mount of Vision! —Tennyson, "The Ancient Sage"

One thing that struck my mind forcibly on my return to the Western hemisphere after an absence of several years in the Orient, was the way we busied and over-busied ourselves, whether in work, pleasure, or movement. Few take life easily; most take it uneasily. Few go through its daily business serenely; most go through it nervously, hurriedly, and agitatedly. Our activities are so numerous they suffocate us. It is a life without emotional poise, bereft of intellectual perspective. We are intoxicated by action. We moderns give ourselves too much to activity and movement, too little to passivity and stillness. If we are to find a way out of the troubles which beset us, we must find a middle way between these two attitudes.

The need of silence after noise, peace after feverishness, thought after activity, is wide and deep today. Amid all the nostrums and panaceas offered to humanity there is little evidence of the realization of this need.

Anyone who can overcome the extroverting and materializing tendencies of our period has to be an exceptional person. Indeed a general turning towards spiritual life is not a hope for the immediate present but for the distant future. This may sound pessimistic. But it will discourage those only who are oppressed by the reality of time and do not perceive its true nature.

The conditions of modern civilized society are not helpful to mystical self-culture, although they will serve intellectual self-culture. What is first needed is a recognition of the value of retreat, of times and places where every man and woman may periodically and temporarily isolate himself or herself whilst withdrawing attention from worldly affairs and giving it wholly to spiritual ones.

These words will make no appeal to the materialist mentality which still regards all spiritual experiences as the outcome of pathological conditions. Such an attitude, fortunately, has become less sure of itself than it was when first I embarked on these studies and experiments, now more than thirty years ago.

The mystic who sits in an hour-long meditation is not wasting his time, even though he is indulging in something which to the sceptic seems meaningless. On the contrary, his meditation is of vital significance.

It is quite customary to relegate us, the votaries of mysticism, to the asylum of eccentricity, crankiness, gullibility, fraud, and even lunacy. In some individual cases our critics are perfectly justified in doing so. When the mystic loses his straight course, he easily deviates into these aberrations. But to make a wholesale condemnation of all mysticism because of the rotten condition of a part of it is unfair and itself an unbalanced procedure.

Wherever and whenever it can, science puts all matters to the test. Mysticism welcomes this part of the scientific attitude. It has nothing to fear from such a practical examination. But there is a drawback here. No scientist can test it in a laboratory. He must test it in his own person and over a long period.

Owing to the widespread ignorance of the subject, there are some people who are disturbed by various fears of meditation. They believe it to be harmful to mental sanity or even a kind of traffic with Satan. Such fears are groundless. Meditation has been given by God to man for his spiritual profit, not for his spiritual destruction.

I would be failing in a duty to those less fortunate if through fear of being thought a boaster I failed to state that my researches have led me to the certain discovery of the soul.

Any man may become an atheist or an agnostic and doubt the existence of his own soul, but no man need remain one. All that is required of him is that he search for it patiently, untiringly, and unremittingly. Reality eludes us. Yet because common experience and mystical experience are both strongly interwoven out of it, they who persevere in their search may hold the hope that one day they may find it. Men will rush agitatedly hither and thither in quest of a single possession, but hardly one can be induced to go in quest of his own soul. Strange as it may seem to those who have immersed themselves heavily in the body's senses, hard to believe as it may be to those who have lost themselves deeply in the world's business, there is nevertheless a way up to the soul's divinity. That the divine power is active here, in London or New York, and now, in the twentieth century, may startle those who look for it only in Biblical times and in the Holy Land. But human perceptions in their present stage cannot bring this subtler self within their range without a special training. Its activity eludes the brain.

Every man who does not feel this close intimate fellowship with his Overself is necessarily a pilgrim, most probably an unconscious one, but still in everything and everywhere he is in search of his soul.

The soul is perfectly knowable and experienceable. It is here in men's very hearts and minds, and such knowledge once gained, such experience once known, lifts them into a higher estimate of themselves. Men then become not merely thinking animals but glorious beings. Is it not astonishing that man has ever been attracted and captivated by something which the intellect can hardly conceive nor the imagination picture, something which cannot even be truly named? Here is something to ponder over: why men should have forfeited all that seems dear, to the point of forfeiting life itself, for something which can never be touched or smelled, seen or heard.

What is it that has turned man's heart towards religion, mysticism, philosophy since time immemorial? His aspiration towards the diviner life is unconscious testimony to its existence. It is the presence within him of a divine soul which has inspired this turning, the divine life itself in his heart which has prompted his aspiration. Man has no escape from the urge to seek the Sacred, the Profound, the Timeless. The roots of his whole being are in it.

We are neither the originator of this doctrine nor even its prophet. The first man who ventured into the unknown within-ness of the Universe and of himself was its originator whilst every man who has since voiced this discovery has been its prophet. The day will come when science, waking more fully than it is now from its materialistic sleep, will confess humbly that the soul of man does really exist.

Men are free to imprison their hearts and minds in soulless materialism or to claim their liberty in the wider life of spiritual truth. Let them pull aside their mental curtains and admit the life-giving sunlight of truth.

What could be closer to a man than his own mind? What therefore should be more easy to examine and understand? Yet the contrary is actually true. He knows only the surfaces of the mind; its deeps remain unknown.

If the mind is to become conscious of itself, it can do so only by freeing itself from the ceaseless activity of its thoughts. The systematic exercise of meditation is the deliberate attempt to achieve this. Just as muddied water clears if the earth in it is left alone to settle, so the agitated mind clarifies its perceptions if left alone through meditation to settle quietly. There exists a part of man's nature of which ordinarily he is completely ignorant, and of whose importance he is usually sceptical.

What is the truest highest purpose of man's life? It is to be taken possession of by his higher self. His dissatisfactions are incurable by any other remedy. Spinoza saw and wrote that man's true happiness lay in drawing nearer to the Infinite Being. Sanatkumara, the Indian Sage, saw and taught, "That which is Infinity is indeed bliss; there can be no happiness in limited things."

Such is the insecurity of the present-day world that the few who have found security are only the few who have found their own soul, and inner peace.

2

Three happenings must show themselves: to be given *direction*, to feel an *impulsion* towards it, and to practise *purification* as a necessary requisite for the journey. Two warnings are needed here: fall not into the extreme of unbalance, and depend not on what is outside. One reminder: seek and submit to grace. It may be imageless or found anywhere anytime and in any form—a work of art, a piece of music, a living tree, or a human being—for in the end it must come from your own higher individuality and in your own loneliness.

3

Before embarking on this teaching, he should ask himself: "What attracts me most in this teaching? What do I hope to get out of it? Am I seeking religious satisfaction or metaphysical truth or moral power or inner peace or psychic faculties? Will I be satisfied with a theoretical understanding or would I go so far as to put it into practice? Am I willing to set aside a half hour daily for the exercise in meditation? How far do I wish to travel in the Quest of the Overself?"

4

The beginnings of this higher life are always mysterious, always unpredictable, sometimes intellectually quiet and sometimes emotionally excited.

5

When first he sets the logs of his raft afloat upon these strange waters whose ending can be only "somewhere in infinity" as the geometricians say, there are no lights to show his frail vessel the way of travel, no suns or stars to point a path for it. But he knows then that his head is bowed in homage to a higher power. Later he will know also how utterly right was the intuition which earlier drove him forth.

6

We walk the Quest uncertainly, human nature being what it is, human weakness following us so obtrusively as it does.

7

The decision to embark on this quest—so new, uncommon, and untried to the average Westerner—becomes especially hard to the man seeking alone, with no companion or relative to fortify his resolution.

8

This urge to discover an intangible reality seems an irrational one to the materialistic mentality. But, on the contrary, it is the most completely logical, the most sensible of all the urges that have ever driven a man.

9

The instinct which draws man to the truths of philosophy, the experiences of mysticism, and the feeling of religion is a sound one.

10

The *fact* of his own self-existence is the innate primary experience of every man. It is clear, certain, and incontrovertible. But the *nature* of that existence is obscure, confused, and arguable.

11

So much happens in the subconscious before they are quite aware of it that only when a new decision, a new orientation of feeling or thought is firmly arrived at, and openly appears, do they discover and define what they have been led to by outer and inner developments.

12

In each man there is a part of him which is unknown and untouched.

13

It is in the region of consciousness below the normal state that the most powerful forces move the human being—and can be applied to move him. Here only can the "radical transformation" which Krishnamurti so often calls for be made.

14

If he believes that these ideas ring true, then his course of duty is plain. To keep aloof in such a circumstance is to write his name in the *Book of Failure*.

15

Man has largely conquered his planetary environment. Now he must begin the sterner task of conquering himself.

16

"Speak, Lord, for Thy servant heareth" is a sentence from that ancient record, the Hebrew Bible. But any man may find that the Lord is still existent and still willing to speak *to him* even today. But to actualize such an encounter he must take to the secret path and practise inner listening.

17

In man, Heaven and Earth unite. He is free to enjoy the one or the other. The first leads to peace of mind, the second ties him to the ego's wheel. Whoever sincerely wants access to divinity may find it, but he must make the first move.

18

If humanity has not been gifted with divine consciousness by the sages, it is not only because such a free gift cannot be made. It is also because humanity prefers other things instead. When a questioner suggested to Buddha that he give Nirvana to everyone, Buddha sent him to ask at many houses what the people there wanted most. All desired some material thing or some worldly quality. Nobody desired Nirvana.

19

The fulfilment of the heart's nostalgic yearning for its true homeland may be delayed, but it cannot be defeated.

20

If experience, reason, or intuition cannot bring him to the conviction that a higher power rules the world, a master's help, grace, or writing may do so. If that fails, he has no other recourse than to keep pondering the question until light dawns.

21

If the quest seems too far from one's environment or circumstances, it is still a good time to start, for the reward will be better savoured.

22

This search after the soul need not wait until death until it successfully ends. To do so would be illogical and in most cases futile. Here on earth and in this very lifetime the grand discovery may be made.

23

The quest upon which he has entered will be a long one and the task he has undertaken a hard one. But the Ideal will also be his support because his conscience will endorse his choice to the end.

24

"O ye aspirant, leave aside wrangling, and take up the quest leading to the true goal, the Supreme Overself, which is unique. Sayeth Kabir, listen O aspirant, push thy enquiry further."—Kabir

25

Is there some particular purpose in my birth here? Is it all mere coincidence? Must we doubt, deny, even reject God? These are some of the questions a thoughtful man might ask himself.

26

If he is to moan over the length of the road opening out before him, he should also jubilate over the fact that he has begun to travel it. How few care to take even that step!

27

If some are immediately and irrevocably captured by the teachings, others are only gradually and cautiously convinced.

28

Those who feel an emptiness in their hearts despite worldly attainments and possessions may be unconsciously yearning for the Overself.

29

So many of us place so much value in possessions, yet we overlook the startling fact that we have not begun to possess ourselves! What man can call his thoughts his own?

30

The conventional measure of a man is his family and fortune, his church affiliation and political membership. What has all this to do with his essential self?

31

Can we build a bridge between this sorrowful earthly life and the peaceful eternal life? Are the two forever sundered? Every seer, sage, and saint answers the first question affirmatively and the second negatively.

32

The echoes of our spiritual being come to us all the time. They come in thoughts and things, in music and pictures, in emotions and words. If only we would take up the search for their source and trace them to it, we would recognize in the end the Reality, Beauty, Truth, and Goodness behind all the familiar manifestations.

33

Those who can no longer confine their thinking within the conventional boundaries of common experience may cross over into religion's reverent faith, into mysticism's deep-felt intuition, or into philosophy's final certitude.

34

Whoever perceives the inferiority of his environment to what it could be, as well as the imperfection of his nature in the light of its undeveloped possibilities, and who sets out to improve the one and amend the other, has taken a first step to the quest.

35

It is better to come late to the higher life with its nobler values and uplifting practices, than not at all. It is still better to come to it when one is comparatively young and foundations are being laid.

36

They will be fortunate indeed if their spiritual longings are satisfied without the passage of many years and the travail of much exploration. They will be fortunate indeed if pitying friends do not repeatedly tell them with each change and each disappointed pulling-up of tents that they are pursuing a mirage.

37

Those who have found their way to this Path leave forever behind them their aimless wanderings of the past.

38

One fateful day, he will ruefully realize that he is octopus-held by external activities. Then will he take up the knife of a keen relentless determination and cut the imprisoning tentacles once and for all.

39

The guiding laws of life are not easy to find. The sacred wisdom of God is also the secret wisdom.

40

The seeker quests until his thought rests.

41

The quest will continue to attract its votaries so long as the Real continues to exist and men continue to remain unaware of it.

42

Title: *The Temple and the Tomb*. (Man, who should be the temple of holiness, is now its tomb.)

43

The mystery of the soul is as formidable and as baffling as any. Yet it is also a fascinating one. If few people have penetrated it today, many tried to do so in the past.

44

Only when they are brought by the discipline of experience to a sense of responsibility, are they likely to seek this knowledge.

45

This does not mean that a spiritual outlook requires an unquestioning acceptance of what man has made of himself and of the world.

46

We do not approach God through our knees, or through the whole body prostrate on the ground, but deep in our hearts. We do not feel God with our emotions any more than we know him with our thoughts. No! —we feel the divine presence in that profound unearthly stillness where neither the sounds of emotional clamour nor those of intellectual grinding can enter.(P)

47

Each man who lights this candle within his own mind will soon begin to attract other men like moths—not all men nor many men but only those who are groping for a way out of their darkness.

48

Can a scrupulously impartial search through world-thought and experience lead to discovery of truth?

49

"Wilt thou be made *whole*?" asked Jesus.

Qualifications

50

Only when this search for a higher life has become an absolute necessity to a man, has he found even the first qualification needed for the Quest.

51

Modern civilization, with its tensions and comforts, its speed and extroversion, its pleasure and treasure hunts, its complicated activities and economic necessities, has trapped its victims so securely that he who would follow an independent path would have to make excessive efforts. It may seem foolish to suggest a scheme of living which involves the sacrifice of time separated out from a pressing day and given up to purposes seldom bothered with by civilized society, whose ways in fact would impede it. It may seem unlikely that people will follow such a scheme when, even if they theoretically accept those purposes, they deem themselves too busy or know themselves too lazy to operate it. It may seem impractical to offer it, especially to those who are dependent upon their work for a livelihood and who lose so much time getting to and from it. And even if they or others could be persuaded into adopting it, there is little likelihood that its exercises would be kept up—for only a comparative few are likely to have the needed strength and perseverance to keep it up. Where then is the spare time out of the modern man's daily program and the continuously driving will to come from? Where are the exceptional persons who would make the requisite sacrifices? No man will take up such a course of self-improvement and self-development unless he is thoroughly convinced of its necessity. And even then he may lack the willpower to declare war against his bad habits, his sloth and complacency, his pessimism and surface-comfort. He may be unable to change his pattern of thought and life, even if he wants to.

52

But the impulse towards a higher life must in the end come from something other than mere escapism or exotic curiosity. It must come from the thirst for truth for its own sake.

53

Without this ever-burning thirst for spiritual awareness, no seeker is likely to travel far.

54

Those whom life has wounded may turn to spiritual teachings for comfort, but too often this is only a passing reaction to sufferings. It has its temporary value and place, but it is not the same as consciously and clearly engaging in the Quest because the thirst for truth is predominant.

55

A passionate eagerness to find the Overself is a necessary basis for all the other qualifications in its pursuit.

56

He needs to have the willingness and preparedness to withdraw every day from his worldly and intellectual life utterly, and then to have the humility to open his heart in fervent supplication and loving adoration of the higher power.

57

If the quest is only an emotional whim or an intellectual fad for a man, he will make little headway with it. If on the contrary it is something on which his deepest happiness depends and he is ready to give what it demands from every candidate, if he is resolved to go ahead and never desert it, he will possess a fair chance of going far.

58

It is an age-old requirement of the higher self that those who seek its favours shall be ready and willing to empty their hearts of all other affections if called upon to do so. Prophets like Jesus and seers like Buddha told us this long ago, and there is nothing that modern inventive genius can do to alter the requirement.

59

To search for truth in its full integrity, putting aside all the pitiful substitutes which content little, less honest minds, requires not only an independence that creates intellectual if not personal loneliness, but also a willingness to abandon egoism and surrender its worldly advantages.

60

The qualifications required from him are love of the highest, desire for truth, conformity of living to the divine laws, and balance in his own person.

61

The seeker who has a strong yearning for Truth and who has a sense of correct values already possesses some of the indispensable qualifications for this path, and should go far upon it. However, the will to continue despite all obstacles, together with a special kind of patience, is also essential—particularly in the earlier stages.

62

He must begin his quest with an attitude of deep veneration for something, some power, higher than himself.

63

A mighty longing for liberation from one's present condition is a prerequisite for the philosophic quest.

64

The ardent desire to establish his true identity needs to be present also.

65

We must bring to the Quest not only all these delicate intuitions and subtle metaphysical concepts, but also a practical common sense and a sturdy, robust reason.

66

This is not a teaching for a little circle of mystical cranks but for more evolved people, that is, for those who are finer in character, more sensitive and intelligent in mind than the masses. It is for people to whom the mind's experiences are not less but even more important than the body's.

67

The Quest will be taken up and taken seriously only by those who have come to see that they must henceforth live as human beings and not merely as animals, if life is to be honourable and their own self-respect retained.

68

Most students of this teaching are not highly intellectual. If they had been, the pride and arrogance of intellect would, in most cases, have stopped them from entering such a mystical field. But neither are they unintelligent. They are sensible, mature, and discriminating enough to appreciate the value of its balanced ideal.

69

To obtain something they greatly desire, men will arouse their will and apply it strongly. Only when sufficient experience of life matures them sufficiently are they likely to arouse and apply this same will to the Quest itself.

70

A would-be follower of this path need not be concerned if he lacks intellect and has had an imperfect education. He should accept what he can understand of the books he studies and leave the rest for some future time. What is needed much more than intellect is humility, intuition, and intelligence, which many intellectuals do not possess.

71

People are needed with intellectual acumen, with emotional control, with balanced reason, with loyalty to ideals and with sincerity and faithfulness in working for them. They are to be undeterred by criticism and unmoved by praise. And lastly, amid the arduous struggles of this quest, its soaring thoughts and serious comprehension of world-sorrows, a sense of humour is needed also.

72

Those who care enough for advanced ideas to seek them out in spite of social rebuffs, as well as those who have the courage to explore what lies beyond already accepted ones, have become a marked proportion of questers.

73

Everyone expects to witness scientific advance made in these modern times but only a few have the mental courage to expect spiritual advance, let alone seek it.

74

It is for those who are ready for the phase of intellectual independence and spiritual individualism, who are courageous enough to face the inner solitariness of the human spirit when it turns from doing to being.

75

That man is excellently qualified for philosophy who has a strong spirit for service, who is well-balanced emotionally, and who is well-equipped intellectually.

76

The Quest calls for men of the world who are not worldly, aspirants with clear minds, endowed with common sense, students who will strive to lift themselves from inner mediocrity to inner superiority, followers who will strive to make worthwhile contributions to their environment.

77

If the faculties of mind and the qualities of character which the successful man of affairs already possesses were to be transferred to the field of understanding and mastering life itself, he could quickly progress in it.

78

It is not for futile dreamers nor neurotics seeking some guru's shoulders to lean on for the remainder of their years. There exist plenty of cults willing or eager to serve them. It is for those who understand there is real work to be done by, on, for, and within themselves.

79

Is he sincerely desirous of receiving truth (rather than comfort for his illusions and confirmation for his beliefs) from the Overself? Is he earnestly willing to obey its leading?

80

It is a mark of the quester that he is utterly sincere in seeking truth, and that he has some depth, enough not to be content with shallow presentations of it.

81

Authenticity of being is a necessary requirement in a would-be disciple. The insincere had better stay away from the quest.

82

If he is as determined as he is sincere, as unselfish as self-disciplined, as sensitive as intuitive, he may expect to go far on the quest.

83

In humility the quest is to be begun: in even greater humility it is to be fulfilled.

84

Until he has become conscious of his shortcomings, his ignorance, and his sinfulness, a man will rest in smug complacency and receive no spur to self-improvement, no impetus to enter the quest. Humility is another name for such consciousness. Hence, its importance is such as to be rated the first of a disciple's qualifications.

85

It is not for the average man but only for the exceptional man—for the one who is determined to pursue the meaning of life to the uttermost.

86

When these words awaken profound echoes in a man's soul, he shows thereby that the intuitive element is sufficiently alive to enable him to profit by further teaching.

87

In every kind of situation he will remember that he is dedicated to this quest, will remember its ideals and disciplines, yet not forget that he is still a human being.

88

They are welcome who are willing to equip themselves with proper and profounder knowledge, who wish to fit themselves by study of fundamental principles, by regular meditation, personal self-discipline, and public service for a higher life for themselves and a valuable one for society.

89

The mass of people are apathetic toward the quest: the poor for one set of reasons, the rich for another. Only the few capable of individual judgement, the defiant and independent thinkers, will be capable of rising up out of the mass.

90

Moral strength is needed by the quester.

91

This path requires something more than a search for righteousness or peace. It requires the aspirant to make himself more sensitive to the sorrows and struggles of mankind, ignorance-born and karmically earned though they may be, to imbue himself with a wise, prudent, and balanced compassion. He must advance from an outwardly-compulsive goodness to an inwardly-natural goodness. Such a way of life, with its chained desires, holy communion, and sensitive compassion, gives any man a higher stature.

92

It is easy to fall into a gloomy pessimism and say that the spiritual life is not for him, that he is unfit to practise its arduous exercises and that he had better abandon what is manifestly only for those blessed with luck or genius. Yet he would be wrong to assume that because the path is not easy he is mistaken in aspiring to it. Because it is not just a matter of daydreaming, nor passing from one thrilling inner experience to another, because hard work and unflagging perseverance are demanded from him, there is still no need to despair.

93

He will need much courage for the Quest because he will be confronted by two powerful enemies. One is himself, the other is society. Within himself he will have to do battle against the great desires. Within society he will have to contend against the great traditions.

94

He can successfully overcome the magnitude of his task if only he possess faith in himself, courage in his vision, and the resolve to shape his life for its higher welfare.

95

If the impulse to embark on this quest is to be something more than an unstable fancy, a calm perception of its stubborn difficulties and a most especially frank recognition of its self-refusing demands, is needed. That man is mistaken who comes to the quest expecting its rewards without its pains, its peace without its emotional crucifixions, its strength without its bodily mortifications.

96

If the quest seems to demand too much from us, that depends on what we ourself demand from life. The statement is true only if we ask for little, but false if we ask for much.

97

The quest is unattractive to sinners and unnecessary to saints. It is for those who are not wholly indifferent to worldly desires nor yet too strongly attached to them.

98

The quest is to be neither an emotional fancy nor an intellectual whim; it has to become something steady, deep-rooted, and strong-sapped in a man's life.

99

He will possess an irrefragable faith in the power of truth, holding that even if it were crushed and obliterated today time will cause it to rise again tomorrow and give it a fresh voice.

100

Whoever comes to this quest is unlikely to stay long with its pursuit unless he comes with considerable devotion and correct evaluation of its spiritual importance.

101

When a man starts on this quest, what work he has called himself to! What discipline of the feelings, what meditation of the intuiting faculty, what study of the thinking faculty, and what sacrifice of the ego must now be undergone at the bidding of no other voice than his own!

102

Those who are willing to take themselves in hand, ready to trample on their lower natures, are alone fit for this quest. They are few. The others, who come to it for its sensational, dramatic, psychical, and occult possibilities, hover around the entrance, but never get on the path itself.

103

The quest is neither for outright saints nor for outright sinners. It is for those who are conscious of having animal passions and human weaknesses, but who are *struggling* against them and *striving* for self-mastery.

104

Just as sickness creates appreciation of the value of good health, so life's anxieties create appreciation of inner peace. But this peace cannot be had without a measure of self-control and self-reform, which calls for use of the will.

105

Those who are satisfied with centering themselves within the ego will not be drawn to such teachings, which educate the pupils to cultivate constantly a withdrawal from the ego.

106

You have launched upon a quest from which there is no turning back. You have embarked upon a journey which will demand from you the utmost patience and deepest faith, the strongest determination and cultivation of the keenest intelligence lying latent within you.

107

This Quest is not an undertaking of a few weeks or months. It is, as I have often said, a lifetime's work: patience is required from us and must be given by us.

108

Yes, you may discover the elusive secret of life—but you must first work for it. "The gods sell anything to everybody," announces Emerson, "at a fair price." Take a few minutes off each day to find yourself, to question yourself, to awaken yourself—that is part of the price demanded.

109

Time and growth are needed before a man can sign that absolute commitment of mind and life for which it asks.

110

Spoiled plans or disappointed hopes may turn a man toward this quest but only appreciation of peace or love of truth can keep him on it.

111

Only such a strong yearning for, and loyalty to, peace or strength or wisdom or truth can carry him through the difficulties and past the obstructions on his path.

112

It has been the best minds, the noblest hearts of the human race which, historically, have enthusiastically given themselves to this quest. For they, with their superior sense of values, could best appreciate its high significance.

113

Only those men who know the value of the Truth are likely to furnish the candidates to search for it, and only those who search for it are likely to produce the few who find it.

114

The mere movement of his body from place to place in the name of adventure will no longer suffice to satisfy him. The only adventure he now seeks is that which will bring him to the wisdom of higher men and to the blessing of inspired ones.

115

Out of his own free choice and his own initiative, the human being has to respond to this divine presence hidden in his mind and even body, has to grow and ripen inwardly as he has already done physically. Here, in this point, he departs from animal existence.

116

He is already on the way to being something more than an animal which has lost some talents or senses and gained some talents or faculties who stops to ponder a single question: what is the source of his consciousness?

117

He may ask himself whether he has any competence for such a great task. But this is to forget that he has been led to this point, to the quest, that the same higher self or power which out of its grace did this can lead him still farther.

118

He who wants to co-operate with the World-Idea, which is inherent in all things, all beings, all the universe, to live in harmony with it and with his fellow-creatures, will be attracted to this quest sooner or later.

119

Useless would it be to thrust these truths on unprepared people and to get them to take up a way of spiritual growth unsuited to their taste and temperament. Persuasion should arise of its own accord through inner attraction.

120

Only when his quest becomes a whole-heartedly single-minded enterprise, working for a solitary end, disregarding all else yet retaining the sense of balance is it likely to succeed.

121

No vow of secrecy will be required of him, no pledge of loyalty demanded from him; he must enter the scattered formless order by a silent act of his whole heart, not by a vocal utterance of his fleshly lips.

122

Is it too presumptuous for an ordinary man to attempt to follow the philosophic path? We answer that no man who feels the need of truth to support or guide his life should be regarded as presumptuous in this matter. He need not be discouraged. He may dabble or penetrate deeply. The path is for him also. But it is so only to the extent that he is willing to pay the cost—no more. He is free to pay as little, and get as little, as he wishes. No one has the right to force him to give more.

123

Men find truth only to the degree that they are entitled to do so. Their aspiration is not enough by itself to determine this degree; their mental, moral, and intuitional equipment also determines it.

124

Whether he is able to follow regular periods of meditation or not, he may still have the basic essential for spiritual advancement. This is the fundamental mood of aspiration, a strong yearning to gain the consciousness of his innermost being.

125

The traveller on this quest is a man who uses his consciousness and his will to better his character and purify his heart.

126

The aspirant who comes to the Quest out of pure disinterested love for it rather than out of a hunger for occult powers or a thirst for occult experiences, who is seeking to know and do the right thing, will go ahead much more quickly and encounter much fewer dangers than the others who are not.

127

He cannot even set foot on this path if he has not become convinced of his weakness and wickedness. For only then will he be really rather than vocally willing to desert the ego.

128

There are not many who are ready for such independence of attitude and life. A certain inner strength is necessary for it first of all, and of course a natural or acquired willingness to desert the herds if necessary.

129

When a man is ready to confess his ignorance, he is ready to begin his study of philosophy. When a man is ready to drop the distorting influence of the emotions and passions which actuate him, he is ready to begin the study of philosophy.

130

He who knows that he has been ignorant of truth, and still is, has begun to enter the knowledge of truth.

131

This is not for those who are so satisfied with themselves that they want to preserve their egos just as they are. It is for those who feel the need of self-improvement, and feel it so keenly that they are willing to work hard for this objective and to take time for it. The Quest is for those who have looked at their own faults and turned their head away from the unattractive and disconcerting sight with downcast eyes. But although their weaknesses have clung in the past to them like limpets, philosophy bids them take hope and take to the Quest which can liberate and strengthen them in the future.

132

Those who have had their fill of society, who have found its gaiety and its friendship to be all on the surface, who have evaluated it as bogus, sham, and unreal, may be prepared to listen more heedfully to the description of a life that is offered as being much more worthwhile.

133

In man's higher yearnings, in his wishes for a better holier calmer self, he shows evidences of intuition.

134

To believe that this quest is only for religious people, or for impractical dreamers, and not for reasonable people or for men active in the world is to believe something that is untrue.

135

The laity, the masses, are entitled to be told that a higher truth exists, that they can come to it when they can cope with it, that it is up to them to equip themselves with the needed qualifications.

136

Just because most people appear to have superficial interests and are not yet ready for the deeper thoughts of philosophy does not necessarily mean that they are not making spiritual progress. On the contrary, they may be doing very well on their own particular levels of development. It will simply be necessary for them to incarnate many more times before they are capable of understanding the more advanced truths.

137

Aspirants come from the low, the middle, and the high strata of life— with most probably from the middle.

138

No age is unsuited to the study and practice of philosophy. No one is too young to begin it, nor too late.

139

Although the middle-aged and elderly, being more experienced, are more receptive to the ideas of emotional control and personal detachment, philosophy is not necessarily a subject fit only for those in their sunset years.

140

Men who are seized by ambition, who want money, prestige, honours, power, will not welcome the idea of detachment, and they are right. For they are not yet ready for it: they need to gain the fruits of their desires, to experience the strivings and accomplishments from which the truth about them can be deduced. Only after the lessons have been learned can they be in a position to reflect properly and impartially upon this idea and appreciate its worth.

141

He who is afraid to touch this study because he is afraid of spoiling his worldly career is unfit for it. Nevertheless, it is an error to believe that those who shed such a fear are called upon to forget their tasks or shirk their responsibilities and duties in this world. They are not. If they become

indoctrinated with the ideas here taught, they can succeed in their tasks
and duties; they need not fail.

142

Those who live in a private realm of far-fetched phantasies which are
caricatures of the real facts, as well as those who betray all the signs of
neuroticism, hysteria, or psychopathy, often talk overmuch about the
quest but do not seem able to apply its most elementary injunctions. To
encourage them to follow it is only still further to build up their ridiculous
egoism and bolster their fool's paradise. For them the quest is unachiev-
able until they become different persons.

143

The unequal balance of the whole psyche is a characteristic of those
seekers who impatiently shun the philosophic discipline. Hence we find
that emotional neuroticism, intellectual disorder, volitional weakness, and
egotistical excess are strongly marked in a number of people who take a
fussy, shrieking interest in mysticism. They seek ardently for teachers but
not for truth, for personalities rather than principles. They surrender
themselves eagerly to visible organizations but not to the invisible Overself. It does not occur to them that the absence of proper qualifications
unfits them for personal discipleship under a competent master. For
anyone to express even a hint of this unfitness is to arouse their anger,
provoke their hostility, and stiffen their conceit. And if he goes on to
suggest, in however kindly and constructive a manner, that their energies
would be more profitably directed towards self-improvement than towards running after incompetent teachers and absurd sects, he is rewarded
by abuse and vilification.

144

Neither a dry pedantic intellectualism nor a sloppy excitable emotional-
ism is desirable in the seeker after truth.

145

It is not for irresponsible persons, those of feeble will or hysterical
nerves.

146

It is wrong to look upon this quest as one for semi-lunatics, emotionally
disturbed persons, or gullible, brainless miracle-hunters. It is not a place
for the deposit of sicknesses, troubles, and deficiencies. Such things must
be taken elsewhere for repair.

147

All too many people take to this quest who are not really ready for it,
who need to become human beings before seeking the more massive

achievement of becoming superhuman ones, who ought to attain personal decency, balance, discipline, practicality, and calmness before losing themselves in the theoretical flights of metaphysical doctrines like Vedanta.

148

Truth is discoverable but not by everyone. It is not discoverable by the criminals who break every *ethical* law, by the lazy who won't pause and look within each day, by the cynics who sneer at the quality of reverence, by those who do not value it enough to cultivate their true intelligence.

149

Does everyone have the right to know this truth? Yes and no. Yes— because all men must do so in the end as a part of the fulfilment of life's purpose. No—when they are as yet uninterested in it and unable or unwilling to receive it.

150

If our thought is to be straight and fearless we ought to fling all prejudices overboard at the very start of our voyage.

151

The prejudiced man wants his prejudices confirmed not contradicted. He is not really looking for truth. Before the quest can even begin, prejudices must be removed. This is a psychological operation which the man cannot perform upon himself, except in part, without a great effort.

152

The fool cannot follow this Quest. He may try to but he will be sent back to learn some wisdom through earthly lessons and through earthly difficulties brought on by his foolishness.

153

Flighty temperaments, which seek the latest novelty rather than the first truth, are unfit for philosophy.

154

The very name "Quest" implies movement, travelling, journey; those who remain stationary cannot be said to be on the "Quest." By this I do not mean those who find themselves stagnating against their will, but those who make no effort inwardly to advance.

155

The truth is sometimes so spiky and so uncomfortable that people hide from it. Entry on the quest is a sign that enough courage has been gathered to face it. Those who assert that they are questers but who are too much in love with their own fancies are incapable of facing the realities behind those fancies. To this extent their quest is a bogus one, although not usually a *consciously* bogus one.

156

Emerson: "People wish to be settled: only as far as they are unsettled is there any hope for them!"

157

No factory can manufacture divine peace for us, nor can any workshop turn out the inspirations which bestow heroism on a man. We may wander the whole length of Oxford Street and find no shop which can sell us a packet of starry truths that might comfort and console. The morning post will bring a hundred letters in the office mail, but it will not bring one word or hint that shall conduct us nearer the higher aims.

Why people come

158

It is because we have the Overself ever present within us that we are ever engaged in searching for it. The feeling of its absence (from consciousness) is what drives us to this search. Through ignorance we interpret the feeling wrongly and search outside, among objects, places, persons, or even ideas.

159

Each man discovers afresh for himself this homey old truth, that he has a sacred soul. He need not wait for death to discover it or depend solely on the words of dead prophets until then.

160

He knows that in striving to fulfil the higher purpose of his being, he is not only obeying the voice of conscience but also approaching the place of blessedness.

161

There are reserves of Power and Intelligence within yourself, of which you live undreaming.

162

In its early manifestation it may show as a feeling of being too limited by ignorance of life's meaning and purpose and the need to get some light in this darkness. But the feeling may be too vague, too generalized and ill-defined to be detected and known for what it is.

163

At intervals, on certain grave, joyous, or relaxed occasions, he may feel a deep nostalgia for what he may only dimly and vaguely comprehend. He may name it, in ignorance, otherwise but it will really be for his true spiritual source.

164

What a bitter irony it is that the soul, which is so near, in our very hearts in fact, is yet felt by so few!

165

Those who have come for the first time to an awakening of thought upon these matters, may grow more enthusiastic as they explore them more.

166

The heart leaps at the thought that life has some higher meaning, some better worth.

167

"I have told you all this," said Jesus, "so that you may have the happiness I have had."—John 15:11

168

In starting this task, he knows that he is not carrying out his own personal desire but following a way chalked out for him by the higher self.

169

They cannot really escape from this inner loneliness by outer means. In the end, and however long put off, they will have to face it. Most often, such an hour comes in with sorrow or bereavement, hurt or disappointment.

170

There are certain rare moments when intense sorrow or profound bereavement makes a man sick at heart. It is then that desires temporarily lose their force, possessions their worth, and even existence itself its reality. He seems to stand outside the busy world whose figures flit to and fro like the shadowy characters on a cinema screen. Worst of all, perhaps, significance vanishes from human activity, which becomes a useless tragi-comedy, a going everywhere and arriving nowhere, an insane playing of instruments from which no music issues forth, a vanity of all the vanities. It is then, too, that a terrible suicidal urge may enter his blood and he will need all his mental ballast not to make away with himself. Yet these black moments are intensely precious, for they may set his feet firmly on the higher path. Few realize this whilst all complain. The self-destruction to which he is being urged by such dread experiences of life is not the crude physical act, but something subtle—a suicide of thought, emotion, and will. He is being called indeed, to die to his ego, to take the desires and passions, the greeds and hates out of his life, to learn the art of living in utter independence of externals and in utter dependence on the Overself. And this is that same call which Jesus uttered when he said: "He that loseth his life shall find it." Thus the sorrows of life on earth are but a transient means to an eternal end, a process through which we have to learn how to expand awareness from the person to the Overself.

171

If a man will not come to this quest willingly, because it leads to Truth and he loves Truth, then he must be forced onto it, unwillingly, because there is no other way to alleviate his burdens and reduce his miseries.

172

Most persons have no inclination to wake up when dreams are pleasant, whereas when they are frightening they soon awaken. So too the dream of worldly life does not impress them with the need of true religion until it becomes tragic or severely disappointing. Only when sorrow drives them to question the value of living do they take a real interest in non-worldly urges.

173

Certain events will so arrange themselves as to put a man upon the quest, or if he is already on it, to prepare him for a further advance. They will not be pleasant events, for they will crush his ego, or render it lame and weak for a time. But it is only through this apparent defeat by circumstances that he is compelled to accept a course which will, spiritually, benefit him greatly in the end.

174

Do men's hearts have to be broken before they yield to the higher power? Often, yes, but not if they heed the teachers, prophets, seers, and sages.

175

Where a man is ready for this Quest but stubbornly clings to his old familiar way of thought and life, the Overself may or may not release karma that will tear him away from it. His ego's desires will then be macerated by suffering until its will to live gets weaker and weaker.

176

A few come to this quest after the shock produced by the unreasonableness and unfairness and stupidity of the treatment they received from the organization, the group, the sect, the church, the party, to which they belonged. Some crisis in their lives, such as the need to get married or to get divorced, blocked by a solemn bleak dogma or decision, became the occasion of the shock. Or, as in Gandhi's case when he was thrown out of a railway compartment by an arrogant member of the ruling race, heartless discourtesy provoked swift disillusionment. A single jarring incident, a single deliberate injustice or hurt or insult was enough to bring on such resentment and indignation—penetrating as sharply as a hypodermic needle—that character change and a new outlook were inaugurated. Some have even come to the quest not because they had any real vocation for it but because they had nowhere else to go, because the world had lost all meaning, all hope for them through some ghastly tragedy or some heart-breaking loss, and this was a better way than committing suicide. But the best way to come to the quest is of course to fulfil the higher possibilities as a human being.

177

Most persons need a drastic shock, an enforced awakening, a sharp arousal from that long sleep which is the egoic existence, if they are ever to come alive spiritually. This is effective only if it breaks old habits, trends, and inclinations, thus making a new man. It may come about through hearing or reading a teacher like Krishnamurti or Gurdjieff, or through harsh events like malignant illness or unexpected bereavement.

178

When a man comes to the point when all his outer life dissolves in tragedy or calamity, he comes also to the point when this quest is all that is left to him. But he may not perceive this truth. He may miss his chance.

179

Either consciously or not, he says to himself, in a sense, "By my I alone I cannot endure this adverse destiny. I must seek help and support from outside myself." So he goes to another man or to an institution, but in the end he must go to God.

180

When one's personal life is miraculously saved during some period of great danger, perhaps in the face of death, it is for a purpose.

181

Before a man comes to this path he may have to grope and stumble and struggle for years.

182

If the man lets others draw him down below his own level, the emotion of remorse and disgust or the logic of suffering and self-preservation may force his return.

183

They need first to discover that they are on the wrong road. Out of the distress or frustration following it may arise the search for a right one.

184

No person makes him take on this task or enterprise, this labour or quest—whatever he wishes to call it. A summons come to him from within, from a part of himself hidden in mystery, and he obeys. Why?

185

It is for those who feel that their lives ought to hold something more than the mere gaining of material necessities or even the mere satisfying of intellectual urges.

186

If he will follow up this intuition, he will be able to move his feet eventually out of darkness into light.

187

When a man becomes tired of hearing someone else tell him that he has a soul, and sets out to gain firsthand experience of it for himself, he becomes a mystic. But, unfortunately, few men ever come to this point.(P)

188

Men will seek to feel the real life only after they have felt the uncertainties of human affection, the transiencies of human passion, and the insufficiencies of human activities.

189

To those who wish to escape from the pressures and tyrannies of contemporary materialism, philosophical mysticism offers the most effective way and the safest road. It seeks to understand the true relationship between the divine and the human. It will enable them to realize their spiritual potentialities. For materialism is and can be only a temporary phase of man's endeavour to comprehend the facts of life.

190

The presence of the Overself within us sooner or later, when the mind is sufficiently developed, creates of itself the craving for truth and the abstract questions about life, God, and man.

191

This knowledge that life in this world can never be fully satisfying makes him commit himself *one day* to the quest.

192

Only when they are tired of the frustrations and obstructions, the spites and cruelties which so often mar worldly life, will they feel ready to turn in real earnest to the Quest. Only then will its perfect tranquillity seem more desirable than the hectic excitement of following desires.

193

The essential point is that the more an executive is involved in the world's affairs, *the more he needs this quest which leads him out of the world*. The more his life is devoted to acquiring money and goods and position, the more he needs a firm base within himself from which properly to use these things as they ought to be used.

194

A time may come when a man may tire of the whole social round, the business or professional rat-race, and desire to turn away from it—when he begins to see through its futilities, vanities, and stupidities.

195

What other recourse can they have, after trying the usual ways—drink, sex, drug, or religion—than to this quest?

196

The first appearance of this sense of futility (in the heart's deeper life), may pass disregarded and unheeded. But it will return again and again, and grow apace, until the unsatisfactoriness of a wholly materialistic life, the transitoriness of a merely earthly happiness, achieve recognition and obtain acceptance. With this negative phase, modern man's inner life begins.

197

They feel vaguely that there are higher laws governing life, that they do not know them. They would like to learn, but in the medley of sects and cults—with their claims and contradictions—they do not feel safe enough to entrust their lives to any particular one, although attracted to some more than to others.

198

To escape from worldly troubles, to assuage the disappointment of frustrated hopes, mysticism offers a way.

199

The smugly complacent, the thoughtless surface-types, or those always immersed in pettinesses and trivialities will have no awareness of a higher need. But the others, relatively a few, will find it gnawing at their hearts and tensing their minds. The very condition which is so satisfactory to the larger group brings misery to the smaller one.

200

No longer is he content to be a straw swept along by the river of circumstance.

201

Those who are tired of the falsities and inanities accepted by so many, who want to come to a true life, must come to the quest.

202

Those who seek a larger meaning to life cannot live like the peasant for bodily needs alone, or like the professional for bodily and cultural needs alone. Their feeling is still the profounder: a peace and harmony, an understanding and strength.

203

They come to this quest seeking something beyond the misery, wretchedness, and cruelty of this chaotic world, something of light, warmth, kindness, and peace.

204

The need to insulate ourselves privately from the shocks of contemporary living, is partly met by mysticism.

205

There are those who come to this quest simply because they are disillusioned with the world. Wearied with the self-seeking disputations of political schemers, repelled by the heartless treatment of non-followers by political extremists, they turn away and look elsewhere for truth, honesty, goodness.

206

Metaphysical subtleties cannot change a man's life. Dull sermons will do it less. We do not find a fresh basis of life in these methods. What then is the way?

207

We seek truth for various reasons. One is because it possesses a certitude that gives us anchorage and rest.

208

Some of those who come to these teachings seeking them only for the sake of getting relief from their trouble end by seeking truth for its own sake.

209

The full-grown person finds in his experience of the world and in the knowledge of himself sufficient subject matter for thought about human affairs. He then asks questions, the great questions, which men have asked since earliest antiquity: What am I? Whither do I go?

210

Every school of thought, variety of cult, sect of religion, and system of metaphysics that has any pretension to spirituality accepts the existence of the soul. Disagreements do not start until after this acceptance. Why not take your stand on this undisputed fact and verify it for yourself?

211

There are billions of forms and of creatures in the universes spread through space. They appear and vanish, they come and go, create and pass away, grow and decay, act and interact. This has been going on for immense periods of time; but in the thoughtful man's mind there must arise the question, "To what end was is and shall be all this?"

212

If mental restlessness, a discontent with ignorance, with the recurring trivialities of a life which does not offer any higher meaning, put him on the Quest, he may find himself suffering from mental loneliness.

213

He may arrive at a true appraisal of life after he has experienced all that is worth experiencing. This is the longest and most painful way. Or he may arrive at it by listening to, and believing in, the teachings of spiritual seers. This is the shortest and easiest way. The attraction of the first way is so great, however, that it is generally the only way followed by humanity. Even when individuals take to the second way, they have mostly tried the other one in former births and have left it only because the pain proved too much for them.(P)

214

Some people come to the quest quickly, under the impulse of a great decision; but most come slowly, by degrees and stages.

215

The world will come to philosophy when it has evolved the necessary prerequisites to do so. Until then it will possess only imperfect expressions of the truth, or caricatures distortions and falsifications of it. Only those individuals who are not satisfied with these substitutes or with the slow pace of the world's evolution, will step out of the mass and enter upon the Quest just now.

216

When a man is thoroughly awakened to the reality of the philosophic goal, he will soon or late hear its summons to him. When that happens he embarks upon the Quest. For example, he starts an activity of conscious self-discipline and deliberate restraint, a process of re-educating the mind, the feelings, and the will.

217

When the interest in philosophic teaching no longer springs out of light curiosity but out of deep need, the desire to embark actively on the philosophic life will inevitably follow.

218

It is the character which he has inherited from former earth lives which makes him susceptible to spiritual urges and attracts him to mystical teachings of this kind. If changing events or changed environments, new contacts with living men or with printed books appear to be responsible, this is only because "delayed-action" tendencies were already in existence but still needed such external changes to be able to manifest themselves.

219

Awakening to the need of the Divine may come through some mental crisis or emotional shock which shakes the whole of man's being to its deepest foundations. It is out of the suffering and grief produced by such a situation that he plants the first trembling steps on the secret path. It is such outer torments of life that shatter inner resistance so that the need for spiritual help is acknowledged. And the more unsatisfactory outward life becomes, the more satisfactory does the blessed inward life seem both by contrast and in itself.

220

Many will be irritated by these thoughts, but some will be disturbed by them. It is only from the last group that a reconsideration of what they seek in life and how they propose to attain it is at all likely.

221

Before a man will undertake the moral purifications with which the quest must begin, and the mental trainings which must complement them, he must have some incentive to do so. Where will he find it? The answer is different with different men, since it depends on his stage of evolution, character, and destiny. If some find it in the sadness produced by world-weariness, others find it in the joy produced by a Glimpse. Still others are prompted by the hunger for Truth or by the thirst for self-improvement, or even blindly by the tendencies brought over from previous births.

222

The hour comes when, prompted by disappointment, bereavement, or revelation, he is driven to find out the reasons for all his activities. He is beginning to feel their insufficiency, their shallowness. Such inquiry, if persisted in, will in the end put him upon the quest.

223

Amongst the multitude of those who are attracted toward such teaching, it is inevitable that there should be those who are only casually interested, those who are tremendously in earnest about it, and those who are to be found somewhere between these two groups.

224

If the teaching favourably commends itself to any individual from the first contact as being requisite to his needs, this is often a sign that he has followed it in earlier existences.

225

One disciple who picked up the Quest again in this life described it as a feeling of reunion, of coming home.

226

If we are curious and interested enough to follow up correctly the clues and hints which life gives us sometimes; if we observe, study, analyse, meditate, and even pray; and if we become sensitive enough, then we shall be driven to become pilgrims with no choice except engagement in a mystical quest. Our supreme need and deep request is then inner work.

227

When he wakes up to the suspicion that the ordinary purposes of human life on earth hide other much more important ones, and that he will have to find them by himself, he may begin to seek out and study the teachings of those who have gone farther along this way.

228

Whether we are guided by human experience or superhuman revelation, by intuitive feeling or intellectual thinking, we must come in the end to the recognition of the great mystery which surrounds us.

229

The mysterious enigmas of the spiritual life must sooner or later challenge the sleeping mind of man into wakeful thoughts.

230

Our so-called intelligentsia, who played with political red fire until they painfully felt its destructiveness on their own persons, played at the same time with intellectual disdain for those who "escaped" from the world into ivory-towers of spiritual seeking. The second world war, however, began the process of making them feel the barrenness of their own fields and the stark coldness of their own outlooks. So quite a number of them have begun to peep into the ivory-towers and to find out what goes on there. The resultant discoveries are opening their eyes.

231

The spirit's beauty has lured men on like a dream of unfound gold. For the heart of man has always seemed to me like a grey galleon moving on the green sea of thought and seeking this world of treasure.

232

Ineffable bliss and serene joy are at the heart of all things and that is one of the reasons why people seek the Overself's infinite happiness even though they are not all aware of this.

233

Those who turn to the spiritual life for material benefits, such as better relations with other people and better physical health are entitled to do so. But they should remember Jesus' counsel: "Seek ye *first* the Kingdom of of Heaven," for then not only will "all these things [material benefits] be added unto you" but they have a chance of gaining the kingdom whereas the other approach postpones such a glorious result. The Overself must be sought for its own sake; otherwise it will not be found or else will be found only in fleeting glimpses. "*That* is the goal, that is the final end," says an old Indian writing.

234

Those who pursue this quest do so because they too want to be happy. Do not imagine that only the worldly pleasure-seekers, the hard money-hunters, the romantic love-dreamers, or the ambitious fame-followers are, in this respect, in a different category. It is only their method and result that are different. All without exception want the feeling of undisturbed happiness, but only the questers know that it can be found only in the experience of spiritual self-fulfilment. Fame, fortune, love, or pleasure may contribute towards the outer setting of a happy person's life but what of that person himself? Who has not heard or known of men sitting in misery amid all their riches or power, of death forcing a well-mated couple to bid each other farewell?

235

Emerson's declaration, "We needs must love the highest when we see it," is quite true of some persons but quite false of many more persons.

236

What lures a man to this quest? It may be that the ideas by which, and with which, he has lived for a long time have proved insufficient, false, or feeble. It may be that bereavement, calamity, or suffering have brought him to cherish peace. It may be nothing else than the simple need for a higher quality of living. It may even be that he comes to this quest, as some undoubtedly do, because he seeks a special benefit—healing, relief, amendment of fortune, perhaps. But in that case he must remain on it because he seeks the Overself, alone. Lastly let it be noted that if for some the first step on this quest is the final step down a long road of increasing desperation, for most it ought to be the first step up a garden path of increasing joy.

237

Some come to this through the joy enkindled by great music, inspired writing, or majestic landscape, or through response to beauty; but others—and they are more—come through being wrecked or crushed, threatened with destruction, left hopeless, forlorn, and helpless. They reach the end of their strength, or discover the falseness and futility of their wisdom.

238

He may come to the need of, as well as the illumination by, the Overself through two very different paths: through joy and sweetness or through suffering and sadness.

239

In the Orient it is the general belief that a man turns toward this quest for either of two reasons. If he is young, it is because he has an inborn genius for it. If he is somewhat older, it is because he is dissatisfied with life, disappointed in it, or bereaved by its calamities. But the philosophical view, while including these reasons, goes farther and wider. For it sees that some, notably those who are aesthetically sensitive and those who are maritally fulfilled, *are* indeed satisfied with their existing form of life. Only, they sense the greater possibilities open to a human being and wish to expand it to realize them more completely.

240

It would be too wide-sweeping a generalization to assert that all entrants on the quest come out of disgust with the worldly life. This may be true of Indians, for several reasons, but it is not so true of Westerners. For among the latter there are those whose approach to life is through art—through sensitivity to beauty and joy—or through science—through the pursuit of truth about the universe. Such persons are not unhappy, not alienated from earthly affairs, but they know that a deeper basis to their present satisfaction is needed.

241

It is not only those who have exhausted all their limited means of attaining happiness who turn away and come to this quest: there are others whose capacity for enjoyment still remains, but having had the experience of a single "glimpse" or understood the pointers given by inspired art, they are attracted towards living on a higher plane.

242

But where some turn away from the world for negative reasons because of their misery and disappointment, others come to the quest for positive reasons; they have sensed or suspected, felt, or been told of, a higher plane of existence: they respond to a divine call.

243

He is not sacrificing so much that is dear to the world for the sake of an empty abstraction, nor trampling on inborn egotism for the sake of a cold intellectual conception. He is doing this for something that has become a warm living presence in his life—for the Overself.

244

Deeper than all other desires is this need to gain consciousness of the Overself. Only it is unable to express itself directly at first, so it expresses itself in the only ways we permit it to—first the physical, then the emotional and intellectual quest of happiness.

245

The impulse which puts a man's feet on this path, is not always an explicable one. It is sometimes hard to say why he obeys it, when it will hinder his ego's natural cravings at the very start and lead to an unnatural self-effacement at the very end. All he knows is that something in him bids him begin the journey and keeps him on it despite its hurts to his pride, his passion, and his ego.

246

Disenchanted with celebrities and disillusioned with the world, they will be more inclined to turn in the end towards the divinity within themselves, to trust its first faint leadings on Jesus' assurance that "the Kingdom of Heaven is *within* you!" Such independence is outwardly a lonely path, but with patience it will prove not less satisfying.

247

Why should anyone be willing to put himself aside, his inclinations and desires, unless he is bidden to do so by a power stronger than his own will?

248

Others are attracted to these teachings through an impulse of feeling unsupported by the understanding of reason. It is safe to say that such persons are being led by their souls into this attraction.

249

Those who conceive of this quest as escapism are neither right nor wrong. They are right when it is embarked upon because of a neurotic refusal to do for and to oneself with effort what it is hoped God or guru will be able to do without it. They are wrong when it is embarked upon because of an evaluation of life that is made above its distorting battle or out of a compulsive, involuntary, and inner attraction toward the Ideal.

250

Only when thought and experience have run deep enough and wide enough are the ego's emotional and fleshly hungers likely to yield to spiritual hunger.

251

He can no more help being on the quest than he can help being on this earth. The hunger to know the inner mysteries of life, and the aspiration to experience the Soul's peace and love will not leave him alone. They are part of him, as hands or feet are parts of him.

252

It is natural and inevitable that, when ripened by experience, men should yearn to be united with their divine Source.

253

Through widely different kinds of external experience, the ego seeks but never finds enduring happiness. Discovering in the end that it is on a wrong road, it turns to internal experience.

254

His own higher self will direct the properly equipped seeker's steps towards philosophy. He may go reluctantly, fighting against its ideas secretly or openly for months and years. But in the end he will have to yield to what will become quite plainly a divine leading. His intellect will have to obey this irresistible intuition.

255

If a man is born with innate tendencies for this quest, nothing will keep him from it and he will surely come to it in the course of time. He may come because he is so satisfied with life that he believes in God's goodness. He may come because he is so disappointed in life that he disbelieves in God's goodness. But, by whatever the road, he will come to it because the urge will be irresistible.

256

One must have suffered to the point of being weary of living, or one must be old and infirm, or one must have reflected very honestly and deeply to believe that it is better to be without the predominance of the personal consciousness. And to be willing to work for this end must seem mad to young eager vital men and women enjoying their lives.

257

The time will come when, under the pressure of the mysterious inner self, this quest will become the most important enterprise of his life.

258

Why are they seeking truth? Because they have at last become sensitive enough to respond to the existence of the diviner self within them, the Overself in which only truth exists. The *fact* of its existence has pressed them subconsciously from within and finally provoked them into feeling a need to become aware of, and co-operative with, the Overself.

259

There is an inner prompting which comes into the hearts of some men, not of all men, which bids them believe in the existence of a higher power. Although they do not know clearly what they are doing when they accept it, they feel that it is then, and will lead later to, something tremendously important. The work is going on inside them.

260

The decision to embark on this Quest may ripen for a long time in his unconscious mind before it is openly and slowly made, or it may explode impulsively in a wholly unpremeditated way.

261

He has entered upon the quest for no other reason than that he has been inwardly and strongly commanded to enter it.

262

The long hard search for the soul asks too much endurance of self-discipline from its pursuers ever to be more than it has been in the past—an undertaking for the few driven by an inner urge. Hence it is not so much a voluntary undertaking as an involuntary one. The questers cannot help themselves. It is not that they necessarily have the strength to endure as that they have no choice except to endure.

263

The urge to follow the Quest, the impulse to find the higher consciousness, comes from the Overself.

264

Whatever be the pull of their interests in their lives, a time comes in the reincarnations when the divine self asserts itself in their consciousness.

265

There is something within us which will not let us rest in what we are, which urges us to think of still higher possibilities.

266

This is the paradox that when you take the first step on this Quest, it is grace which impels you to do so. Yet you think and act as if you have never been granted the divine gift.

267

There comes a time when the unfulfilled possibilities of a man begin to haunt him, when his innermost conscience protests against the wastage of this reincarnation.

268

He must come for a while to the position that T.E. Lawrence of Arabia came to when he wrote: "The truth was I did not like the 'myself' I could see and hear."

269

All this work on the Quest is directed towards discovering himself, his best self, and to bringing its influence into whatever it is that he does or thinks. He ought not to enter into it for the sake of ego enhancement—that is for the worldlings—but for the sake of something that transcends the ego.

270

With the coming of middle age a man begins to appraise his life's course, work, fortunes, and in the end—himself. Quite often the results are not very satisfactory, perhaps even disappointing.

271

Too intelligent to accept the narrow short-sighted view of life, too idealistic to accept a merely animal satisfaction of desires, he needs guidance. This is what the quest is for.

272

He feels that he must enter irrevocably on the quest for moral self-perfection, however unattainable it may seem. For he does so in obedience to the inner voice of a conscience the ordinary man does not hear. And his feeling is a right one. The *destination* may be only a glorious dream but the *direction* is a serious actuality.

273

He may come to see the grave contradiction between his ideals and his actions, his mental world and his actual world, and the sight may disgust him. Out of this chagrin, the desire to renounce a senseless existence and withdraw altogether from it may take hold of him.

274

So long as men feel the need of inner support and mental direction, of moral uplift and emotional consolation, so long will they continue to study, to follow, and to practise philosophy—that is, to enter upon the quest.

275

The consciousness of his own imperfection sooner or later awakens in him an urge to seek perfection, that is, to enter on the Quest.

276

When they awaken to truer values, they will desire a truer kind of life. They will want one that brings God into it, and they will view with remorse the past which left God out of it.

277

Only after he has received what he has desired, and come up against its limitations or defects or disadvantages, will spiritual desire begin to take meaning or offer higher value to him.

278

When he is no longer content to be wise and happy and good only for moments but foolish and miserable and weak for periods, he will firmly resolve to begin the process of self-changing and self-deepening that is the Quest.

279

The man's distress over his personal shortcomings and the loathing for his personal weaknesses goad him in the end to do something to improve the one and conquer the other.

280

He sees now at long last that he has acted against his own best interests long enough: the time has come to redress the balance.

281

He feels the call to dedicate himself to higher ideals.

282

Men pass their whole lives in error when they might pass them in truth. They do wrong when they might do good. The result is suffering when it might be peace. When all the chief decisions of a man's life are made in a condition of spiritual ignorance, what other results may be expected than unfortunate ones? It is a bitter moment—and the consciousness of his error falls painfully upon him—when he discovers that the aims he pursued have led him up a blind alley and that the ambitions he nurtured have yielded only ashes for his hands. The parable of the Prodigal Son now assumes an intimate meaning for him. He may derive an astringent wisdom from all these unpleasant consequences of the lower ego's activities. It has indeed been like a blind man tremblingly feeling his way and moving from one mishap to another, making one false step after another.

283

When he sees how the little personal self has brought him so much pain sorrow disappointment and waste of years, that even when it brought him success the latter turned out to be false and deceptive, he will become disgusted with it. He will not want to live with the ego any longer and will yearn to get away from it altogether.

284

Because something deep down in the subconscious knows that the ego is destructible, sooner or later, in one incarnation or another, a longing arises for that which is indestructible. From this moment he begins, however feebly, to cease indulging the desires, the wishes, of his ego, and to replace them by something new and higher. This is the beginning of the Quest, and it may take a religious, a mystical, or a philosophic form, according to man's maturity.

285

They seem to believe their entry into the mystic quest would set their life in order and solve their problems forever. This is, of course, mere wishful thinking. It is not their entry but their completion of the quest that could ever do these things for them.

286

He should guard against being unconsciously insincere, against protesting his love of the divine when it is really a mask for love of himself. "Beware lest you call desire of the world search for God," warned Al Hallaj, a Sufi adept. But more often his quest is inspired by mixed motives. On one hand, he is interested in the personal benefits he hopes to get from it. On the other hand, he is also interested in learning the impersonal truth about life.

287

To the young neophyte the quest, with its mysterious traditions and magical promises, is an enchanting and glamorous enterprise.

288

Men of rank, fortune, influence, or power may become complacent, satisfied with what they are or have or where they are. But this is a condition which cannot last. Why? Because the higher purpose of life, embodied in the World-Idea, is also present and will make appropriate change or exert appropriate pressure at the destined time.

289

There is always a number of enquirers who interest themselves in the teaching to a certain extent and then drop it altogether. Why? Because they are not primarily seeking the Overself for its own sake but only the Overself along with hidden powers or personal success or something else, or sometimes, these things only and the Overself merely as a means of obtaining them.

290

Many come to this quest in the beginning because of some personal desire. This personal satisfaction is their primary goal. It may be that later, with growth, harmony with the Overself becomes not less important. A few in the end will come to see that nothing short of pure devotion to the Overself *for its own sake* is their proper goal.

291

The Quest has different attractions for different people. Some find that it replaces the very ordinariness of their lives by exotic, unusual, even dramatic ideas or experiences. Some draw near because of its promise of help sorely needed to cover up their weaknesses. Others need its intellectual concepts to support their withdrawal from orthodoxy. Still others are delighted to get its help in the reinterpretation of orthodoxy, and in its reasonable replies to reasonable questions.

292

If the philosophical code attracts some by its moral nobility, it attracts others through their personal necessity.

293

It should not be thought that all those who read some literature, or attend such lectures, or even join such movements, are seeking more than a simple glimpse. Perhaps most are ordinary people who are satisfied with having a credo to support their lives which enlarges their traditional religion or belief.

294

All sorts of people come to this quest—the truthseekers, the halluci-nated, the ambitious and the meek, the highly intuitive and the utter imbecile, the joyous and the embittered failures, the really intelligent and the merely curious—but few stay on it. Most are caught soon or late on the detours, the sidetracks, and the return-tracks.

295

If many come to this Quest because they are discontented with living or even despairing of it, some come because they feel the joy of living or even exalt in it. There are a few, however, who come because they seek truth or reality.

296

There are those today as never before whose deep but unconscious spiritual loneliness remains unsatisfied by religions.

297

If some come to this quest because of disgust with the world and its ways, or of disappointment with life and its experiences, others come to it because of disgust, disappointment, or dissatisfaction with themselves. Only a few come because of the hunger for truth for its own sake, or because of the sense of incompleteness of a merely materialistic existence.

298

The reasons which men give for coming to this quest are widely dif-ferent. If suffering brings many, joy brings others. If a kind of ambition brings not a few, satiety with ambition brings a few.

299

Men come to this quest simply because they seek truth, because they want to learn what their life means and what the universe means and the relation of both, which is the best of all reasons. But others come because of shaken self-respect or after a bereavement which leaves them without a dearly loved one. Still others come in reaction to disillusionment, frustra-tion, or calamity. And lastly there are those who come out of utter fatigue with the senseless world and disgust with its evil ways, which is the second best of all reasons.

300

Human lacks, human sufferings, and human failures drive most of the people who come to it, to the quest as compensation. But there are a few whose human circumstances are satisfactory, yet who come to the quest also. They are the seekers after truth, the explorers trying to find a higher consciousness. Both classes are welcome, of course. But the second class exemplify the quest at its best.

301

We may come to this change of view by strict philosophical reflection alone, which is the easiest and pleasantest path, but which demands certain intellectual and moral capacities, or we may come to it by the path of bitter pain and external compulsion.

302

Some people seem hungry for Truth. This is because society has starved them and given them no satisfaction other than a surface one.

303

Some people are slowly brought to the quest by the inescapable conclusions of reason, others are brought into it more quickly by the natural guidance of instinct.

304

For some people the Quest begins with a feeling that something is missing from their life, a need that none of their possessions or relations can satisfy.

305

Sometimes—do you lie awake at night? Thinking about "what you might have been"? Watching the procession of your past life move like a cinema film before your eyes? Reading anew the whole tale of time born and dead, a few joys, many tears perhaps, and long barren years of drought? Waiting for something bigger, better, brighter to turn up? But it has not come yet. The road is hard and the field you are tilling is sterile.

306

Among those who come to the quest for reasons other than the search for truth, which usually means for emotional reasons, there are those who come to it at the end of a period of mental depression and those who come at the beginning of a period of mental elation. The first kind may be unhappy because of past personal experiences and seek comfort, consolation. The second kind is prone to exaggerated hopes because of a somewhat neurotic enthusiastic temperament. The one may find its peace and the other its joy but both may overlook the need for determined work and self-discipline as the cost.

307

Few people come to this quest by choice; most come by necessity. Its invitation, addressed to a reluctant world, is heard and considered only when under great pressure and suffering, or after great moral or mental or aesthetic growth.

308

Some propulsive force from within or some compulsive condition from without must come into existence to make him undergo the self-discipline needed to open him to the divine influx.

309

With this event a new era opens in his personal life. He feels that, for the first time in his life, he has touched real being when hitherto he has known only its shadow. It is the first link in a whole chain of good consequences. Consequently it is in reality the most important one. Whoever once gives his allegiance to the Overself as affirmed and symbolized by his entry on the quest, undertakes a commitment of whose ultimate and tremendous consequences he has but a vague and partial notion.

310

When the Overself sounds the mystic note, its echo is heard within the man and he awakens from spiritual stupor.

311

A time comes when we see at last that all the mind has gathered from its schooling is information, when what it needs and hungers for even more deeply is revelation. The faintest clue or hint from a higher source would be enough; how much more the fullness of a glimpse.

312

A correspondent in America wrote: "I awoke in the middle of the night to discover the room filled with bright light. I could see all the furniture. A marvellous peace pervaded me. I said to myself, 'God is that You?' and instinctively, I knew that it was. After a while I got up when the experience was fading to check its extraordinary nature and confirmed that none of the electric lamps were switched on. Since then thirteen years have passed. I have a loving husband and loving children, enough money for the basic things of life. But for some time life was not meaningful and I felt empty. I looked at my friends, so willing to accept this hollow life, but I could not. It became intolerable. Five years ago I was shown the spiritual quest of truth and this has since become my mainstay." Was there a connection between the vision of Light and the subsequent restlessness until she turned to the quest? That there is such a line, is confirmed by many other instances scattered around the world.

313

Every man who catches such a glimpse of his diviner possibilities will be haunted forever after by them until he tries to catch up in actual thought and life with them. The endeavour to do so brings him sooner or later on the Quest.

314

In that moment of first meeting with his Higher Self the quest is laid open to him in reality. He has to see the opportunity and to take the first step by an act of intuition and a venture of faith. There will be many more succeeding steps if he is to continue the quest and most probably a number of missteps, but it all begins with this initial recognition and reaction.

315

He who meets for the first time the challenge in an adept's eyes, meets his fate, did he but know it. For he is at once presented subconsciously with a choice between two courses: the one leading to a higher kind of life and aim, the other continuing on normal lines.

316

When the truth explodes suddenly like a blast of dynamite beneath the traditions or beliefs or habits which held him captive in untruth, the light may dazzle and bewilder him or it may set him free from them in a way and with a speed which could not have existed ordinarily.

317

It is this faith that there is a World-Idea and that we must adjust our lives to it or suffer unnecessarily which marks him out from the herd.

318

It is the desire to do for himself what Life wishes him to do, to realize his higher potentials, that puts him on this Quest.

319

It is this feeling that he is not in his true place that pushes a man into this search for a teaching or a teacher.

320

Men whose lives have been so endangered and whose minds so troubled will either turn for relief to gross sensuality or search for wholeness in new spirituality.

321

The sickness of the world wants something much more than a mere philosophy of the lecture-room to cure it; no bottles of verbal drugs can prove potent in the present desperation.

322

Not all men understand just at what time, what date, their quest of the Overself was started. This may be because it did not happen all at once.

323
There are others, however, who are not satisfied with such ignorance and such indifference, who want certain and assured knowledge of the spirit, by penetrating the secrets of their own being. And it is the promise of the satisfaction of this want which attracts them to mysticism.

324
It is a tradition in mystical circles that anyone who has ever felt the truth power or beauty of mystical teaching, however briefly, will not be able to escape being drawn to its practical consequence, the Quest, one day, however long deferred it may be.

325
A mind which is no longer satisfied with shallow consolations will naturally turn to mystical experience or metaphysical study for deeper ones.

326
All that has happened before his entry upon the quest has really been converging towards it.

327
It is as inevitable that some men should come to the Quest because of their sorrows and difficulties as that other men should abandon it temporarily for the same reasons.

328
Mysticism offers the surest path to the mind's peace and the heart's satisfaction.

Why many people don't come

329
Reading about these truths has a revelatory effect upon certain minds but only a boring or irritating effect upon others. Why? It is because the first have been brought by experience or reflection to a sufficiently sensitive and intuitive condition to appreciate the worth of what they are reading, whereas the second, comprising for the most part an extroverted public, will naturally be impatient with such mystical ideas and contemptuous of their heretical expounder. Indeed, some of these writings must seem as incomprehensible to a Western ear as the babblings of a man just awakening from the chloroformed state.

330
The masses would show no interest for they possess insufficient mental equipment to understand it.

331

How can large principles find a resting place in such little persons?

332

The incomprehension of the undeveloped minds and unrefined hearts puts up a barrier between them and philosophy. To ignore it is first to bewilder and then to frustrate them.

333

It is not fair to ask them to accept and believe in teachings which seem to be contradicted by all their experience and by all the experience of the society around them. How can we demand that they violate their own thinking and their own feeling by doing so?

334

They are not necessarily more materialistic. It is simply that they have not begun to think about life, to question its meaning and ask for its purpose.

335

The call to a higher kind of life may sound absurd to the lower kind of mind.

336

It is often said in criticism that its doctrines are unreasonable and its techniques impracticable.

337

It is a subject which the arrogant intellectuals of our time, being unable to cope with it, find irritating or bewildering.

338

The seeming failure to get these truths accepted more widely, still more to get them practised, is no failure at all. Men are what they are as a result of what they were in the past.

339

It is easier for most persons to lay down their distressing burdens at the door of faith in formal religion than turn to the quest which explains the very presence of these burdens and prescribes the technique to remove them.

340

Too many people who are ordinarily supposed to be good people with some religious side to their character, hide behind their duties and responsibilities to avoid the Quest. They find in these two things sufficient excuse to disregard the larger questions of life. They keep themselves busy supporting themselves and their family or keeping up a position in the world of activity, following an occupation, or maintaining a business. In this way they are able to ignore any self-questioning about why they are here on earth at all or what will happen to them after death or whether these practical duties and responsibilities are all that is required from them by the god they profess to believe in.

341

"All the world complains nowadays of a press of trivial duties and engagements which prevents their employing themselves on some higher ground they know of; but undoubtedly, if they were made of the right stuff to work on that higher ground, they would now at once fulfil the superior engagement and neglect all the rest, as naturally as they breathe. They would never be caught saying that they had no time for this when the dullest man knows that this is all that he has time for."—Thoreau, in a letter.

342

There are now so many activities calling for his interest and energies that modern man thinks he has no time to devote to finding his soul. So he does not seek it: and so he remains unhappy.

343

The discomfort of being confronted by the fundamental questions which we must at some time, early or late, ask of life can be evaded—as all-too-many persons do evade it—by deliberately turning to more activity, or by reinforced egoism.

344

Some reject the whole system for such reasons as "I do not want to become a saint," or "I have to earn my livelihood." This is an unwise attitude.

345

Their minds are mostly occupied by personal matters, both petty and large, leaving little or no space in them for thoughts about life in general. How then can there be interest in the quest?

346

They dismiss the teaching in a few seconds under the erroneous belief that its expounder is just another cultist. It is easy to fall into such a gross misconception since they know nothing about it, or about the ancient tradition behind it.

347

The fact is that, in the ordinary consciousness, many people are not interested in the question of truth, nor in the discovery of what seems without personal benefits of a worldly kind; they are certainly not willing to practise various controls of thought, emotion, speech, and passion.

348

The yogic quest of *samadhi* (cessation of thinking leading to object-free awareness) like the Zen quest of *satori* (enlightenment) has suffered miscomprehension in its own land by its own people, much more therefore in the West by those unfamiliar with or unable to cope with Oriental intuitive perceptions.

349

The assumption that these truths are fit to be studied and the Quest to be followed only by a few elderly, gullible, or eccentric persons is wrong.

350

For too many Western minds the terms "mystic" and "yoga" have either unpleasant or derisive connotations attached to them. Too many quacks, incompetents, fanatics, charlatans, fools, or lunatics have brought reproach and opprobrium on them. Only a small handful of persons employ them deliberately to express the lofty, the admirable, and the honourable meanings.

351

Few are willing to undergo the philosophical discipline because few are willing to disturb their personal comfort or disrupt their personal ease for the sake of a visionary ideal. The eagerness to improve oneself, the willingness to cultivate noble qualities are uncommon.

352

If some joyfully recognize the truth as soon as they meet with it, others shudderingly turn away from it.

353

The materialistically minded persons are too sceptical to take up this training and re-education of the mind; the self-indulgent ones are too lazily unwilling to disturb their comfort with it and come out of the groove in which they have sunk; while the egoistic are too uninterested in merely long-range, far-off, and intangible benefits to see any value in it.

354

Many people, especially in the working and the petty bourgeois classes, find their felicity at the beer table or the television, in idle chatter or in the particular successes of ambition. The notion that anyone could find it by means of nothing that can be measured in materialistic terms would seem foolish to them, while the Quest of the Overself would seem the highest point of all foolishness.

355

They accept the futility of materialism because they have never known the vitality of transcendentalism.

356

This is not the atmosphere in which those minds which are satisfied with the shackles of dogma or the pretensions of mere opinion can thrive: hence a few glances at philosophy are often enough to keep them away.

357

Most men devalue themselves, although they do not know it. A part of them is divine, but it is ignored and neglected.

358

The first trouble with us today is that we have not enough faith in the higher power; the second is that we have become too soft and will not submit our lives to the higher purpose.

359

Amusements, sports, gossip, theatres, even sex protect the thoughtless masses from having to confront the higher challenges of life, from having to let into their minds basic questions. It allows them to escape all through the length of their incarnation from the one thing they were put here on earth to face. In short, they hide from the Quest.

360

It would be too much to expect the mass of people to take to this quest in its fullness. They are unable to make more than an elementary effort to confine the lower nature within the required limits.

361

"Philosophy is of no use to me!" exclaimed a businessman. If knowing more about himself as a human being and living better than would be likely otherwise are of no use to him, then he is right.

362

Most people are like sleep-walkers, caught up in their own illusions. Their belief that they are awake is the biggest of these illusions.

363

The poor are overpowered by their grinding poverty, the rich by their fortune; both find neither the time nor taste for spiritual enquiry.

364

Easily stupefied by sensuality, thoroughly bewitched by constant repetition of the same pleasure, they shrug aside the disturbing thoughts and visible reminders of life's transitoriness and the body's infirmity.

365

After the work done to gain livelihood or fulfil ambition, there is usually a surplus of time and strength, a part of which could and should be devoted to satisfying higher needs. There is hardly a man whose life is so intense that it does not leave him a little time for spiritual recall from this worldly existence. Yet the common attitude everywhere is to look no farther than, and be content with, work and pleasure, family, friends, and possessions. It feels no urge to seek the spiritual and, as it erroneously thinks, the intangible side of life. It makes no effort to organize its day so as to find the time and energy for serious thought, study, prayer, and meditation. It feels no need of searching for truth or getting an instructor.(P)

366

People who find their own company boring, their own resources empty, their own higher aims non-existent, must needs flee from it to some form of escape, such as the cinema, the radio, the theatre, or television. Here they are not confronted by the uncomfortable problem of themselves, by an aimless meaningless drifting "I."

367

Humanity ordinarily shirks this enquiry into truth partly because of its difficulty, partly because of its apparent personal unprofitability, and partly because of its loneliness.

368

There are those—and they are many—who do not want such a quest: its disciplines frighten them away or its studies bore them or its isolation makes too daring a demand on their gregariousness.

369

It is easy to understand why so many persons have little faith in such teachings, but it is hard to understand why so few persons take the trouble to investigate them.

370

Most people are too shallow—for which they are not to be blamed, since living itself is a fatiguing job—to be able to mine successfully for Reality, or for Truth, which is the knowledge of Reality.

371

It is hard for the moderns to appreciate the Buddha's declarative sentences about the illusory goals of desire, hard to see that their years, when measured against Jesus' teaching, are often spent in futile activities, hard to understand with the mystics that they merely exist and do not really live.

372

They bow too quickly before the mystery of life and being, resign further search and enquiry, make no more effort to develop and use their mental and intuitive faculties. Faith and patience are deserted too soon.

373

Quite a number seek understanding of life's meaning, but few seek a *true* understanding. Most want a partisan or prejudiced one, an endorsement of inherited ideas or personal satisfactions.

374

Too many are married for life to their personal views: they are not seekers after Truth and are not really willing to learn the New and the True.

375

It is a wrong and yet common notion to believe that one is not in a position to start out on the Quest. The businessman pleads his business cares, the sinner his sins, the old man his age, and the young man his youth as excuse for failing to make any beginning at all.

376

Only seldom during a lifetime, and that very briefly, will men give a thought to these larger features of their existence—to its unreality, to its changeability, and to its mortality.

377

Few women succeed in making the self-disciplinary grade which the quest of philosophy calls for. This is because they are more easily distracted from the quest by their personal feelings than men are.

378

Men who live unaware of why they are here consequently live unconcerned with what seem like mere abstractions lacking any utility at all.

379

They could not face truth for they would be embarrassed by the Goddess's unshrinking gaze.

380

Too many persons will have nothing to do with the Quest when they learn about it for the first time. This is not because they find it impossible to believe some of the ideas on which it is based, such as the idea of reincarnation ("I find it incredible" was Somerset Maugham's comment about it). Nor is it because the metaphysical side is too abstruse for them to go through the needed labour of troubling their minds with it. No—it is because the ideal set up for the questers is, they claim, completely outside their horizon and quite unreachable by most, if not nearly all of them.

381

Its peak seems so austere, the climb up it so demanding of all the bravery that a man could ever possess, that few even venture to approach it.

382
They hear of saints and yogis who seem to achieve the impossible—a happiness which eludes their fellow denizens of this planet and a self-control which puts human desire and passion easily underfoot. What these spiritual supermen can do, in temptation-free Himalayan heights or European monastic retreats, they see no prospect of ever doing in their noisy busy cities.

383
It is not possible, they think, to live on such a high godlike plane in a world where meanness and violence are everyday patterns. This is a plausible view but it is not the only one.

384
It is impossible only if they think so. No victory can ever be won when it is already lost in the mind.

385
There are those who feel that the Quest is an enterprise which is more than they can undertake. Very well. The simple acknowledgement of this apparent fact is itself a beginning. But it is not an end.

386
His values depend upon the five bodily senses which is acceptable, and upon them alone, which is not.

387
For most people it is an ideal which seems so distant that to talk of attaining it is to mock them.

388
Those persons who are satisfied with substitutes for Truth could not appreciate or recognize it even if it were offered them. In short, they are not ready for the real thing.

389
Those who seek neither moral elevation nor spiritual teaching do not thereby show their indifference to thought about life. They show only that they are smugly satisfied with the little thought they have managed to do.

390
Those who are content with a life of nothing more than sitting down to meals, going out to make money, and coming back to make love—that is, with a solely materialistic life—find nothing in such inspired messages and get nothing from such mystical teachings.

391
There is no large idea in their petty lives.

392

It will not engage the interest of the spiritually indolent.

393

So long as we keep ourselves focused wholly in the physical world, thoughts such as these may be read but will not reach our minds.

394

The man who sees no need for a higher concept of his nature than the merely physical one will see no need for a higher goal than feeding, clothing, sheltering, and amusing his body. In letting the senses, the passions, the intellect, and the ego take sole charge of his life, he quite naturally sees only mere emptiness beyond them. He doubts and refutes the intuitive-spiritual and denies and rejects the mystical. The Infinite is nothing to him so long as he prefers to remain shut in within the sense-bound outlook. This is why he dismisses mystic experience, religious feeling, and philosophic insight as mere hallucinations. But all this opposition takes place only in his conscious mind for there is unavoidable recognition in his subconscious mind. He wants to escape from himself, however, and fears the ordeal of facing himself. These words will make no appeal to the materialistic mentality which still regards all spiritual experience as the outcome of pathological conditions. Such an attitude, fortunately, has become less sure of itself than it was when first I embarked on these studies and experiments, now more than thirty-five years ago.

395

People neglect the Real because they believe they already have it (in sense-experience of the world outside) and for the same reason they do not seek truth.

396

The unfortunate who have been unable to manage their affairs or to recover from the blows of destiny may turn to religion for comfort: they seldom turn to philosophy. For this fails to comfort their emotions: its appeal is only to those who are learning that emotions need to be checked or balanced or controlled by reason.

397

The mass of people do not want, and may even fear, the spiritual and intellectual freedom to search for truth. They are more comfortable inside the gregarious protection of a ready-made group tradition.

398

It is not only that so many people are not capable of comprehending the truth but also that a large number of them do not want to comprehend it. The truth hurts their ego, contradicts their desires, and denies their expectations.

399

Most people are contented with their chains or even strongly attached to them—such is the awesome power of desires, passions, infatuations, and especially egoisms.

400

They fear the quest because they fear that, if they get involved in it too seriously, they might have to repress some inclination in their nature or renounce some habit in their way of living. So they take from it only what appeals to them, and discard the rest.

401

The freezing temperature of those snowy peaks of thought frightens away some who might otherwise venture on the Quest. It is the ego which is so frightened, knowing that its own end would come with the end of the journey into this elevated region.

402

A man may stay at his present level or try to rise in character to a better one than he was born with. If ideals and values do not stir him, if he is ruled by undisciplined animal appetites, these truths will not appeal to him.

403

Even if a man is qualified to receive truth he may not be in the mood to do so, that is, he is not ready and willing to meet the cost. His interests or his desires or his emotions at that particular time lie elsewhere.

404

When they learn the price—disciplining and reducing the fattened ego—that will have to be paid for this higher consciousness, they are more hesitant to embark on the Quest.

405

Men who are uninterested in affairs other than their own personal ones, in matters other than their own work and pleasure, position and fortune, men who are preoccupied with the trivial round of external, selfish activities only, will naturally regard the study of philosophy as a waste of time, the practice of meditation as a form of indolence, and the endeavour after self-improvement as a needless trouble. No higher yearnings enter their hearts, no reverent feelings touch them.

406

Because of their unwillingness either to look within or to think more deeply for any higher purpose or obligation that they might have, people live largely in delusion and deception, especially self-deception. "Why am I here on earth?" is a question for which they can only find one answer: to satisfy their own material desires.

407

Not everyone is prepared by temperament, or past history, to seek the higher truth, much less has the time and will for it. Not everyone among the seekers is ready to make the sacrifices that a conscientious re-adjustment of character and behaviour wants from him.

408

I believe in a higher power behind the universe. Call it God, if you like. I believe in a higher power behind man. Call it the soul, if you like to. Such beliefs do not appeal to the cocktail-soaked cynics and sophisticates of our era.

409

Such teachings are ignored or rejected as being of interest only to dreamers, idlers, or misfits. There is some truth in this criticism, some basis for this attitude. Plain normal people who have to make a living, who are busy with the world's work, politics, and economics, who have personal and family problems most of the time, find all this to be unrealistic, out of touch with things as they are, humanity as it is and has been.

410

So long as the objects of their existence remain small and circumscribed, selfish and materialistic, so long will the meaning of their existence be denied them.

411

It is not that they are contemptuous of truth but that they are indifferent to it.

412

The opinions of most people about mysticism are either totally or partially worthless. This is because they are not informed either by accurate or by sufficient knowledge of the subject. They know next to nothing of its true history, nature, and results.

413

Lack of concern for higher values reveals men's frailty or malice.

414

To the diseased mentality, mysticism is an attempt to cripple progress by weakening intellect and inhibiting needed action.

415

The word "mystic" is not the perfect one to convey my meaning, but it is at least the handiest one. It has been so ill-used that spouters of errant nonsense have taken shelter under its roof whilst oracles of the loftiest wisdom have not hesitated to call themselves by this name. The partisan approach to this name has caused it to become either an abusive or else an adulatory word rather than a precise description. Whereas some use it in contempt, others use it in praise! Again, how many are scared by its very sound! There are even persons who feel a shiver run down their back when they hear the word "mysticism" uttered!

Postponing the choice

416
It has been stated at the end of the appendix to *The Hidden Teaching Beyond Yoga* that they who do not feel in possession of enough strength or desire to tread the ultimate path need not do so, and that if they remember and sometimes read about it even this will yield good fruit in time. We have been asked to be more explicit on this point. We deeply sympathize with all those who do not feel inclined to tackle the mental austerities involved in the ultimate path. If, however, they will just dip into its intellectual study from time to time, a little here this week and a little there the next, without even making their reading continuous and connected, there will slowly take shape in their minds an outline of some of the main tenets of this teaching. And however vague this outline may be it will be immeasurably better than the blank ignorance which covers the rest of mankind like a shroud. These new ideas will assume the characteristics of seeds, which under the water of the student's own aspiration and the sunshine of visible and invisible forces, will grow gradually into fruitful understanding and deeds. For the karmic consequence of such interest will be one day birth into a family where every opportunity for advancement will be found.

417
The yearning for spiritual light wells up in the heart spontaneously. It is a natural one. But desires, egoism, and materialism cover it for so long a time that it seems unnatural.

418
At least it has aroused them to awareness that there is such a thing: they have later the chance to think about it, still later to try it, and perhaps in the end to appreciate it.

419
The ideal may appeal, coming as it does from the Overself, but the ego will put up obstacles, resistances, to its realization.

420
The images of the Ideal formed in the early years of adulthood may get broken or smudged or even lost.

421

The clamour from outside—by which I do not mean heard noises alone—is so insistent that the summons from inside is seldom heard or, if heard at all, is taken to be a summons to culture, art, poetry, and music perhaps or to intellect and its development.

422

This dream of eventual illumination will haunt the background of his mind as a hope to be fulfilled in some far-off future life. He is too aware of his own weakness to bring it into the foreground.

423

How many men think and say that when their material fortunes improve, or their family problems are solved, or their living place is changed they will be able to give time and effort to the spiritual quest, but until then they must wait! But in actual fact this seldom happens. For when the improvement, solution, or change does take place, new matters call for their attention or new attachments are formed for the ego, and so the spiritual effort gets postponed again.

424

Those who believe that it is better to wait for more propitious circumstances before they begin the Quest, deceive themselves into an unavailing and lugubrious pessimism. Neither tomorrow nor the next year will be any better.

425

Procrastination may be perilous. Later may be too late. Beware of being drawn into that vast cemetery wherein men bury their half-born aspirations and paralysed hopes.(P)

426

It often happens that aspirants put off the sacrifice of time which prayer and meditation call for because, they complain, they are too busy with this or that. Thus they never make any start at all and the years slip uselessly by. In most cases this involves no penalty other than the spiritual stagnation to which it leads, but in some cases where a higher destiny has been reserved for the individual or where a mission has to be accomplished, the result is far different. Everything and everyone that such a person uses as an excuse for keeping away from the practice of meditation, the exercise of devotion, and the communion of prayer may be removed from his external life by the higher self. Thus, through loss and suffering, he will be forced to obey the inward call.

427

Human beings are given more than one chance to redeem themselves. Such is the mercy of the higher power.

428

Time-backed and earth-bound as he is, it is not surprising that he often tries to evade the Quest, to ignore it in various ways such as always keeping busy trying to fulfil increasing ambition, cultivating scepticism disguised as "practicality," or demanding instant and demonstrable proofs. But most often he deflects the thoughts of it or changes the conversation abruptly. The very idea makes him nervous if pursued by himself or others. He is uneasy at the thought of higher laws to be obeyed. He is fearful of what he will be asked to do and of the discipline to be practised.

429

It is sadly human to want to digress from the straight path of the Quest at times. This happens to many and a proportion of them yields to the desire. Invariably, however, the passing years bring them back to either the leaving point or even the starting point. Experience always points up the lesson that the initial urge faith conviction or reasoning which put them on the path was a wise and necessary one. The picture of life grows a little clearer to them when they learn at first hand with sorrow, loss, or frustration what the teachers offered free without such unpleasant consequences.

430

If a man is born with spiritual capacity but refuses to use it, and even deliberately shuts it away, a day will come when it will thrust itself up into his conscious self for acceptance and use. If he continues to deny it, the capacity will then operate against him, until his sanity becomes questionable or his fortunes become adverse.

431

No man can afford to fail to heed the summons to the Quest. If he does, it is at his own peril and he will then fail in everything else, for this is an imperative call coming from the highest part of his being.

432

Those who have been personally confronted by an illuminated man with the Quest of the Overself and reject it to continue their quest of the ego instead, are destined to suffer.

433

The warning which *Light on the Path* gives to disciples, "But if thou look not for him, if thou pass him by, then there is no safeguard for thee. Thy brain will reel, thy heart grow uncertain, and in the dust of the battlefield thy sight and senses will fail, and thou wilt not know thy friends from thy enemies"—this warning is apposite here and should be taken deeply to heart.

434

Necessity will with time force this comprehension on them. Prophets and teachers will disclose this truth to them but if they do not listen then hard experience must disclose it.

435

How long can a man withstand this silent call of the god within him? — as long as his hopes and desires can find some measure of satisfaction, as long as frustration does not crush them, or until destiny itself overrides his indifference and compels him to heed it.

436

The "Call of the Quest" once heard may be lost for a while, even a long while, but it will return.

437

The need of truth is an irrepressible one but it may take a long time to come through in all its force and clarity.

438

He is left free to save or destroy himself, to accept the truth or turn his face away from it.

In what sense is there a choice?

439

The longer I live and the more I observe in the lives of others, the more numerous become the illustrations of higher laws—the factuality of karma and the universality of the Quest. This is only as it should be for both are parts of the World-Idea. Thought and action are reflected back by karma. All people in all lands are seeking nostalgically for their homeland—the multitude unconsciously, the few consciously—this is their Quest.

440

Let no one make the mistake of separating out the quest from everyday life. It is Life itself! Questers are not a special group, a labelled species, which one does or does not join, but are all humanity.

441

This is not merely a matter for a small elite interested in spiritual self-help. It is a serious truth important to every man everywhere.(P)

442

The inability to measure up to these ideals does not carry a stigma. All men at this level come to earth with their imperfections.

443

All men seek for truth either consciously and deliberately or unconsciously and blindly, but they can seek only according to their capacity and ability, circumstances and preparedness.

444

It is not a question whether questers are happier than non-questers—for that is an individual personal matter: the division itself is an artificial one. The ascent to Consciousness is for all men, not for a few only.

445

Mankind is so near to God and yet so far away from God! Every fresh day is a fresh call from the Overself to man.

446

Hidden away in every man there exists a being immeasurably superior to the ordinary person that he is.

447

It is there in all, whether it be latent or patent, this impulse in each man to improve and better himself into a person of worth. Ultimately it develops, in this body or a later one, into the aspiration to transcend himself.

448

The divine soul dwells in every man. Therefore, every man may find it, if only he will apply the faculties he possesses.

449

Each man must someday take to this quest. This is as certain as the sun's rising, for is it not said on high authority that we can not live by bread alone?

450

The work of opening up to his inner being, and to its best, not worst, side is both the duty and the destiny of every man. He may evade the first and retain the second for a time but cannot do so for all time.

451

What the quester does of his own free choice today, the generality of men will be obliged to do tomorrow.

452

The hour of awakening must come to every man, even if it has to come at the hour of death; and when it does it will be with utter amazement and stupefaction at best, or else with all the force of an explosive shock. For he is a member of the human species, not of the animal one, and shares its destiny.

453

The Quest cannot be evaded: in the end all must come to it; otherwise they will be pulled or pushed along it however unwilling or reluctant they may be.

454

More and more people are moving, albeit at a slow pace and with suspicious minds, into mystical teaching—but they *are* moving.

455

Nature is trying to teach them to equilibrate themselves. The sooner they learn this lesson, the better for their happiness and success.

456

The multitudes who people our planet will eventually travel the same course that the philosophic aspirant now travels. But they will do it slowly through the lapse of numerous centuries; they will move lightly, imperceptibly, and without the intense pressure he puts upon himself.

457

Man is made in God's image in the sense that he latently possesses certain godlike qualities. But these have to be developed by evolution, which can be slow, through the path of normal experience, or swift, through the Quest.

458

All people are trying to find their Overself, to feel its love and sense its peace. Those who are in flight from worldly things do so consciously; those who are in pursuit of them do so unconsciously.

459

Life compels no one to enter upon this conscious Quest, although it is leading everyone upon the unconscious Quest. Even among the students of this teaching, not all are following the Quest, many are merely seeking for an intellectual understanding; their interest has been attracted and their curiosity aroused, but they have not felt called upon to go any farther. This may be due to inner weakness or to outer difficulties or both. Such men and women do not have to pledge themselves to any moral tasks or mystical exercises. Nevertheless, their studies and reflections upon the teaching will not be without a certain value and will place them on an altogether different level from the unawakened herd which is bereft of such an interest.

460

Shall we say that *all* humans are travelling on this quest of the Overself but most humans do so unconsciously and unwillingly? For then the person technically called a "quester" simply differs from other persons by his awareness of the journey, the demands it makes upon him, and his willingness to co-operate in satisfying those demands.

461

Man unconsciously seeks his freedom and enlightenment, as he consciously seeks his welfare and happiness.

462

It is because God is hidden in all creatures that all creatures are searching all the time for God. This remains just as true even though in their ignorance they usually mistake the object of their search and believe that it is something else. Only on the quest does this search attain self-consciousness.

463

The uninformed man is blind to the work of spiritual evolution which goes on within him and consequently thwarts and obstructs it unwittingly. The informed man sees the work and co-operates with it consciously.

464

How sad, how foolish that so many people turn their heads away in indifference, in apathy, and in inertia when they hear of these truths concerning the inward life and the universal laws! They believe that, even if there were any truth in them, these ideas are only for a handful of dreamers, for an esoteric cult with nothing better to do with its time and thought than to entertain them. There does not seem to be any point of contact between these ideas and their own lives, no applicability to their personal selves, and hence, no importance in them at all. How gross this error, how great this blindness! The mystic's knowledge is full of significance for every other man. The mystic's discoveries are full of value for him.

465

Man's hope of a happier existence and need of a faith in universal meaning has led him to try so many wrong turnings which brought him only farther from them, that it is understandable why cynicism or indifferentism should claim so many votaries. But this is not yet the end result. The few who today have found both hope and need adequately satisfied are presages of what must happen to the others.

466

Even those men who do not believe in the Overself are unknowingly seeking to find it or waiting for it.

467

Every man has within him this divine possibility. But if he refuses to believe it, or puts his faith in a hard materialism, or fails to seek for it, it will remain only latent.

468

It is the thought of attaining happiness in some way which induces men to commit most crimes, just as it is the thought of attaining truth which induces them to hold the most materialistic beliefs. Although they see both happiness and truth from a wrong angle and so are given this deceptive result, still the essential motivation of their lives is the same as that of the questers. The segregation in thought of a spiritual elite as being the only seekers is valid only for a practical view, not for an ultimate one.

469

Like blind men they seek the unseen. Like mystics they want the unknown centre of their being, but the conscious mind does not yet share in this desire. Everything else they try must in the end fail them, since life itself fails them at death.

470

Those who do not choose to tread the path of mysticism need not therefore tread the path of misunderstanding it.

471

This wisdom is latent in the bad as well as the good man. Any moral condition will suffice as a starting point. Jesus spoke to sinners as freely as to those of better character. His words were not wasted as the sequence showed. Krishna promised salvation even to those who had committed great crimes.

472

Was it for the sake of a small withdrawn spiritual elite that Jesus walked in Galilee, that Buddha wandered afoot across India, that Socrates frequented the Agora in Athens?

473

There is hope for all, benediction for the poor and the rich, the good and the bad, for every man may come into this great light. But—some men may come more easily, more quickly, while others may drag their way.

474

Those who feel no call to develop themselves spiritually, no obligation to follow the quest, are nevertheless unwittingly doing both. Only, they are doing so at so slow and imperceptible a pace that they do not recognize the activity and the movement.

475

All the experiences of life are in the end intended to induce us to seek wholeheartedly for the Overself. That is, to lead us to the very portal of the Quest.

476

In a fairly wide experience, we have found that most people who are interested in this subject are still very far from having achieved the mystical goal, and that not one in a hundred has been successful in travelling the mystical path to its end. Of the many who have started on this quest in modern times, few have reached the goal, most have gone astray. Of those who have stood on the temple's threshold, only a very small fraction were able to make their way inside. This is a significant fact that requires explanation.

477

Few people have either the interest or the wisdom to carry these thoughts through persistently to the true conclusions.

478

Men who live enclosed within their own little egos naturally feel no call either to pursue truth or to practise service. And such are the majority. Therefore, it is said that philosophy's quest is only for the few.

479

Not all men are disposed to look for truth, rather only a minority.

480

Prophets and teachers, sages and saints have come among us in all times to speak of that inner life and inner reality which they have found. But only those who cared to listen have profited by these revelations, communications, and counsels, and still fewer have profited by being willing to follow the path of discipleship.

481

Because the Higher Power is present in the whole world, it is present in everyone too. Because few seek the awareness of It, fewer still find it.

482

Those who are seeking personal help are immeasurably more numerous than those who are seeking the impersonal Truth.

483

Those who seek philosophic achievement are today, as always, necessarily few since it belittles the ego and incites aspirants to overcome or crush it.

484

Those who are willing, or who are able, to put themselves under the quest's discipline are few. The unwilling find it irksome, the unable impossible. Those only who come to it with a passionate devotion and an eagerness to advance, can muster up enough power to submit to the discipline and practise it. But they are a small group: the others are a large one.

485

Most men are happy enough with the flesh, satisfied enough to live in the body alone or the body and intellect together. Few want the Overself; most are not even ready for it and would be blinded by its light.

486

Not many are willing to submit themselves to the performance of exercises, for most modern people and almost all city people feel they have enough to do already.

487

Although salvation is open to all, it is not free to all. The price must be paid. Few are willing to pay it. Therefore few actually claim salvation, let alone receive it.

488

The Biblical saying, "Many are called . . ." does not refer to the general scheme of evolution, but only to the few who seek to quicken it by taking to the Quest. And few of these succeed in achieving quick realization although many attempt to do so. This is because the path is subtler, harder, and more hidden than other paths; because the adverse elements bestir themselves to mislead aspirants and take them off on sidetracks where they eventually get lost; and because it is next to impossible to find correct guidance, since many are directed to the wrong teachers by emotion, desire, egoism, and wrong preconceptions. The way for humanity is long and dark, but the few who want to shorten it may do so.

489

Only one man here and there among thousands takes to philosophy. Yet in some ways the world is better prepared to understand it now than in earlier times.

490

Few people breathe the clear, keen air of truth; most prefer the impure air of prejudice and illusion.

491

The high goals with which, at an impressionable and idealistic age, youth started adult life, have not remained. Many have settled for less. But not all did so. A minority has refound its way, the better way.

492

Only a few sufficiently appreciate its teachings and fewer still put them into practice.

Implications of the choice

493
The Quest will make demands upon him if he is to reach to its farther bounds. It will call for strength to steel himself against unwanted passions; it will call for reason to judge persons, situations, and circumstances; and it will call for aspiration to go one better than his best.

494
The position of personal responsibility in which he finds himself may pass unnoticed or be evaded, but it is present in each important decision, each serious action. Whether knowingly or unwittingly, he pronounces judgement on each occasion: the faculty of discrimination is always exercised, even by taking shelter under the rigid dogmas of ancient institutions. They may rob him of this *feeling* of responsibility but its actuality remains.

495
Once committed to the Quest, he will find that it is no light relationship. It exacts obedience, imposes responsibility, and demands consideration in the most trivial and the most important departments of this business of living.

496
Only time and experience will bring him to consider the fuller implications of the Quest and its graver consequences. He may then feel alarm or even repulsion; or he may find gratification and even joy.

497
He has not chosen an easy way of life. A future of strenuous self-discipline stretches before him.

498
The complete acceptance of philosophy involves a complete reordering of a man's life. His conduct will be motivated by new purposes which will themselves be the result of his new values. He will stop acting impulsively and start acting rationally. But in actual practice we find that the acceptance of philosophy is never so complete as this. The individuals will bring it into a part of life but not into the whole of their lives. It is only gradually absorbed and the ideals which are sought to be realized are only gradually set up.

499
Those who embark on the quest must pay for their journey with personal self-denial and unceasing self-struggle.

500

Knowledge of the higher laws, consciousness of the higher self, bring special obligations. To apply them carries new responsibilities to live according to them.

501

Once he has engaged himself in this quest there is no rest or happiness for him unless he obeys the laws that govern it and carries out the duties that pertain to it.

502

There will be murmurings, complaints, and disheartenments; there may even be short or long lapses; but he will understand sooner or later that he will have to go through with this quest till the very end. Something that is certainly not his ordinary self drives him to do so. Indeed, his power of choice or freedom of will have become irrelevant to this particular matter.

503

He must remember that he has set his feet upon a path, and he has begun to move on that path. He must continue to do so. He must not desert the Quest under any circumstances. He must go on until the goal is reached. It is impossible in life to avoid at some period or other difficulties, trials, handicaps, obstacles, temptations, and so on. They must come, but that is no reason why anyone should give up the Quest. One should stick to the Quest in spite of all that is happening to one. If he gets a sense of failure—and he may get it—or a sense of intense depression, he may think that the Quest is too difficult and its rewards remote, and he may be tempted to give it up. He must understand what is happening. He should understand that he is expressing a mood, a mood of depression and a sense of failure. But he should remember that it is just a mood; it will pass away. And so he can say to himself: "Very well, I will not occupy myself with thoughts of the Quest for the present. I can feel no enthusiasm for it." Very well, but he must not give up the Quest. He should realize that he is doing it just for the present, that tomorrow or next week or next month or even next year he will take it up and continue, that he is not giving it up, that he is just "lying low," so to speak, for a while, but keeping in the back of his mind that he is sticking to the Quest, even though for a while he has to give up conscious effort. If he feels that he has failed, if he feels that he has sinned, even these are no reasons why he should give up the Quest. He may fall a thousand times. That does not justify his giving up the Quest. He must pick himself up and try for the thousand-and-first time. There is no steady, smooth progression to the goal. It is not an easy path. He walks, and there is no possibility of moving towards the goal without meeting with hindrances and rebuffs. And he has to learn to be patient and to be tolerant with himself, not to withdraw because he meets with those rebuffs or because he becomes dissatisfied with himself. He must not give up. He can wait, and then he can continue, and even if he falls, still he can say he will try again. Although he may really fail a thousand times, it may be that he is destined to succeed the thousand-and-first time. So he must try, because he never knows which of his efforts is going to be a successful one; and if he persists, there will come a time when this effort will and must succeed. It is as though the gods like to play with him for a while to try his patience and endurance, just to see how keenly he wants this attainment. If he gives up at the first few hindrances or rebuffs, it means that he is not so very keen after all; but if he can endure and keep on, and keep on, and still keep on, no matter what happens, well then, the gods say, here is someone who really wants truth, so we must give it to him. That is the attitude which he must develop. It doesn't matter how troubled he is personally or how dark circumstances are: they will change because they must change. The wheel of destiny is turning all the time. So he must not let circumstances or his own inner moods deter him from continuing on the path. As a matter of fact, once he has begun on the right-hand path, there is no turning back. He has accepted the responsibility, and he will have to go on with it—and if he tries to turn back, what happens is that he meets with nothing but suffering and disappointment in order to force him to return to the path. So, it is really a serious undertaking to enter upon this path, because he has to continue, and the gods will give him no rest if he runs away from it once he has really set his foot on it.

504

If he allows other people to influence him to abandon a worthy endeavour, he must blame only himself, only his own weakness, not them. If, too, he allows obstructive circumstance to influence him in the same way, he is again to blame. This fault is harder to see and to admit than the first one. But the Quest cannot be played with, nor undertaken only for his easier and more comfortable hours. It is a master to whom he has been indentured for lifelong obedience. It is a duty from which he must let nothing swerve him.

505

If the quest becomes too arduous he can always take a holiday. It would be foolish, in the end futile, to give it up altogether.

506

Hope is the instinctive turning of the flower to the sun. It bestows inspiring strength on the weak and gallant endurance on the sorrowful. It is a way up from flinty tracts to the level plateau where the worst troubles vanish. And those of us who have planted our feet on the grander path that shall lead one day to ultimate wisdom, have to go on—whether it be through sorrow or joy, weakness or strength, world-turmoil or world-peace. For us there is no turning back.

507

Once he has solemnly made this momentous decision and has reverently dedicated himself to the quest, he has to remain loyal to it under all the experiences of pleasure and pain, temptation and tribulation which will henceforth be brought to bear upon him. To desert the quest at any point will only delay his movement and increase his suffering, for he will find in the end that no other way is open to him except the way of repentance and return.

508

He is indeed free who, unpossessed by his own possessions, unswayed by his own family, undeflected by his own desires, remains ever loyal to the quest.

509

Once he has started on this quest in earnest, he will never be able to leave it again. He may try to do so for a time and to escape its claims but in the end he will fail. For some power which he cannot control will eventually and often abruptly emerge in the midst of his mental or emotional life and control him.

510

This quest is an irreversible journey. Once you have really started on it there is no turning back. You may believe that you have given it up in despair or turned away from it for a worldlier existence, but you are only fooling yourself. For one day either a deep repressed hunger will suddenly reassert itself or else a cataclysmic turn of events will drive you back to seek this last and enduring refuge of man.

511

Where is the truth to be found in all this bewildering array of doctrines, creeds, claims, systems, and beliefs? That is the reaction of many young aspirants toward a life higher than the materialistic one offered them by society today. *Theirs* is the choice: the responsibility cannot be evaded. There may be long mental struggle or easy swift emotional acceptance but the consequences belong to them. Through all these things they learn, develop, discover, and find their way in the end.

3

INDEPENDENT PATH

General description

What am I? is such an ancient and perennial question only because it has to be answered by each individual for himself. If he finds the true answer, he will find also that he cannot really transfer it to another person but only its idea, its mental shadow. That too may be valuable to others, but it is not the same.

2

Surely the human race has by this time, by this late century in history found the truth? Why, then, does the man who wants it have to make his own personal search all over again? It is because he must know it for himself within himself.

3

It was Ramana Maharshi of Arunachala who said, "You yourself are your own guru. Be that."

4

He who seeks the truth about these matters will discover that it is contrary to current opinion, and therefore he will have to discover it by himself and for himself.

5

He should verify the truth not by reference to book or bible but by reference to his own private experience.

6

There is no room in this school for those who are ready to dispose of life's problems with secondhand judgement. The need of individual thinking is vital here.

7

Humanity will not be saved in groups or by organizations. It will be saved individual by individual.

8

The Quest begins with, and ends in, himself.

9

Being true to oneself brings happiness. Being indifferent to the criticisms of those who misunderstand brings freedom from anxiety on their account. Walking the streets in a spirit of independence, enables us to walk as a millionaire! Let others sacrifice themselves to snobbery, if they will; let us be free. Only when the feet rest can we bring the mind to rest—unless we are Attained Ones!

10

We can be devout and dignified but we need not therefore be dull. I do not deny that the drift of several movements which are in the world's eye today, is toward this idea of greater spirituality. But whereas they are confined in their search by attachment to a set creed, or a particular philosophy, or even some one person, we propose to pursue an absolutely independent quest—one limited in its width by no qualifications or conditions.

11

The individual need to escape from rigid formalism into intellectual freedom comes only to a minority. But it is from this minority that the real truth-seekers emerge.

12

Taking no theoretical position, not committed to any beliefs, not wearing any labels, not putting himself in any categories, the philosophical student starts his search for truth in intellectual freedom and ends it in personal inner freedom. He is then what he is.

13

The independent self-reliant attitude of Saint Paul set an example which, had it been followed by succeeding generations, might have changed the history of his religion. He refused money gifts and followed his craft of tent-making throughout his wide travels.

14

To become a follower of this quest there is no master or organization whose permission he must ask: he is free to do so just so far as his aspiration and capacity permit him to.

15

Has he refused to submit to his own ego only to submit to society's? Shall he conform to the world and its ways out of fear of the world's opinion of him? Is he to have courage enough to reject his neighbour's religious ideas but not to resist his neighbour's foolish habits?

16

If a man cannot find in society or surroundings the standards which suit his character, then he must find his own. It is this that makes him a quester.

17

A man must stay in his own orbit and take his directives from within. If through fear of loneliness, intimidation, or suggestion, he joins the marching groups of his time, he will not reach his best.

18

Christianity, as it has become in its organized and institutionalized state, presents the good citizen as its model. Taoism, as it originally was, presented quite the opposite nonconforming citizen as its own model. So long as society is itself ignorant of where it is going wrong in its appraisal of the nature of man and mesmerized by institutional prestige while neglectful of inner light, so long ought its demand for conformity to be treated with cold reserve, asserted the Taoist sages.

19

So long as so many men live in error or compromise with wrong, merely because both have been established by tradition or custom, so long must a few among them do the greater and nobler thing by following a bold nonconformity.

20

Without making any fuss and avoiding unnecessary friction, he may pursue his independent path and choose his own goals.

21

The average, the "normal," is not to be taken as the true standard.

22

He must walk at his own pace, not society's hasty trot. He must choose his own road, not the most trodden one. The way of life which his neighbours follow does not suit him, so he must alter it. He holds the desire to fashion himself creatively into something better than he is at present, something nobler, wiser, and more perceptive. But they hold no such desire, are content with static existence.

23

He must be willing and even determined to think and feel differently from those around him. How can it be otherwise when his goal is different from theirs, too?

24

So far as a convention is reasonable and helpful, he will respect it, but when it becomes a hollow formality or stuffy pomposity, he will not.

25

So far as conformity connotes pretense and insincerity and timid blind imitation, he is not one to favour it; but so far as it connotes decency in behaviour, consideration for others, and experience-tested proven standards, he is for it.

26

He must accept the fact that he is not, and does not want to be, like the majority of people.

27

The superior person always has a choice facing him: is he to live in the way others live in order to please them or is he to live in the way his own standards call for? If he lets them pull him down he loses what has taken him many, many years to develop. Somewhere at some point he must take his stand, must plant his feet and refuse to budge any farther.

28

The ideal world will be one in which the seeker can live without becoming worldly, where he can fulfil his social obligations without becoming a slave to social conventions.

29

The philosopher's brave defiance of stuffy herd thought has a positive spirit behind it and not a negative one.

30

When a man falls away from the false standards set by materialism, he falls into conflict with the crippling conventions of his time.

31

Whatever peculiarity he may have shown in the past he need not look like that today, need not wear bizarre dress or assume theatrical postures. His dress may be ordinary and inconspicuous, his behaviour normal, his demeanour simple. But one thing he may do and that is cultivate some individuality in his attitude toward life.

32

Most men live as prisoners of ideas which are not even their own but which have been suggested to them by other men. Independent thinking is rare.

33

Consciously or unwittingly, most of us are suggestible. We accept the thoughts which other persons want to put into our heads. And we do so to such an extent that we live vicariously: we do not really live our own lives. This is quite fitting and proper to the childhood and adolescent years, but how can it be worthy of the adult ones?

34

Where is the man who has his own self, and not one made for him by others? Heredity and environment, society and suggestion, convention and education heavily contribute to forming an "I" that is not his own "I," to making a pseudo-individual that is not himself but passes for it.

35

As he goes deeper and deeper into himself, his private acts become more and more independent of other people's suggestions and resistant to their influence.

36

The longer I live the more I am impressed, to the point even of awe, by the tremendous power of suggestion on the human mind. Where is the person who is able to cultivate his own intelligence without being conditioned by ideas and examples put into it by his environment or by his reading, by his religion or his family, by his social tradition, or by the personal fears and desires connected with others? It is *others*, whether of the long-dead past or of the living present who partly or wholly imprison him in their thoughts and imaginations, their conflicts.

37

An inner life not entirely directed by or dependent on another person is an adult one. No one is such who has to seek another's approval of his actions or shrinks from disapproval of them.

38

We do not have to accept all the burdens which others try to put upon our shoulders. We are free to choose and to be sure that we are not merely surrendering our own ego to the other person's.

39

Of what use is it to ask or accept the opinions of those who are inexpert in this subject because they have yet to study it thoroughly?

40

A truth which is born out of personal knowledge, or hammered out of personal experience, has more value for a man than other people's hearsay.

41

Whatever form his outer life may have to take under the pressure of destiny, he will keep his inner life inviolate.

42

It is not necessarily an unstable mind which pushes him from guru to guru, or from belief to belief, or from group to group. It may be that he is really seeking the one Truth and has not by his own standards found it in any of these yet.

43

It is the individual who refuses to be cast in a mold who brings inspiration, inner contact with the divine, not the institution.

44

There are a few who rise above the crowd to this level by their own self-ennoblement and self-interiorization.

45

The philosopher is not discouraged because the number of those who adopt philosophical ideas is so small. He is not seeking the success of a movement, group, program, or sect. Even if he were the only man who held these ideas he would still not be discouraged. For he knows that he has not been put in the world to reform it but to reform himself.

46

He makes his own world-view rather than inherits it with his body, that is, he thinks for himself, without inherited bias and prejudice.

47

It is sometimes beneficial to throw away the manuals of spirituality, the textbooks of holiness!

48

The seeker must be distinctive and not accept conventional views or orthodox religious notions. He must judge all problems from the philosophic standpoint for he should not believe any other will yield true conclusions. This standpoint has the eminent perspective which alone can afford a true estimate of what is involved in these problems.

49

We turn away from a teaching which does not satisfy our inmost spirit, which leaves our deepest thirst unslaked.

50

In this matter our wisest course is to follow the scientist's example and test the truth of these theories, either by ourselves carrying out experiments or by observing the experiences of other people.

51

One may complain about a sense of depression which comes to his mind after meeting with certain people. He should reduce such meetings to the least number possible, and where it is necessary to deal with them, to do so by correspondence as much as he can. It does not matter that such people may have spiritual interests and may also be on the Quest. The Quest is an individual matter; it is not a group Quest. One finds God by oneself, alone in the privacy of his heart and life, not with the help of a group nor in public associations.

52

Be yourself, your own divine self. Why play a part? Why be an echo? Why follow the world in its pursuit of the trivial, the stupid, the pain-bringing?

53

He should not permit himself to be re-entangled by others in past contacts which have outserved their purpose and which now will only keep him down.

54

This freedom to search for and find truth as well as to select one's own path of approach toward it, is a precious prerogative.

55

He refuses to accept a label; he feels himself to be outside all the common categories.

56

The divergence of opinion among leading individuals on every subject is extraordinary and emphasizes once again the necessity of thinking for oneself.

57

Remember that custom and habit are the great tyrants who enslave the mass of mankind. Real freedom is possible only when one is true to one's own self. Do not permit yourself to be hypnotized by the common indifference to these high matters, but be loyal to the promptings of the spirit.

58

With this decree he runs up his personal declaration of independence. No school can hold him. His loyalty is henceforth given to global thought. Nor is this all.

59

The mystic life depends on no institution, no tradition, no sectarianism. It is an independent and individual existence.

60

Without falling into the vacuity of scepticism, the intelligent and independent seeker shuns dogmatic sectarian intellectual or emotional positions. But his openness of mind, his semi-detached stand, do not prevent his forming favourable appreciations or accommodating unflattering impressions.

61

Let others follow whatever path attracts them, but do not let them impose their path upon you if you do not feel any affinity with it.

62

As a man walks through life keeping a secret loyalty to his inner spiritual self, he is likely to make a few friends among those who are keen-sighted enough to perceive this loyalty, and a few enemies among others who misconstrue his actions and misunderstand his motives. And because he firmly believes in complete payment for all deeds by the Higher Powers set over mankind, he will remain indifferent without resentment and without hatred to the latter, while silently returning a benign love to his friends.

63

Mysticism is not concerned with those who depend on traditional forms of worship and current religious creeds for the satisfaction of all their inner needs. It is not for them and could do nothing for them. But those to whom such dependence is merely incidental or mostly provisional may find further nutriment in mystical teachings and practices.

64

Spiritual pride can take different forms. One of them is a studied intellectual independence, a refusal to be committed, the maintenance of a so-called open mind which never comes to a decision. Any good thing overdone becomes a bad thing and although independent judgement and thinking for oneself is necessary, if pushed to an extreme it merges into mere pride—egoistic pride.

65

It is only as he gets released from all the self-pictured, self-made, much-limited imaginations provided for him by ignorant but well-meaning men that he can begin to let in the grace-bestowed new understanding of the Overself.

66

The person, young or old, who has his mind set on higher things than pleasures of the moment and is willing to sacrifice a fragment of time, attention, and interest to such studies and such meditations, will find his refusal to conform to other people's ways is repaid in inner growth on the quest.

67

Attainment of sanctity must not be bought at the price of relinquishment of sanity.

68

If men would learn to accept the authority of the Voice of Inspiration whenever and wherever it spoke to them, they would not need to cramp and confine themselves within the narrowing walls of any sect or section, any cult or organization.

69

The Real Self dwells above time and space, matter and form, inviolable in its perfect liberty. If that be the goal and ideal state, he must sooner or later make a beginning to come into closer relations to it and to grow by the radiance of its Light. Therefore he does no wrong in standing aloof from the confinements of discipleship to one particular man, and the restrictions of membership in one organized group.

70

No longer is he willing to accede to the world's demand for his loyalty, for his conformity, for his surrender. He is recovering his own individual identity and is determined to keep it.

71

It is to the Overself that he must give his ultimate allegiance.

72

If his mind is filled with other people's teachings, it may give no attention to his own Overself's teachings, leadings, and intuitions.

73

There is a teaching principle in every man which can provide him with whatever spiritual knowledge he needs. But he must first take suitable measures to evoke it. These include cleansing of body and mind, aspiration of feeling and thought, silencing of intellect and ego.

74

As an expression of the divine life-power, he is unique. In the end, he will always have to take his guidance from within, that is to say, direct from that life-power which has made him what he is.

75

The independent seeker, uncommitted to any cult, may be a sheep without a fold but he is not necessarily without a shepherd. The inner voice can guide and care for him no less than a man in the flesh.

76

Those bewildered by the doctrinal differences between the established or traditional creeds, theologies, liturgies, and customs, yet still seeking some mental satisfaction, finding similar differences between the religious heresies, the non-established or modern cults, have a way out of their problem. This is to apply themselves to direct personal practices which can give them their own experience, their own teaching, from within. These standard practices include self-purification and meditation. For this inner work they do not have to join any group or organization, do not have to search for, follow, or cling to any guide. The god within them becomes, with faith, patience, persistence, and practice, the light on their path.

77

If he finds the same tenet in ten different religious creeds or metaphysical codes he is glad to get their repeated confirmation. But in the end he must get it for himself from within his own self—the Overself. It is the firmest base of life.

78

Although it is quite true that each quester must travel the path for himself, must move on his own two feet, this does not mean that he is travelling completely alone, or on his own. If he has no personal guide to accompany him, the Higher Self is still there, within him, pulling, drawing, leading, or pointing, if only he can learn how to recognize it.

79

He wants to be faithful to "the Glowing Light" within, as it has been called by Far Eastern mystics, not subjected to or obstructed by an outside authoritarianism.

80

If the Infinite Power is everywhere present, it can surely make itself known to its ardent seeker in any place, even though that place be bereft of masters.

81

He is original in the true sense of the word: he does not have to copy others, only to express his own individuality, mostly his higher individuality. He takes care to remain what he is or in Shakespeare's words to be true to himself, his higher self.

82

Insofar as he lets his happiness depend on another person and loses his independence, he becomes weakened. Even if the other gives him knowledge or love or support, he should still not cease to look within as deeply as he can for the idyllic Peace.

83

In the end a man must come to himself, his diviner self, his essential being. And where shall he look for it if not there where Jesus pointed, within? —not outside, not to some other man, however high his repute as guru, not to some book, however sacrosanct its scriptural authority. Both man and book *must*, if loyal to the highest, also direct him inward.

84

The Kingdom is within you, not somewhere else, not in an ashram, not even at the feet of a guru: Jesus' declaration is literally accurate.

85

The writer suggests that the individual seeker should take his own soul—his higher self—as his guide. By prayer and meditation, he may attain glimpses of it occasionally and receive the needed guidance. This is safer than tying himself to any institution or a so-called master. If he can put as much faith in the existence and power of his soul as most seekers put into their blind following of these masters, his efforts should prove sufficiently effective. (In this connection, the reader should read the last two pages of the first section of Chapter 15 in my book, *The Wisdom of the Overself.*)

86

Just as Emerson returned disappointed from his European search for a master, so George Fox returned from his British search. But just as Emerson came to understand that he would have therefore to find a higher self-reliance, so did Fox. "Then the Lord did let me see why there was none upon the earth that could speak to my condition, namely, that I might give Him all the glory," he wrote in his diary.

87

We regard Ralph Waldo Emerson as the perfect example of spiritual independence. He seems beholden to no man and draws all his light from within. How did he arrive at this condition? For in his early thirties, he wrote to his Aunt Mary, "A teacher . . . when will God send me one full of truth and of boundless benevolence?" This question was written soon after he came to Europe. There were four literary heroes across the Atlantic among whom he hoped to find his teacher. They were Carlyle, Landor, Coleridge, and Wordsworth. But when he met them in the flesh, Landor severely disappointed him. The Coleridge visit was "of no use beyond the satisfaction of my curiosity." Emerson's interview with Wordsworth was more successful but still so fruitless that he was glad to end it. The first glance at Carlyle made him believe that his search for a teacher was over, that here was his man. The actuality was that he found a lifelong friend, even a fellow-pilgrim and seeker. But he did not become a pupil. He had gone in search of a master. He failed to find one. Indeed he tells his aunt as much, that he seeks a man who is wise and true but that he never gets used to men. "They always awaken expectations in me which they always disappoint." He left Europe, writing in his journal on shipboard the melancholy after-reflection, "I shall judge more justly, less timidly, of wise men forevermore." And it was there, in his little cabin, that he received the illumination which he could not find in Europe. He need look outside himself no more. Out of his illumination, whilst still afloat on the ocean, he wrote down such sentences as these: "A man contains all that is needful within himself." "Nothing can be given to him or taken away from him but always there is a compensation." "The purpose of life seems to be to acquaint a man with himself."

88

His attraction toward this or that teacher may weaken and die but his attraction to the Inspirer of all teachers, the Overself, will keep on growing stronger in him.

89

He alone must answer this question, and he can best answer it by listening for and obeying that deep inner feeling which is called intuition.

90

The rarity of competent teachers in the world, and especially in the Western world, forces seekers to practise self-reliance and cultivate independence, unless they are willing to accept substitutes for competence or join organizations making unsubstantiated claims. The Overself will not neglect determined seekers and through circumstances, events, books, or otherwise gives them the particular guidance or instruction needed at a particular time.

91

The aspirant of today who is thoroughly discriminating will generally fail to find the support of a competent teacher. Usually he will have to depend on the inner Self alone.

92

He need not accept any human leadership if he will listen to the voice of the Silence and accept its invisible leadership.

93

What he learns from outside himself, from teacher or tradition, will never lead to his true fulfilment until he joins it with what he learns in the stillness from inside himself.

94

People tie themselves to some one man, living or dead, and worship him. Yet he is outside themselves, and the divine is within themselves. They contemplate his form, surrender to his personality, refuse to look within. As long as they do this, so long does the Consciousness elude them.

95

When a man recognizes that all he really needs comes to him from the higher self, and not from other men, and in the measure that he uses his own efforts to complete his development and so come closer in consciousness to that self, in that measure will he gain what he needs.

96

Books however sacred, ceremonies however impressive, lectures however learned, even Masters however wise are still only outer helps and as such must in the end be discarded.

97

Despite all the high idealistic talk of oneness, brotherhood and egolessness, each of us is still an individual, still has to dwell in a body of his own, to use a mind of his own and experience feelings of his own. To forget this is to practise self-deception. Each will come to God in the end but he will come as a purified transformed and utterly changed person, lived in and used by God as he himself will live in and be conscious of the presence of God.

98

His inner self has the capacity of making its own revelations to him. These got, he will find himself increasingly independent of those which come from outside, from the hearsay of other men or the writings of dogmatic traditions.

99

What a number of men and women can no longer get from church or temple, they must get from their own selves through mysticism.

100

He needs to realize that his greatest power will come to him through his own Overself and not through any other source, such as the overshadowing by spirits, and so on. Through this eventual realization, he will attain to greater progress and render much deeper service. Thus he will fulfil his own highest destiny.

101

Let him stand in his own place, and not seek to occupy that of another. Let him find a life that is real, and not copied. But such admonitions are good only so far as he has already come into communion with the Overself.

102

Ultimately, there is only one real Master for every spiritual seeker, and that is his own divine Overself. The human teacher may assist him to the extent of giving him a temporary emotional uplift or a temporary intellectual perception, but he cannot bestow *permanent* divine consciousness on another individual. All that the teacher can do is to point out the way through the labyrinth; the journey must be made by the seeker himself. For example, an individual living alone on a desert island could travel through all the stages of the Quest and attain the highest realization even though he had no visible teacher. The Overself will give him all the guidance and help he needs. However, he is likely to mistakenly believe that his own ego is making the progress.

103

All that he needs for the management of life can be had from within.

104

If a man is to remain forever the mere appendage of another man, if his mind is to echo back only that other man's idea, the question arises: When will he come to himself, his *Atma*? For is this not the final purpose of our life here? He who has reached this stage when he must cease being the shadow of others, will not fall into proud deceptive self-assertion if he humbly yields and follows the inner voice.

105

All efforts that take him outside of himself are only halting and temporary concessions to human weakness. The soul being inside of himself, he must in the end turn within.

Take truth where you find it

106

Welcome the truth on whatever horizon it appears, look for it in all four directions, and do not leave any of them unvisited. In short, do not become narrow-minded or fanatical.

107

Let him not be intimidated by history and believe that truth has appeared only in the past, or by geography and look for it only in an Oriental location.

108

In whatever place you find truth, with whatever name it may be labelled, take it.

109

In his endeavours after a better life, he should welcome the help that could come to him from every right source.

110

He should always be receptive to ideas and practices which might enrich those he already knows.

111

No single path will lead of itself to the full truth.

112

There is no one group which has captured the monopoly of truth, for its recognition is a universal experience. Let us refuse to listen to those who insist upon our travelling one way and one way alone.

113

Truth is not confined to any sect but fragments of it may be found scattered here and there.

114

We may learn from everything and everyone, from every event and happening something that is new or a confirmation of something that is old, something affirmative or something negative.

115

When a teacher of a teaching, a book, or a mystical exercise is itself being used as the indirect expression of the Overself's own movement to shed grace, then it is sheer blindness to denounce it as useless.

116

Why limit the help you are willing to receive to a single quarter? All men are your teachers. Truth, being infinite, has an infinite number of aspects. Each spiritual guide is inclined to emphasize some only and to neglect the others.

117

Inspiration has manifested itself in many lands and in different forms, through widely spaced centuries and various kinds of channels. Why limit culture to one contribution, one land, one form, one century, and one channel alone? This applies not only to intellectual and artistic culture, but also to its religious aspect. We may go even farther in this matter and apply the same idea to personal gurus. Must we always be moored to a single guru? Cannot we respect, appreciate, honour, venerate and receive light from other ones in addition?

118

During his Egyptian studies Pythagoras visited every man celebrated for wisdom, so eager was he to learn. He did not follow the Indian custom of sitting down only at one man's feet.

119

"Study everything but join nothing" is the best counsel. But alas! naïve enthusiasts seldom heed it.

120

He must make a stubborn reservation of his ground and run the flag of independence in the quest of truth, of nonattachment in the relationship with the teachers of truth. He will humbly and gladly accept whatsoever good he can find in their teachings, but he will not do so under a contract of pledged discipleship. In this matter he must be eclectic, taking the best from every available source and not shutting out any source that has something worthwhile to offer. It may not be the way for most people, for they cannot walk alone, but it is the only way for him. Self-guidance also leads to the goal.

121

It is only through free, independent, truth-seeking research that there is any hope of success in this Quest for ultimate truth. Naturally each vested interest tries to limit the search to its own fold for obvious reasons, but he should refuse to limit his studies to any single school.

122

If he keeps his intellectual liberty, he is less likely to fall into narrow sectarianism. Today, as in ancient Alexandria, he can study the world's teachings, taking truth eclectically, but not making himself a disciple.

123

Learn some of the basic truths each system contains without identifying with the system itself. Keep the mind open and free to acquire worthwhile ideas and practices from other cultures and avoid the closed-in sectarian attitude.

124

To become liberated from sectarian, conventional, and authoritarian narrowness is to regard every inspired book as a bible.

125

Such an isolated position, outside groups and without labels, offers this advantage, that he is able to take from all, to accept and reconcile fragments of widely different and apparently contradictory teachings.

126

Take whatever is of value to you personally, in your present mental condition, from all these teachings and discard the rest. This is the eclectic way, and better than the commoner one of entering a single doctrinal cage and staying there. Hesitate well before committing yourself to join this or that organization. Remember that there are more aspects to truth than one, and it may well be worth keeping yourself free to learn something of these others.

127

I have always recommended to those who feel strong enough to be able to do so, to refrain from joining any organization, to keep their freedom, while at the same time studying the doctrines of whatever organizations interest them, whatever religions engage some of their attention. This freedom enables them to look anywhere, to study everything, to question courageously, to keep breadth of view, depth of thought.

128

Only such independence can reach out to the new without losing what is worthwhile in the old; all others are committed, fettered, captive.

129

By remaining open to truths from different sources, and fitting them together like mosaics, we get eventually some sort of a pattern.

Intelligent nonconformity

130

No man comes to the knowledge of his divinity through a crowd of other men. No human entity can discover its own relation to God through any group method. The way to spiritual *awareness* is entirely individual, essentially lonely, inescapably within oneself. That is to say, it is mystical. Insofar as religion succeeds in showing the way, it ceases to be religion and becomes, or rather, consummates itself in, mysticism.

131

Nothing is final and absolute. All is relative. Nobody need obey any mandate to bind himself forever to any single group of ideas, need follow any sectarian flag. If he is to surrender his allegiance at all, it can only be reasonably done to the perfect synthesis of all that is needed for human living in all its departments.

132

If the man of letters is to hear and pronounce the word of truth, he must be independent of groups, organizations, parties, and institutions. He must be at liberty to play with many different points of view without committing himself forever and finally to any of them.

133

They must try to work out interpretations of scripture and life for themselves, not remain tied to obligatory ones imposed from without. They must begin to stand on their own individual resources or they will never rise to the level of direct spiritual communion at all. The tendency to look to one man or one organization as the sole repository of spiritual wisdom may become dangerous to their further progress. In *The Wisdom of the Overself* it was mentioned that the currents of evolution and the circumstances of modernity have created new cultural values which in turn have lessened the need of such dependence. One proof of this assertion lies in the fact that the same line of change may be seen also in the social, political, and economic spheres.

134

To seek knowledge from unprejudiced sources is a rule hard to fulfil, because such sources are rare. The next best thing is to be an unprejudiced seeker, and this is the ideal I have tried to follow. Sectarianism is everywhere, because institutions and organizations are everywhere. There is a better chance for the truth seeker when flying the flag of independence.

135

There are those in India who have made a sect out of Vedanta, even of Advaita Vedanta. The intolerance, the fanaticism of the narrower groups and religions has been brought in here too. Let the Western student of philosophy who takes it seriously enough to think, breathe in remembrance, and live actively by it, be warned and stay free, unjoined, unlabelled, spacious in outlook, understandingly tolerant in practice.

136

"Study both sympathetically and critically the other contemporary mystical movements *but do not join them*." Such is my general answer to the seeker who questions me about them. He should certainly examine and study other teachings, not necessarily for his acceptance, but for his broadening. Be a good student, but a bad joiner! For he will find it difficult to recognize the lineaments of full perfection either in the teaching or the practice of any existing institution or movement. However, the danger here is that he may overconcentrate on their study or practice, elevate side-routes into the main one, and finally get so absorbed in them as temporarily to abandon the original quest altogether. So there are certain reservations in my advice, a certain watchfulness is needed during such studies. He should take care to be only an enquirer into these cults and not a follower of them. He should be first a sympathetic enquirer and then only exercise the philosophical right of severely critical examination. In the end, every aspirant must find his "own." "The path of another is dangerous," says the *Bhagavad Gita*. Unless a spiritual teaching has enough inspiration behind it to help him successfully tackle his gravest personal problems, it is not the right one—however much it may be so to others. For he needs grace, and does not call in vain.

137

With so many cults, creeds, religions, sects, and societies claiming that their teaching is the only true one or that their path is the only path to salvation, the seeker will either get bewildered or be forced to do the right thing—which is to exercise his own independent judgement and not to accept any claim on its mere face value.

138

Whoever loves truth in its fullness cannot put on the chains of a partisanship and stay confined in a church, a temple, a mosque, a synagogue, a "school of thought," a theism, or an atheism. Therefore he cannot become an adherent to any one belief only, a convert to any one religion, a member of any one group, or a follower of any one man but must remain an independent, that is to say, a philosopher (philo = liker or lover, sophia = wisdom). He sees that all doctrines, all ways of belief and thought are steps on the way, satisfy some need of some persons, and hence are of service at some time. But he sees not only that truth's fullness is allied to his own freedom: it is also allied to namelessness.

139

The fellowship of philosophy requires no ritual, no immersion, no dogmatic confession, no creedal test. It is free and non-sectarian. It shuts no one in, no one out.

140

Philosophy is for the free mind, willing to live without organizational bondage, and understanding that what it seeks must be found and grasped for itself.

141

Since the real essence of philosophy has only an inner content, which must be felt intuitively and grasped intellectually, but no outer form, it cannot become material for a cult, an organized group. It must lead each person on his own individual way, letting him grow naturally from within. His quest will then take the independent course proper for him, not made to conform to one suitable only to others.

142

He who can commune with his soul by himself does not need a church, a labelled religion. Society has no right to impose it on him. In their naïve adolescent gropings, the young who discard their traditional form of religion, feel something of this truth.

143

How can he who loves the Spirit, who feels Its goodwill which excludes nothing, associate himself with an enclosed group or community which excludes everyone who is not an adherent of its particular faith?

144

The refusal to join any ecclesiastical church or religious society does not leave a man spiritually homeless. If he faithfully exercises himself in meditation and seeks to practise the presence of God, what better "home" could he have?

145

There is an independence which gives a man special strength for it allows him to possess complete purity of motive. It does not come easily, for he has to stay clear of all attempts to organize the truth, of all orthodoxies, groups, factions, parties, and sects which claim to be united with it. He may align himself with none of those. Therefore he can take up no defined position, no particular program. Is he then a neutral? No and yes. Is he an individualist? Yes and no.

146

Only this total independence of all cults, creeds, groups, and organizations can enable him to find the facts as they are, rather than imaginary pictures of the facts.

147

If the independence of the philosophic position stops him from speaking for any particular established religion or mystical cult, it allows him to view all religions and all cults with fairness and detachment.

148

It is to be found in the privacy of your own mind: no cult, group, or church will provide it.

149

Philosophy stresses the need of development's being individual. Students of other teachings may grow in groups, but not students of philosophy.

150

It is not an essential part of the outer conditions of his life that he should subscribe to any particular institution or organization, but if he is led to do so that will be acceptable also if it is an honourable one.

151

Mind in its ultimate condition is free and infinite. We, as humans, are at the very beginning of its discovery. Let us not set up false steps to our journey or ignorantly put up fences to block our view. Let us avoid the ill-informed littleness of sectarianism, the common eagerness to huddle under a label.

152

For several reasons he is not a joiner. Most sects have only partial and limited views, most mix some error with their truth, and most develop ugly dogmatic tyrannies. Furthermore, their adherents, believing that they alone possess the truth, generally exclude all others from the warmer temperatures of their goodwill—if they do not openly dislike them. But the largest reason for his refusal is that the Overself is unlimited, unconfined; he wants to express this freedom.

153

The orthodox way of looking at these questions will no longer serve. A new way is needed. The right answers will be found only if we reorient our thinking and free it from the dogmas of established institutions.

154

He is not a joiner because of several reasons: one of them is that joiners are too often too one-sided in approach, too limited in outlook, too exclusive to let truth in when it happens to appear in a sect different from his own. Another reason is that too frequently there is a tyranny from above, imitated by followers, which forbids any independent thought and does not tolerate any real search.

155

Man's search for truth cannot be properly carried on unless he has full freedom in it. Where is the religious or religio-mystical institution which is willing to grant that to him? Is there a single one which lets him start out without being hampered by authoritarian dogmas, taboos, limitations, and traditions which it would impose upon him?

156

Lectures, societies, and group-movements are of limited value: they can never replace nor achieve what is gained by one's own individual efforts made in the right way.

157

The seeker after truth will not find his way easy to travel. He may find that an institution, an authority, or an organization is suffocating him mentally or oppressing him emotionally. This may be the hour when he must claim his freedom.

158

It is illusory to believe that, by blindly handing or humbly submitting his character and credo, his standards and values, his spiritual purposes and practices, to any organized group or established church, to a teacher, guide, or guru, to form and formulate, a man can evade the responsibility of judging them for himself, accepting or rejecting by himself. It is required of every fully human being that he be individual, not a parasite, and that he be himself, not someone else.

159

The prestige of institutional mysticism, like that of official religion, mesmerizes nearly everyone interested in the subject. The independent mystic, who refuses all affiliation with any sect, school, ashram, monastery, group, or society, is suspect and finds himself left almost in isolation. But although this may seem unfortunate, it is so only in some ways. In other ways, it leaves him entirely free from the bonds of dogma, free to remain faithful to truth irrespective of all other considerations, free to speak in a voice whose authority comes not from worldly power but from spiritual status.

160

He should not change his chains by going from one master or one sect to another. Rather should he drop all chains.

161

He is entitled to be set free from his former dependence on the church so that he may live his own individual inner life.

162

How can he bring himself to join any group, cult, or sect when he believes all of them to be right, only some are more right than others, and all of them to be wrong, only some are more wrong than others? There is not one whose limitations he does not see. He prefers the truthfulness of being uncommitted to any "ism," and the freedom of being unjoined to any group.

163

He is not likely to be a member of any organized movement because his mind is too large to be exclusive. He is outside all organized groups because, in spirit, he is inside all of them.

164

Far from the din and disparagements of jarring sects, he lives unlabelled and free.

165

He belongs to no particular named, classified, and indoctrinated group, and this keeps his own freedom while excluding none from his general goodwill. At the same time he stays open to truth and avoids the closed mind, fixed only on its own dogmas opinions and beliefs.

166

The only group he is likely to be a member of is the human race!

167

He is unwilling to be tied to any sect or coterie, established orthodoxy or organizational unorthodoxy. He may even refuse to fit into any of the accepted patterns. He has to follow a light of his own. Such an anarchistic attitude is likely to provoke hostility and create detractors.

168

I have an Emersonian love of spiritual freedom and intellectual independence, a Krishnamurtian urge to keep away from all restrictive, limiting, and narrowing groups, organizations, and institutions. I have seen so many lost to the cause of Truth by such constrictions of the mind and heart, so much of its good undone by this harm, that I shrink from the idea of becoming tagged as some one man's disciple or as a member of some ashram, society, or church. If this man has found the Right, why not let his natural expression of it—whether in writing, art, or life—be enough? Why create a myth around him, to befog others and falsify the goal? Why not let well alone?

169

Having no official connection with any group, sect, organization, or church leaves me free to help anyone, anywhere.

170

A strongly individualistic temperament cannot be at ease in the collective membership of an organization where dogmas are set up like fences and where patriotism rejects salvation for those outside. Such a temperament needs the free air of unfettered thinking and uncircumscribed goodwill. It can sympathize intellectually with many different points of view without losing itself in any one of them, but it can do so only because it belongs to none.

171

The routine devotions of an institution do not appeal to this type of temperament—sensitive, moody, and independent as it is.

172

The man who has seen the light and experienced its warmth will prefer his own way of living if it is the consequence of his awakening.

173

His mind is bound by no religious dogmas, his conduct by no prohibitions or commandments. But this does not mean he is free to do what he pleases.

174

One man and one God are all the organization needed. More is a superfluity. The seeker who cherishes his independent path and individual thought cannot comfortably fit into a group where all alike must be pressed into the same shape.

175

It seems historically inevitable that every spiritual movement should sooner or later become organized and institutionalized. In that way it reflects the need and serves the tendency of average human nature. But where a person is not average and refuses to be taken up into it by that means, preferring to keep his independence and his allegiance, he is just as much entitled to do so.

176

Those who feel tempted to do so, may study the public cults and listen to the public teachers but it would be imprudent to join any of the first or follow any of the second. It would be wiser to remain free and independent or they may be led astray from the philosophical path.

177

By rejecting the easy way of joining a particular sect, a labelled group, he rejects at the same time the withdrawal of sympathy or understanding from all other groups which usually or often accompanies the joining. If the universal character of truth requires him to keep his mind uncorralled, the personal need of strength confirms the requirement.

Pros & cons of independence

178

The follower of a labelled cause, movement, or party tends to become unfair to competing causes, exaggerating their weak points but minimizing or even shutting his eyes to those of his own. He who refuses to attach himself but remains independent is more likely to judge without prejudice and after genuine investigation of both sides.

179

The advantages of being in a position of intellectual and social, religious and personal independence are several. The chance of finding truth and, if luckily found, of expressing it, is surely larger.

180

If he has to analyse problems for himself and has no one else to do it for him, the endeavour may help him to learn discrimination and good judgement.

181

It is better to make one's own decisions independently. This is not the case, however, if one feels too incapable of thinking out an issue, or too ill-informed about it, or too vacillating to make up one's mind on its pros and cons.

182

If his understanding of this teaching delivers him from excessive dependence on another man or on external methods, it will clear his path and help his self-reliance. But if it outruns itself and makes him cocksure, proud, arrogant, and irreverent towards the masters, then it has degenerated into misunderstanding. This will block his path.

183

A man can achieve his independence by grades without rebellion but he is seldom so wise as to do so. More often, he lacks patience, takes the more foolish violent way, and attains his freedom at a cost, to himself and to others, that could have been much less for the same result by evolutionary ways.

184

The passionate contempt for organized authority, or its complete rejection, may be only a cover for weakness: the inability to undergo a course of discipline, much less undertake it for oneself.

185

The danger of walking alone is also the danger of identifying his own private judgements, impulses, desires, and thoughts as intuitions from the higher self.

186

But independence of mind has its own perils, for it may lead to stubbornness in error, to arrogance in behaviour, and to fanaticism in attitude.

187

He who depends upon his own personal intellect and personal strength alone, deprives himself of the protection which a higher power could give him.

188

The endeavour after independence can achieve only a partial success, never a total one. We find that we are tied to other people.

Requirements

189

As much as anything else, one needs personal freedom in this search after truth. Every form of interference and obstruction comes from sources which have acquired only a partial or false insight into truth. But such freedom is permitted only insofar as one is good enough, wise enough, balanced enough, judicious enough, and discriminating enough to use it properly. Otherwise it leads to non-truth and self-deception.

190

He must learn to think for himself and to practise discrimination for himself, if he wants to find his way to truth.

191

If a seeker finds no one in his surroundings, contacts, or society near enough to his level of spiritual interests, then he must accept his loneliness, because he has chosen to draw away from the common preoccupation. For in order to be a working philosopher, a man must go his own way. This demand for individuality requires courage and wisdom. If he lacks higher knowledge, intuitional feeling, and intellect—whose combination is wisdom—then he must seek to develop them and this demands work. Meanwhile, he can take help from personal guides and superior books. Without wisdom, or at least genuine efforts to work towards it, his course could be wrongly set and he could arrive at disaster.

192

To withdraw from sectarian community life and walk alone requires qualities that only few possess. There is security, comfort, moral and worldly support in it. To be able to abandon these things a man must have a strong inner urge as well as a continuous clear perception of philosophy's meaning.

193

The weakling cannot walk this path. A man needs strength to follow out what his deep intuition tells him to do, especially where it departs from the allegedly rational or the socially conventional. If his guided attitude or action meets with criticism or opposition, what is that to him? He is not answerable for what other people think about him. That is their responsibility. He is answerable only for what he himself thinks and does.

194

Only the man who has a passion to acquire the certainty of truth, who has the courage to hold unorthodox views and come to independent conclusions, who lives in an atmosphere of original thought, and to whom the charge of heresy is no charge at all, is at all likely to find his way to the truth.

195

Their duty is to act as pioneers; but if they are to be successful pioneers, they will need courage to forget outworn ideas and to free themselves from dying traditions so as to cope with the new conditions which are arising. In this connection, the suggestion that it is also a duty to co-operate with existing spiritual movements would be acceptable if it were practicable; but experience will show that most of these movements are unable to enter that deep union of hearts which alone can guarantee success to any external union. Such a plan would end in failure and it is better for them to pursue their own independent course than waste time and force in attempting what would not succeed and is not really needed.

196
The freedom to command one's life in one's own way can be got only by first getting the fearlessness to disregard the criticism and to ignore the expectations of other people.

197
He who would follow an independent path must, to some extent, be fearless. He must refuse to be intimidated by the power, prestige, claims, or size of established organizations, just as he must refuse to be deluded by the idealizations of themselves which they hold before the public.

198
Few people know what a free existence really is; most people live caged in by fear of, or enslavement to, the opinion of others. Even the rich do not know it for their cages are gilt and comfortable. Even the spiritual do not know it for they merely echo back what these others want them to think about God. Complete freedom is possible only to those who have a special character, one that is devoid of tyrannizing ambitions and despotic cravings, and even of unworldly strivings.

199
Such is the strange paradox of the quest that on the one hand he must foster determined self-reliance but on the other yield to a feeling of utter dependence on the higher powers.

200
Those who are self-sufficient and prefer to learn and develop by themselves, are those who especially need to practise this inward listening and waiting.

201
What we mean is that modern man has to become more self-reliant, has to throw off the remnants of tribal consciousness which still rule him, has to learn to think for himself.

202
But if he must stand aloof to live his own way, with his own free thoughts, it remains a benevolent, amiable independence. He wishes all beings well while knowing they receive, suffer, or enjoy the results of their own physical, emotional, or mental action.

203

His desire to express individual views, character, and personality must be respected so long as he does not try to impose them aggressively or tyrannically on others.

204

It is not necessary to be surly and irritable in order to be an individualist. One can still be affable, genial, civil, and courteous—even radiant with goodwill. It is all a matter of inner equilibrium.

205

He must refuse to violate his intellectual integrity or sacrifice his spiritual independence.

206

If he is unable to continue in this quest without the association, encouragement, or sympathies of others who are also following it, then he had better not enter it at all, for quite obviously he is not ready for it nor sufficiently appreciative of its values.

207

If "being different" is an honest result of the search for higher truth, it must be acceptable. But when it is merely a disguised egocentric exhibitionism, it becomes reprehensible.

208

He must try to keep his life in his own hands if he would keep it free from influences that would take away the ideals which he has specifically set up for it to follow. If he values freedom, he must refuse to put himself in a position where he will be compelled to echo the views of those who do not share his ideas. He may have to choose between the trials of sturdy independence and the temptations of enervating security.

209

It does not ask him to make harsh sacrifices but it does ask him to make reasonable ones. If they seem harsh to him that is only because he has been kept until then in a state of so-called normality by the powerful suggestions of organized society. This normality is merely the pooling of common ignorance and the sharing of common weakness.

210

If the mind is to engage with success in the quest for truth, it must first be unfettered and then unprejudiced.

211

It requires moral strength or mental power to refuse the gregarious support of the crowd—be it sectarian church, a mystical group, or some other combination. It requires faith in oneself and the courage to resist the pull of others and be an individual.

212

To venture so far afield from the common way and yet keep quite sane and practical, and not become a human oddity, a social freak, is something indeed.

213

He has to pick his way through mistaken teachings, among provisional standpoints, and between ambitious gurus.

214

The self-sufficiency of his ideal, its remoteness from popular ways, may be boldly and openly expressed in action or kept as an interior and hidden thing. For most the first may prove to be an imprudent course but for others it may be a necessity.

215

Mentally he cannot fit himself into any of the accepted categories which the society of his place and time provide, so an independent and solitary path attracts him. Physically, he may have to make an uneasy compromise with society, with the result that both benefit by their mutual services. Thus without doing violence to his chief principles he yet finds a way to live among those who have no use for them.

216

Before anyone can carry out an independent investigation of truth, he must first possess the capacity to do so. To develop this capacity where it is lacking, the philosophic discipline is prescribed.

217

He is not prepared to relinquish individual expression, however much he is only too understanding of the need to relinquish the ego's dominance—which is not the same thing.

218

It is what he expects from himself that will be more effective than what someone else expects from him. Rules and regulations thrust upon him from outside which he is unwilling or unable to enforce will be of much less use.

Is monastic discipline needed?

219

The way to full realization of the Overself may lie through a monastery or a nunnery for one person and through a family home or a career in the world for another. If any man asserts that it must lie solely through a particular one of these two, he is mistaken. If he insists on forcing this idea on all aspirants, he is sinning. If he claims illumination as authority, it could be only a partial, limited, and incomplete illumination.

220

Whether a man stays within the household and secular society or whether he enters the monastic and ascetic one, his enlightenment is neither guaranteed by the second choice nor blocked by the first one. The god within him is his secret watcher, be he layman or hermit. He can defile or purify himself in either state, grasp the truth or miss the point whether active in the world (as most of us have to be) or enclosed in a religious order, ashram, or temple.

221

The notion that a man who marries, has children, lives across the same road, and catches the commuter's train is unfit to receive the grace of God, whereas a man who wears a priest's dress or a monk's robe is alone fit, is one of those ideas sedulously fostered by priests and monks themselves. The fact is that grace is no respecter of clothes, status, or social activities; that it happens to alight on those whose hearts and minds seek it most, and in the right way; that today Christ is militant, is working *inside* man wherever he may be and whatever garments he wears and however he chooses to pay his debt to society; and that His true followers are not easily distinguishable by any outer labels, but are easily measurable by their own conscience, in their degree of consciousness. They are not professional exhibitionists eager to display their spirituality, to talk about it and impress others with it. They may be passive in a monastery or active in an office—that is not the point. What is going on inside them?

222

There is no special superiority in either of the two conditions of life— the monastic or the householding. Whoever praises the monk's state as being the highest open to human beings, errs. Whoever praises the house-holder's as being the best, also errs. What can rightly be said is that for certain persons at certain times and under certain circumstances, one or the other state is better. For the same persons at different times and in different circumstances either may be worse. So it is the setting up of universality, the claiming that one alone is the most spiritual or the most satisfactory ideal, which is wrong.

223

Each must find the way uniquely ordained for him, and not passively, imitatively, accept the way ordained for another man. Although it is true that some have realized the goal while living a normal life in the world, married and active, others have been able to do so only while freed from the world's ways. It is therefore essential for him to be himself, an individual, and let his own inner voice guide him to the particular path suited to his destiny.

224

To the householder taking on a family life is a joy; to the monk it is an encumbrance. Neither man is wrong. It is all in the point of view. Each has inherited his own attitude from his former selves.

225

He need not abandon the householder's life unless the divine command tells him to do so.

226

They are not necessarily strong and heroic who stay in the world and disdain flight from it. It may be that pleasures and possessions keep them there. Equally, those who have nothing worth renouncing—the poor, the unlucky, the disappointed, and the frail—make no sacrifice in passing to the cloister's shelter, the monastery's peace.

227

There are those who flee the world, its futile tumults and doings; they do well. But we who hold to philosophy may flee or stay, just as we choose. For we can make of it a pathway to the Ever-Peaceful.

228

The man of independent temperament cannot fit easily into monastic existence with its formal patterns and clock-timed bell-signalled regularity.

229

If the book *Mahatma Letters* says that a married man cannot become an adept then the author of it must be thinking of a special kind of adeptship belonging to his own particular school of thought and training which is, as a matter of fact, a school for monks only. But this school is not the only one which is able to find truth. There are others and they are intended not for monks but for people who have to live in the world and earn their livings and live the family life. The real celibacy is in the heart and mind and has nothing to do with external social customs like ascetic monasticism.

230

The solution of the world's problems does not lie in renouncing the worldly life itself. If every man became a monk and every woman a nun, they would merely exchange one set of problems—worldly ones—for another set—monastical ones. It is probably correct to say that the first kind are harsher and grimmer than the second kind. But whatever type of life is adopted, problems will inescapably be there.

231

Whether the ideal is a hermit's existence or a householder's the same qualities have to be developed.

232

"If this doctrine should be attainable only for Lord Gautama and the monks and nuns, but not for his male and female adherents living the household life, then this holy life would be incomplete, just because of this. But because this doctrine may be attained by the Lord Gautama and the monks and nuns, as well as by the male and female adherents living the household life, therefore this holy life is perfect, just because of this."

— Buddha, in *Majjhima Nikaya*

233

When Subba consulted Buddha about the question of renouncing the world, Buddha frankly admitted that he had no basis for judging that every hermit was ethically or intellectually superior to every householder, or vice versa. Therefore, he concluded, each man, whether he be monastic, recluse, or worldly householder, could best be judged only on his individual merits. Buddha's general and most reiterated reason for asking his followers to become monks was, as he has here confessed, not because their way of life was spiritually superior but because, in his own words: "Painful is the life of a householder and free is the life of renunciation." This is not an ethical reason, therefore, but a purely practical one. He recommended external renunciation because it relieved a man of domestic troubles and family burdens; it was a rule of expediency rather than an absolute principle of spiritual method.

234

I was glad to find these ideas confirmed by a great yogi and sage of Bengal, Paramahamsa Narayana Tirtha Dev, so that it cannot be said they are Western notions grafted on Indian trees. The yogi, who was the head of a secret fraternity with more than a thousand members living near the Assam frontier, was dead before I came to know him, but to glean more details of his techniques and doctrines I made a special journey to the group of intimate disciples who survived him. He said, "In the coming nation, there will be no place for *Sannyase*. To realize the Self through the householder's life shall be the grand ideal of the future of the world. It is not by giving up all, but by realizing the Self in all, that one has to realize the object of the world-evolution and be free. The path is not through negation of the Universe to the affirmation of the Supreme Self, but through affirmation of the Supreme Self to the mergence of the Universe in the Supreme Self. The mission this time is educational and not religious. Spread education in the name of the Highest Truth enshrined in the *Upanishads* and religions will grow of themselves on the sure foundation of the Highest Truth."

235

The belief is that in the world a man's activities are usually, and mostly, devoted to the benefit of himself and the sustenance of his family, whereas in the monastery they are devoted to seeking God. But this is theory. I once heard Ramana Maharshi rebuke those who were sitting in the Ashram Hall. "Some of you are really householders wearing the sadhu's robe, while some of the householders living in the world are really sadhus!" he said.

236

Must a man take formal vows in order to discipline himself? Can he not be loyal to his ideal, which in the end is self-chosen or he would not have turned his back upon the world, without making promises and uttering pledges which it may not be possible to redeem? Are the tonsured head and the coarse robe essential to ensure the practice of self-control in act and thought? If he is to persevere in the purification of character, is it not enough that he himself wants it?

237

If he chooses to do so, he is free to live in the normal human relationships, to follow a career in the world, to marry and beget children. Of course this will necessarily entail certain disciplinary conditions. But he will not be obliged to flee from all possessions into jungles, monasteries, or the like.

238

Whether he be outside in the world or inside in the cloister is not so important to a man as whether his thoughts and feelings, his character and consciousness have right direction. Either of these environments may be a hindrance or a help to his spiritual aspirations, depending on its particular nature. Yes, even the world may be a means of advancement if he uses it for this specific purpose.

239

It is less important whether or not we live under monastic rules than whether we live faithfully in the purpose which prompted those rules to be formulated. The purification of the mind may be accomplished at home or it may be accomplished in an ashram-monastery. Do not be carried away from truth by the bigots who denounce the one or the other place!

240

The monks who have stepped out of the world may have stepped into a vocation which is proper and good for them, but it is not necessary and not right to suggest that everyone else should do so. First of all, everyone else could not do so.

241

It is not a matter so much of staying with the worldlings and doing their work nor of fleeing to the monks and following their disciplines, as of comprehending the mentalist secret and of keeping an inner detachment.

242

Detachment from the world is an absolute necessity for the man who seeks authentic inner peace, and not its imagined counterfeit. But renouncement of the world is not necessary to any except those who have an inborn natural vocation for the monkish life.

243

It is immeasurably more important to have inner detachment than to wear a monk's robe.

244

We ought not, in our appreciation of a spiritualized worldly life, minify the value of a monastic life. Let us not forget that the man who becomes a monk to the extent that he sincerely and understandingly embraces the new ideal, exhibits admirable qualities. In taking the vow of poverty he shows forth his tremendous faith, for he will rely upon the infinite life-power to sustain him henceforth. In taking the vow of obedience, he shows forth his great humility, for he confesses that he is unable to guide his own life and thought wisely, but will take his guidance henceforth from those who stand nearest to God. In taking the vow of celibacy he makes a magnificent gesture of defiance to his own lower nature, against which he will henceforth fight and to which he will not willingly succumb.

245

He need wear no distinctive robe nor display a tonsured head. He need pursue no special tradition, enter no monastic establishment, nor cut himself off from ordinary life. That he is a philosopher is not to be advertised by such outward signs. Yet if he feels a personal vocation to follow these customs, he is also free to do so. It is simply that there is no necessity in the general sense.

246

Asiatic mysticism has been well nigh suffocated under the weight of monkish traditions which have accumulated around it. The consequence is that the present-day student who lacks the spirit of critical research, will not know where the philosophy begins and where the monkishness ends. If we study the available texts today without the expository guidance of a competent personal teacher, we shall almost certainly fall into a number of errors. Some of these are merely contributory towards a superficial understanding of the texts and no harm is really done but one of them is crucial and much harm may then be done. For it must be remembered that in the days before the art of writing was widely used almost all the earliest texts were handed down from generation to generation by word of mouth alone. This entailed wonderful feats of memory which we must admire but it also entailed the possibility of conscious or unconscious alteration of the texts themselves, against which we must guard ourselves. It must also be remembered that the texts were customarily in the possession of a segregated class of men, either priests or monks or both types united in the same man. Quite humanly, too, new passages which praised their own class and idealized their mode of living were slowly if surreptitiously introduced into these same texts. It may be said that an honest man would not do this but it must be replied that an honest yet well-meaning man may do it. Anyone who really knows the East knows that this has demonstrably happened right through its history even until our own era. Whether it happened or not, however, one thing was psychologically unavoidable. This was the interpretation of passages, phrases, or single words according to the unconscious complexes governing the minds and controlling the characters of those who preserved and passed down the texts. It is perfectly natural, therefore, to expect to find that sacerdotal and monastic interests, characteristics, and practices are idealized whereas the interests, characteristics, and practices of all other classes are minimized and criticized. This indeed is what we do find to be the case. The inevitable consequence is that words which bore one meaning when they were uttered by the original author came bit by bit to receive a modified or altogether different meaning when they had passed through the mouths and pens of monks and priests. Our semantic study alone would indicate such a historic probability. The result for us who live today is somewhat unfortunate. For we learn from the text that if we would live a higher life, if we would pursue the quest of the Overself, we must put away our duties, cast aside our responsibilities, and deny our physical natures. We must discourage interest in the improvement of this world or the betterment of mankind's miserable lot. We must flee from society and hide in retreats with other escapists. We must regard the world as a trap cunningly invented by Satan for our downfall and the body as a tomb dug for our divine soul. Whoever refuses to accept the path outlined by monkish and sacerdotal editorial interference is shamed by having the very word-meanings or passage-quotations born of such interference hurled at him in proof of his error! The divine quest, which was originally intended for the study and practice of mankind generally—so far as their worldly status, class, or profession be—has now become something intended for the study and practice of monks and ascetics only. Men obsessed by a persistent complex which made them fuss anxiously over their bodily life to the detriment of their mental life; men who failed to perceive that the real battlefield of human life is internal and not external; men who could not comprehend the unity of Spirit and matter; men, in short, who had yet to realize that they were virtuous or sinful primarily as their thoughts were virtuous and sinful—these are set up today as the arbiters of how we twentieth-century persons shall live in a world whose circumstances and systems are beyond their own narrow imaginations. The quest indeed has been turned into something impossibly remote from us, something only to be talked about at tea-tables because we cannot implement it. Such a situation is unacceptable to the philosophic student. Better ostracism, abuse, slander, and misunderstanding than this.

247

No church, no monastery, no ashram can shut in the divine life behind its walls. THAT is for all.

248

Kabir:
Why put on the robe of the monk, and
live aloof from the world in lonely pride?
Behold! my heart dances in the delight of a
hundred arts; and the Creator is well pleased.

249

The point is that holiness is not necessarily limited to hermits and monks: it may also belong to householders. Whether it be the Long or the Short Path, both may be practised in the daily routine of life.

Independence and teachers

250

The problem is to take advantage of outside help and yet leave the student individually free. Its solution is simple. He can get this help through books written by seers, sages, and philosophers.

251

Those who can only advance by hanging on to a teacher make only a pseudo-advance and one day their house of cards will come tumbling about their ears. But it is equally true that those who can only progress by dispensing with a teacher, progress farther into the morass of ignorance. He alone who can take a teacher's guidance in a free spirit; who comprehends that while the teacher points out a path, it is for him to strive, toil, and adventure forth; such a man will derive much from his discipleship.

252

When he finds that he can go no farther by himself, the time has come to look within for more grace or to look without for more guidance. He needs the one to get away from his own selfishness or the other to get away from his own darkness.

253

There is sometimes conflict between submission to authority and obedience to conscience.

254

To rely wholly on oneself is not so wise as to rely both on oneself and on the teachings of illumined men. Such teachings exist in abundance in the whole world's great literature—sacred, philosophical, and ethical.

255

One of the most valuable philosophic character qualities is balance. Therefore the student should not be willing to submit himself to complete authoritarianism and thus sacrifice his capacity for independent thinking, nor on the other hand should he be willing to throw away all the fruits of other men's thought and experience and dispense with the services of a guide altogether. He should hold a wise balance between these two extremes.

256

I will humbly bow before the revelation of a superior truth and submissively study his teaching, but I will not regard that as sufficient reason to abandon the free, full, and autonomous growth which I am making. For only if such growth remains as natural as a flower's and is not artificially shaped by another man, can I fulfil the true law of my being.

257

The young want and ought to have gurus and doctrines. The adult should learn to discriminate for themselves, collect their own doctrines from a wide field, and become their own teachers. But in this matter of understanding life, one does not become adult and acquire a sense of responsibility precisely at twenty-one.

258
Authority and individuality need not contend with one another in a man's mind.

259
It makes man responsible for his own life while duly honouring the helps and influences outside him. He must rely on the force of his aspiration and devotion, work and discipline instead of leaning on guru or avatar or turning primarily to dry academic scholarship and depending on book learning for final judgements. The master is not rejected but then he is not given the place of God.

260
I deeply admire the genius and humbly respect the attainment of each guru, but do not feel that it is proper to let him, or any other man I so far know, have a *controlling* influence over me.

261
When it is hard to form a correct judgement by oneself, the wisdom of consulting another person becomes obvious. But if one consults the wrong person, one gets wrong advice. His conviction that he knows what is right does not make it necessarily so. One is unable to escape from the need of judging the other's advice. So in the end one has to practise some degree of self-reliance.

262
If he refuses to seek and cling to the human personality of any Master, but resolves to keep all the strength of his devotion for the divine impersonal Self back of his own, that will not bar his further progress. It, too, is a way whereby the goal can be successfully reached. But it is a harder way.

263
Be a disciple if you must but do not be a *sectarian* disciple. Keep away from such narrow alleys.

264
Both an inspired church and a qualified master have their place but it is only a limited one. Beyond those limits, nothing outside his divine soul can really help the spiritual seeker. For its grace alone saves and enlightens him. The religious man who depends on a church for his salvation thereby delays it. The mystical aspirant who depends on a master for his self-realization also delays it. He will have to learn to rely less and less upon other people for his spiritual and worldly advancement, more and more upon his inner self.

265
It is well to seek and accept guidance. The error and exaggeration creep in when you become too concentrated on a single source of guidance.

266

He is perfectly entitled to clear his own pathway to the Spirit for himself, and without the help of any contemporary, any neighbour, or any leader who lived in the past centuries. But will this independence and this isolation be a gain or a loss? The answer must always be an individual one: it cannot always be one or the other alone. It depends on what sort of a man he is, what sort of teaching and what sort of teacher he has access to.

267

But parallel with this practice of self-reliance and this assumption of self-responsibility we may receive the help of a more advanced person if it is available to us. It should of course be received only if it leaves our freedom untouched and only if it is competent. Thus we do not take advantage of such help to *sink into* lazy forgetfulness of the work that must be done upon and by ourselves.

268

There is room in life for the element of revelation equally as for that of realization. Guidance or instruction from another person is not to be rejected merely because it is external, but only if it emanated from a dubious source. If an aspirant is going to ignore *all* the signposts, he will wander around for a very long time before he gets started on the right road.

269

Not knowing where to find the right path, he may easily enter by mistake on the wrong path. Indeed, he may take several false steps before he reaches surety or, more often, some right ones mixed up with some wrong steps. And not having the strength for the true ideals, he may slip many a time. Thus his quest may need harder efforts and take a longer course than the quest of a competently guided disciple.

270

Without qualified guidance, the labour of the aspirant becomes a process of trial and error, of experiment and adventure. It is inevitable, consequently, that he should sometimes make mistakes, and that these mistakes should sometimes be dramatic ones and at other times trivial ones. He should take their lessons to heart and wrest their significance from them. In that way they will contribute towards his growth spiritually.

271

The duty of the aspirant to cultivate his moral character and to accept personal responsibility for his inner life cannot be evaded by giving allegiance to any spiritual authority.

272

Contrary to the common Hindu teaching, the Buddha taught that although this would necessarily be the slower path, still it was possible for anyone to attain Nirvana (as a Pacceka Buddha) by relying on himself alone and remaining independent of any master's help. And his statement to his personal disciples is significant: "Treat my doctrine as your Teacher when I am dead."

273

That an aspirant *must* join a particular group or attach himself to one teacher is questionable. This helps many beginners, the vast majority of whom usually do it anyway. But they are of the ordinary sort. When anyone begins to make real advance, he emerges into real need of an individual path unhampered by others, undeflected by their suggestions. The inner work must then proceed by the guidance of his own intuitive feeling together with the pointers given by outer circumstances as they appear.

274

The necessity of a teacher is much exaggerated. His own soul is there, ready to lead him to itself. For this prayer, meditation, study, and right living will be enough to find its Grace. If he has sufficient faith in its reality and tries to be sensitive to its intuitive guidance he needs no external teacher.

275

It is not really necessary to have the guidance of an adept if one has sufficient inner resources from which to draw. For those who have such inner guidance, spiritual progress may be made quite satisfactorily.

276

But each aspirant has in the end to find his own expressive way to his own individual illumination. Outside help is useful only to the extent that it does not attempt to impose an alien route upon him.

277

Listening to someone else's teaching, or reading it, will only be a temporary makeshift until the day when he can establish communication with his own intuitive self and receive from it the teaching which he, as a unique individual, needs. From no other source can he get such specially suitable instruction.

278

All Nature shows the self-evolution which is going on. Each of us is part of it. Each of us can carry himself further into the next phase and beyond. The Force and Intelligence are present, but the faith in them must be drawn on. Otherwise, we shall have to look outside for help, probably for someone to guide, lean on, and be carried by. But held too long and too far, the hope proves illusory.

279

When the excess of guru-worship and priestliness became too prevalent in India, Buddha tried to reproclaim the truth and to counterbalance the superstition. He taught in many places, said on many occasions, "No one saves us but ourselves; no one can and no one may. Each alone must tread the path." In our own time we hear echoes of these beliefs that Buddha tried to reform.

280

The risk is too great. The pitfalls are too deep. The snares are too dangerous. If I cannot find a genuine indication of the presence of God-consciousness in a man by some fleeting or permanent reflection in the mirror of my own internal experience, then I must perforce abandon my would-be discipleship to the care of the divinity that lies hidden somewhere at the back of my mind.

281

In the absence of a master let him follow a lone path, welcoming whatever he can learn from competent authorities but attaching himself to none.

282

Nothing that I have anywhere written should be regarded as meaning that instruction can be dispensed with. But in view of two factors—the rarity of competent instructors and the over-emphasis of Indian-originated suggestions upon the need of a teacher—I have tried to show aspirants that the way to success is still open to them.

283

Nobody should overrate the help which a spiritual guide is able to give and underrate his own resources. The quest is a work whose continuity goes on for a whole lifetime, whereas the personal contact which is needed to make a guide's help effective can only be gotten occasionally at most and then only for limited periods of time. I give the warning because I know from several of my correspondents that this is a common tendency among beginners and even among those who ought to know better.

284

The importance of a teacher is somewhat overrated. If one continues his program of study, prayer, and meditation, and if he appeals to his own higher self for guidance, he will certainly continue to progress. Earthly responsibilities will not interfere, for the time spent away from prayer and meditation is also part of the spiritual life.

285

Beware of professionalism in this field, of the professional expounder of truth and the professional seekers of it. Both Way and Goal are far simpler than most of them seem to think it is, and markedly unlike the impression left by many writings and lectures, books and teachings, whether ancient or modern.

286

First at the beginning of the Long Path, and again at the beginning of the Short Path a master, a spiritual guide, is really required. But outside these two occasions an aspirant had better walk alone.

287

The teacher himself has to go to this inner source for his own enlightenment, why not go to it directly yourself?

288

It may be slower but it will be much safer, present-day conditions being what they are, to teach oneself and liberate oneself.

289

To find out the truth little by little by oneself is to make it really one's own. To be pushed into it with a plunge by a master always entails the likelihood of a return to one's native and proper level later on.

290

We must find the Overself through our *own* perceptions, that is, through our *own* eyes—or never. It will not suffice to believe that we can go on seeing it through the eyes of another man—be he a holy guru, or not.

291

The seeker must elicit these things for himself, and from within himself: reading about them is not enough, hearing about them from gurus, or at lectures, is not enough.

292

Something more is needed than what books or even gurus can give him. This can only be found within himself. The courage needed for such a standpoint must also be found, and can be, within himself.

293

He may well be a bit suspicious of all these offers, much less of guarantees, of salvation by a guru. How this can be done without thwarting Nature's intent to develop us fully on all sides is difficult to see. We shall be robbed of the important values implicit in self-effort if we are granted absolution from such effort.

294

The searcher who is undeceived by fine phrases and knows when to look for the self-interest behind them, will know also when emphasis on the need of a master is cunningly or emotionally turned into exaggeration of the need.

295

I will be the most deferential of men before the teaching and in the presence of a truly illumined man. But I will stubbornly resist, and stand firm on my ground, when I am asked to surrender my intellectual freedom and become his bonded disciple, open no longer to the teaching or influence of any other man.

296

He has to detach himself—or let himself become detached by book or teacher—from false ideas, conventional fallacies, or blind leadership.

297

There is no contradiction between advising aspirants at one time to seek a master and follow the path of discipleship, and advising them to seek within and follow the path of self-reliance at another time. The two counsels can be easily reconciled. For if the aspirant accepts the first one, the master will gradually lead him to become increasingly self-reliant. If he accepts the second one, his higher self will lead him to a master.

298

When this craving for a guru becomes excessive, inordinate, it is a sign of weakness, an attempt to escape one's own personal responsibility and to place it squarely on somebody else's shoulders, a manifestation of inferiority complex such as we are accustomed to see in races that have been long enslaved by others.

299

Although it is true that he must find his own way to the goal, he need not do so as if he exists alone on this planet! He may be helped by drawing creatively on the experience gained by others even while he critically judges it.

300

Gautama tried teacher after teacher and left them after a time because he found their doctrines deficient or their practices defective. If he had not had the courage to do so, the world would never have had its Buddha. Even Sri Krishna did not ask Arjuna to follow him blindly but tried to dispel his doubts by reasoned discussion, so that only at the *end* of the *Gita* do we find Arjuna saying, "My doubts are gone."

301

They run hither and thither, from teacher or teaching to a different teacher or teaching, from Euramerica to India, to Japan, to Indonesia, looking away from their own being for that which is the essence of that being. They are like the man who looked everywhere for his spectacles. At last he gave up the search—only to find the spectacles resting on his own nose. But his attention had first to be drawn to his nose by someone—or by the book of someone—who could see them there. These seekers are not ordinarily aware of what is continually present within them, the stillness of the centre of their being, and instead of looking there for it, they look elsewhere, or to other men. The real service which is rendered them by these others is to tell them where to look; the rest is for them to do. But the lazy, or those who want something for nothing, expect or want the gurus to do it for them—a false idea. The other great error of these confused minds is to seek from Asia what Asia is now rejecting. The best Asiatics are not rejecting its spirituality but its ignorance, superstition, unbalance, futility, narrowness, and excess of conservatism. The Westerner who adores Asia's past wants to copy it, picturing it as a golden age (which it never was). He tries to restore it for himself and in himself, becoming an ape and a parrot.

302

If some have found their way to this illumination by following slavishly the details of a special teaching, others have found it by following no teaching at all.

303

It is not uncommon for inexperienced beginners on the Quest, who are ignorant of the serious and often harmful results of such associations, to turn to untrustworthy so-called occult teachers. In most cases, it would be far safer, and more satisfactory in the end, for them to depend solely upon their own unaided efforts than to follow such a dangerous method.

304

Enactment of the master-pupil relationship, with the subordinate and submissive role allotted to him, is far better if it happens within his own person than if it is objectified without. Then the lower ego will have to play this role.

305

Only when he is beginning to find his own way to the inner reality and feel its support, only when he is lessening his dependence on some other human being (call him guru or what you like), can it be truly said that he is a disciple of the Holy Spirit itself—not some particular man's disciple.

306

To lose his own ego in some other person's is not to conquer it. And although this is clear enough in ordinary cases, it is not so clear in reference to losing it in a guru's person, in total surrender to him. Yet the direction is still external, still taking him away from the god within himself. He exchanges one kind of dependence for another—but both share this limitation of being outside himself. Then why has this way been prescribed so often and so much in the Indian spiritual systems? Because it is useful for beginners: it is a step forward towards separation from their own will into at least a better one. But for the man of more development, there is no other way than to turn round and look within, to depend on the Light and Power which is there and which, with enough patience, will be found there.

307

We all ought to be happy at the mention of certain names of contemporary spiritual guides—whether those who have now passed out of the body like Mary Baker Eddy and Sri Ramana Maharshi or those who are still with us. Human culture is ennobled and enriched by what these people have given it. Human existence is better because they existed. Not only their immediate followers but we also have gained by their presence or their work. Each has given his or her own special gift to us and in his or her individual way. This said, it is needful to add that we all ought to follow what is true in these spiritual leaders' teaching as we ought to imitate what is good in their conduct, but we ought not do so quite uncritically. They are still human and therefore still fallible. We ought not to follow them in their mistakes nor imitate them in their misjudgements.

308

Only arrogance will reject the experience of other men, but only weakness will support itself solely on such experience. A wiser attitude will use it discriminatingly.

309

How does the average seeker come to his particular teaching? He rarely makes, or has the time to make, a complete investigation of all the teachings offered. And even if he does, his judgement may be too poor or too inexperienced to be relied on. So the basis on which he selects the favoured teaching is the emotional reaction aroused, that is, the degree to which he personally likes or dislikes it. Or he joins a teacher who is either well-publicized in books and journals, easily accessible, and much talked about, or else one who does his own advertising, often exaggerated. This again is an insufficient basis for proper selection and immensely inferior to a careful analysis of sufficient data made by a cool impartial judgement. If the seeker makes any advance at all, it is really due to his own merits, which would have enabled him to make it anyway and with whatever method he adopted. Yet the credit goes to the teacher or the method, although they do not deserve it!

310

This looking to, and leaning upon, one man, may come to dominate the mind to such an extent that the creative powers and discriminative judgement of that mind may be wholly suppressed.

311

If you rely on an external teacher you rely on something which you may have to drop tomorrow or on somebody you may have to change the day after.

312

All this is not to be misunderstood to mean that we suggest that everyone ought to acquire every item of his spiritual knowledge afresh through his own personal experience, ignoring all the experience of the whole race. On the contrary, we would strongly suggest that he avail himself of this experience through the form it has taken in great literature throughout the world.

313

To sum up: a competent spiritual director of his way is certainly worth having, but unfortunately the problem of where to find such a man seems insuperable. If an aspirant is lucky enough to solve it without becoming the victim of his own imagination he will be lucky indeed. If not, let him exploit his own inner resources. Let him appeal to the divine soul within himself for what he needs.

314

The two schools of thought, one of which says that spiritual attainment depends on self-effort and the other that it depends wholly upon the Grace of God, do not really clash, if their claims are correctly and impartially understood. When a man begins his spiritual quest, it is solely by his own strivings that he makes his initial progress. The time comes, however, when this progress seems to stop and when he seems to stagnate. He has come to the end of a stage which was really a preparatory one. The stagnation indicates that the path of self-effort is no longer sufficient and that he must now enter upon the path of reliance upon Grace. This is because in the earlier stage, the Ego was the agent for all his spiritual activities, whilst it provided the motives which impelled him into these activities. But the Ego can never be really sincere in desiring its own destruction, nor can it ever draw from its own resources the power to rise above itself. So it must reach this point where it ceases self-effort and surrenders itself to the higher power which may be variously named God or the Higher Self, and relies on that power for further progress. But because the aspirant is living in a human form, the higher power can reach him best through finding a living outlet which is also in a human form. So it bestows its grace upon him partly as a reward and partly as a consequence of his own preparatory efforts by leading him to such an outlet, which is none other than a Master or Guide in the flesh. No man is wholly saved by his own effort alone nor can any Master save him if he fails to make effort. Thus the claims of both schools are correct if introduced at the proper stage.

Loneliness

315

There is little place today as ever for the spiritual individualist, the man who cannot betray himself and deny truth for the sake of peaceably settling down in one of society's organized groups or established institutions. The climate is hostile to him. He must remain a lone thinker, self-exiled, paying a price but getting his money's worth.

316

The independent mind which does not wish to commit itself to any creed or group or cult must accept its loneliness as the price of its independence.

317

The fact may be noted without reproach and without antagonism, without surprise and without arrogance, that men are the victims of the very institutions they have themselves created and maintained. The individual who refuses to be lost in their mesmerized surrender to the false prestige of these institutions must go forth alone into an arid and empty wilderness, must set himself apart from the world around him.

318

He has entered a world of being where few men will be able to follow him. Their lack of understanding will be the bar.

319

He will find that few of his kind are settled in this world, a discovery which he may meet either with disappointment or with resignation.

320

The man who is travelling this inner way soon finds and feels its loneliness. He may try to get rid of the feeling by joining a group, but this can give only a partial liberation and, in the end, only a temporary one. But this loneliness need not be a cause of suffering. Rather he may come to enjoy it.

321

The feeling of being isolated, the sense of walking a lonely path, is true outwardly but untrue inwardly. For there he is companioned by the Overself's gentle ever-drawing love. He has only to grope within sufficiently to know this for himself, and to know it with absolute certitude.

322

The higher the peak one climbs, the lonelier the trail becomes. There is a paradox here for the loneliness exists outside the body, not inside the heart, and the more it grows outside the less it is felt inside.

323

The quest is to be walked alone. Yet although this means that one must have a solitary and creedless path if the Word is to be said, the Touch is to come, the Glimpse is to be seen, or the Feeling of the presence is to enter awareness, the gracious revelation is the sacred compensation.

324

Because of the soul's own infinitude, its expressions in art and culture, its manifestations in society and industry, will always be infinitely varied. If we find the contrary to exist among us today, it is because we have lost the soul's inspiration and forfeited our spiritual birthright. The monotonous uniformity of our cities, the uncreative sameness of our society, the mass-produced opinions of our culture, and the standardized products of our immobilized mentalities reveal one thing glaringly—our cramping inner poverty. The man who possesses a spark of individuality must today disregard the rule of conformity and go his own way in appalling starving loneliness amid this lack of creativeness, this dearth of aspiration.

325

In the end he must inwardly walk alone—as must everyone else however beloved—since God allows no one to escape this price.

326

As he climbs towards the ideal he finds himself drawing farther and farther away from his fellows who herd on the plains below. That which draws him to itself, also isolates him from others.

327

He may wander through the low haunts of life, seeking the smiling figures of Fortune and Love. He may go, too, into the higher abodes of better people. In both places he finds illusion and frustration. So it comes about that he ceases his wandering and sits silently by a lone hearth. He knows then what he had always dimly suspected.

328

Emerson (in a letter to a young seeker): "A true soul will disdain to be moved except by what natively commands it, though it should go sad and solitary in search of its master a thousand years. . . . I wish you the best deliverance in that contest to which every soul must go alone."

329

If he is really to attain Truth, he will have to learn how to stand solidly by himself, how to live within himself, and how to be satisfied with his inner purpose as his only companion.

330

From the moment that he has embarked on this quest he has, in a subtle and internal sense, separated himself from his family, his nation, and his race.

331

He must be prepared to accept an appalling loneliness if he wishes to walk this path. But the loneliness will be limited to his novitiate. For a new presence will slowly and quietly enter his inner life during its advanced stage.

332

There is a point at which no aspirant can surrender his ideals under the compulsion of a materialistic society, can no longer come to terms with it. Such a point will be vividly indicated to him by his own conscience. It is then that, of his own free will, he must accept the cup of suffering.

333

The disciple must not shirk the isolation of his inner position, must not resent the loneliness of his spiritual path. He must accept what is in the very nature of the thing he is attempting to do.

334

The aloneness that he feels must be accepted. Only then, only when he understands and dwells calmly in it, will the great power of the Saint come forth and dwell with him in turn.

335

It is most pleasant for a man to feel himself at one with the crowd, most uncomfortable to feel himself at variance with it. Yet the seeker who has heard truth's call, has no other choice than to accept this intellectual loneliness and emotional discomfort if he is not to find what, for him, is the worse fate of violating his spiritual integrity.

336

The cure for loneliness is company; but if there is no affinity in the company, then it is only a quack cure. This prescription is true for everyone, even for the sage, for he finds his company in the Overself's self-presence.

337

The attempt to follow a lone path may well make him wonder at times whether or not he is making a mistake. It needs more than ordinary stubbornness to remain in a minority of one or two. He will certainly need at times, and gladly welcome, some reassurance from others.

338

He must be willing to stand alone, although that may not prove to be necessary.

339

"Is there not an unnatural air about the quest?" This is a question which is sometimes asked. The answer depends, of course, upon a definition of terms. The multitude of non-questers are certainly not living close to Nature. What the questioner really wants to say is that the quest seems to lift a man out of the herd, to make him no longer average, to mark him different from the other men around him. Its goals do not accord with the ordinary human desires and the common instincts.

340

There is only one real loneliness and that is to feel cut off from the higher power.(P)

4

ORGANIZED GROUPS

Benefits for beginners

Should he join an organization, a community of students, or a group of seekers? Some are hindered by such a move, others feel they are helped; all in the end will have to come to themselves, will have to look inward rather than outward.

2

The usefulness of organizations makes them a necessity. The appointment of men to administer those organizations is unavoidable.

3

In the arrangements of human society, there is a necessary place for human institutions.

4

In his earlier years, the seeker may try one kind of institution of a religious or mystical character and then move to a different one if it does not fulfil his expectations. In this way he may experiment with different creeds and different forms of practice. This may be useful so far as it exposes him to the influences which are needed to balance one another. But it may be bewildering if he overdoes it.

5

Most traditional forms, or the newer organizations which have some sort of spiritual teaching, are useful in the beginning to most people. But this is not to say that they're going to be useful always. They have their limitations, and at a certain stage may prevent further advance.

6

But those who can stand alone are always smaller in number: most persons will frankly admit that they cannot, certainly most young and most old persons. This is the justification for the need of organizations, groups, churches, and priesthoods. They offer what seems fixed support in life, stable in doctrine, superior nobler holier and wiser than what the ordinary person finds in himself. This is why philosophy attracts the few, those who are, or who can be trained to become, strong enough to walk a lonely path.

7

I have never forgotten the statement made to me somewhere in India by a young man who had recently joined the Society of Friends and had been sent out to what was then a famine-stricken tropic country on a Quaker relief project. "Why, when you admit to all these queries and doubts, and feel you are searching, do you then make yourself a member of a sect, admittedly one of the noblest and finest of all, but still a sect, with all the limitations which go with it?" I had asked him. He thought for a while and then broke the long silence to reply: "I quite understand and admit what you say about sectarian limitations. But I feel my youth and inexperience and weakness. At my age there is need for some kind of support from outside, some group to give me not merely fellowship but also a feeling of solidity and stability, something to lean upon, in short." What he said taught me a lesson and made me understand sympathetically that the love of independence to ensure a free search, and the desire for self-reliance do not belong to everybody, and that others, certainly most people, have other needs, prefer other ways, for which there is also room in human life.

8

Despite these criticisms, however, he sees also how organizational life was helpful to his early efforts and guided his early steps. He knows that there is a place for it, but he also knows that that place is a preliminary one. If the final work of a seeker is to be done for and upon himself, that does not displace the necessity of an institution in assisting him to do the preparatory work. Therefore, even the advanced mystic, who has no need of its services, cannot in principle be hostile to an institution. He readily admits its necessity and denies only its all-sufficiency.

9

These groups led by a guru may be quite useful to a beginner who is stumbling in the dark. But to join one without knowing the limitations and dangers would be foolish.

10

Religious followers begin to organize themselves either quite spontaneously when unled, or quite obediently when a leader appears, for several good understandable reasons. The coming together in a compact group affords some protection, offers them a mode of expression and the teaching a mode of preservation.

11

The strength of such a group must lie in its quality and not in its numbers. It must be the result not of propaganda activities but of the spontaneous association of like-thinking people.

12

It is true that there are many eccentrics among these believers but there are also many serious sensible and well-behaved people among them.

13

Membership in a group, be it a vastly spread religion or a small minor sect, gives each member a feeling of correctness in their joint beliefs; each supports the others. But this may begin to weaken when some drastic and unexpected event may prove hard to bear.

14

There is nothing wrong with the group idea if its members meet for fellowship.

15

If he joins a monastic order he will usually have to take a vow to practise certain restraints and renunciations. To a lesser degree this also occurs with joining certain groups and circles in the world outside such orders. The value of the vow is that it sets up a standard to be followed, a course to be travelled, and a goal to be reached. He may fall from the standard, deviate from the course, and fail to approach the goal, but their existence may help him come closer to the object of the vow than he might otherwise have come. On the other hand, the layman who is not interested in vows but simply resolves to improve himself lacks their stimulus. There is nothing but the inner force of his own ideal to keep him from abandoning the self-imposed rigours of his discipline. He depends on the power which he will have to summon up from somewhere within himself. The weakness of binding himself to the new regime which he himself has imposed is that it can easily be shirked at any time, that if he yields to the inclination to do so, the restraints upon it will be weaker and fewer.

16

Whatever church, organization, or cult to which he commits himself, he should always make for himself at least the reservation that he should retain the freedom to leave and go elsewhere or to cease seeking among outer organizations and to search within.

17

But there is a place and a need for the cohesion of a group, for the sustained teamwork of an organization, and for the discipline imposed on individuals by a church.

18

Any institution dedicated to training for the life of the Spirit will always keep out the Spirit. It cannot be found through any formal performances, nor through any organized group work. And all that training can do is to open a way wherethrough, *if It is already coming or willing to come,* it may pass.

19

The need to identify himself with an organized group, established religion, or particular sect, or indeed with any cause, is at base the need to identify himself with the God within. He unwittingly wants to belong to something larger than his own little ego. Such membership helps to achieve this because it removes the sense of separateness and the feeling of loneliness. But it does so only at the surface level. With the efflux of time, he finds it necessary to search for satisfaction at a deeper level. For the group, the church, or the institution are outside him and give it only temporarily, partially, or spottily. A durable and fuller result is possible only by turning around and looking within his own being. For there, in the hidden presence of the Spiritual self, he will find that larger Cause, Source, Mystery, with which he can identify himself in the perfect way.

20

In joining a society or group he joins mostly those who are not more advanced than himself in the capacity to meditate. There are certain hindrances to progress which accompany membership in such organizations. If, however, the social value of finding other persons interested in spiritual subjects outweighs the immediate need of making inner progress, then membership would of course be most helpful.

21

My advice is often asked about forming a little group of people to study my books. Ordinarily, there is no objection to a few people meeting together for such study, as they might help answer mutual questions. But it is best not to let the group increase its size. There are several reasons why it is better to restrict the class to a small number than to let everyone who wishes enter it. Quality should be the only consideration in such admissions; quantity would in the end disintegrate the group. Let the effort be limited to study, clearing up questions, and talks. Group meditation should not be practised among beginners if there is no powerful uplifting leader in their midst to protect them. There is a right time and a wrong time for personal endeavour to lead and assist a spiritual group. The right time will come only with competence. Until then there is the ever-present task of the student's own self-improvement. That is above all else.

22

It is only as group allegiances are slowly widened that goodwill can be established towards those who are outside such borders.

23

The desire of an individual to join a group can never be given more than qualified approval. But if he feels certain that something may be gained by associating with other seekers, and if he is successful in finding a group devoted exclusively to the search for the highest Truth, it may be all right for him at that particular phase of his development.

24

There is need of a school where an effective form of service would be the giving of practical initiation into meditation for inexperienced beginners, and the guidance of development for experienced intermediates. This could do much good. A single meeting for meditation is usually enough: individuals could then be left to work out for themselves the contact thus given, returning to the school periodically for further and more advanced instruction.

25

Instead of being found out, the particular needs and special tendencies of the individual seeker will be ignored and even suppressed in the endeavour to conform him to the system. There is both good and bad in this. Which of these he will receive depends upon the competence of the teacher, if he has one, or the mental attitude he takes toward the system itself—upon his blind slavish adherence to it or intelligent, open-eyed use of it.

26

He is under no obligation to stay fixed in an ashram or group merely because he once entered it.

27

The time comes when the aspiring philosopher feels that he will get no actual benefit from his studies and make no personal progress unless he enters the second stage and begins to work on himself. It is then that he will perceive, if he is not too foolish, that most of these groups and cults are of no further use to him.

28

We must be prepared in advance not to expect too much from human institutions, for the simple reason that they are administered by or composed of human beings, that neither they nor the institutions are perfect, that any claim to the contrary is a roseate dream, any belief in the affirmative is naïve, and the person holding it is inexperienced.

29

I am not criticizing those who follow such ways or advocate such teachings, nor venturing to judge their rightness or wrongness. The need for, and the usefulness of, group organization is admitted. But I feel there is an equal need for a different approach, for independence from all group organizations; there is room for a path which avoids "joining." This need not be misunderstood. There are those who like the first way and they will have to follow it. There are others who will prefer the second way. I am among them. Both ways are needed but by different people.

30

Those who feel their own path or school or cult calls to them should heed it. It is right for them. But they should not be so narrow as to proclaim it to be the *only* way to God.

31

To find out that his way does *not* lie through such cults is a useful compensation for the time spent in following such a way, although life is hardly long enough to spend much of it in such negative pursuits.

32

The beginner who ventures on a tour of these cults, in the hope of finding one to suit him, ventures into a danger-beset field, where lunacy is often mistaken for illumination and where exaggerated claims substitute for solid facts.

33

The desire for power over others, for authority, is a form of personal ambition which has, in the past, mixed easily with a spiritual glimpse. A new sect, a new movement, has then come to birth. The seeker after truth who comes in contact with it would be far safer to take some of the teaching without sacrificing his freedom, without joining the group.

34

If any work, institution, or organization is centered in the Overself it cannot fall into the base, negative, or selfish currents which, in the historic past, have polluted, poisoned, and sometimes destroyed so many tasks and enterprises.

Problems

35

The pressure to make all people members of organizations, to herd them together and affix labels, is a kind of mania. Why should there not be room for untrammelled, independent minds, who prefer to remain free and uninfluenced, untied to any one group?

36

It is a common but fallacious belief that by joining a group we get at the truth more quickly, or progress to spiritual reality more easily.

37

When men act together in a religious or political organization, they often act worse than they would as individuals.

38

Why is it that the eagerness with which so many disciples flock to join an ashram ends so often in a deterioration of character after they have lived in it for a while? The answer is that there is a fundamental fallacy behind the thinking which draws them into it. It is the fallacy that they have any business with the other disciples. Their true business is with their master alone.

39

The disadvantage of adhering to a single system of belief or joining a single organization teaching religious, mystical, or hygienic principles is that the sound truths given out are usually one-sided; they ignore others equally sound and valuable but outside the purview of the system's founder or the organization's leader. This neglect prevents attainment of the full truth about the subject.

40

There is indeed some perception of this but it is quite a confused one. That which ignorant aspiration accepts as the necessity for joining some group, is much more the awareness of its own spiritual helplessness than of the group's spiritual strength.

41

Most groups of human beings, most of their associations, societies, and organizations suffer at some time from troubles caused by human weaknesses and shortcomings. These include divisions, jealousies, malices, and personal dislikes or hostilities. This is as true of idealistic and religious groups as of business and professional ones.

42

Those with experience of the cults and organizations know how unsatisfactory they are in the end. The passage of truth from mind to mind has always been a personal matter and cannot be otherwise, just as the training in meditation is equally personal.

43

The teacher soon finds that he is faced by a new problem: the temperamental incompatibilities of the students. They cannot study together without coming into disagreement and they cannot work together without coming into conflict. They take offense too easily and do not realize that the teacher has duties toward many other students besides themselves. They can't even discover that the teacher has sent more letters or given more interviews to another student without becoming jealous of the latter. Thus the personal factor cannot be eliminated from any group. In the end, the teacher finds that he has to advise each student not to concern himself about the others. So the teacher concludes that he can get better results by dealing with each individual separately than in a group.

44

Those who serve the interests of their institution, those who mold its policy and become its instrument, will have to choose between such activity and the Ideal.

45

To overreact against the misuse of power or the deficiencies of an institution is to commit a fresh error.

46

Whilst men are imperfect and whilst power makes them drunk, it is foolish to entrust the government of any religious institution, any religious organization, or any human life to a single man.

47

The organization of a church, group, or society along the usual lines is too often motivated by a mixture of urges—some creditable but others not. If there is the desire to spread what is believed to be true, there may also be the desire to occupy a prominent leading position in the organization, the ambition to dominate others.

48

Men try to escape their responsibility in this matter by handing it over to an official Church, or Spiritual Guide, or referring to Scripture. But they fail to see that in the end *it is they themselves* who judge between doctrines, decide upon beliefs, choose spiritual paths, request ceremonies and accept observances, and finally and personally pronounce the words: this is Truth! To accept belief is unconsciously or consciously to pass a judgement, one's own judgement, on that belief.

49

The idea of introducing Questers to other Questers has generally failed to effect the original purpose and has not seldom had disappointing results. It is better to recognize that this is an individual work, not to be identified with any group effort, even so small a group as two or three, let alone the larger ones of several dozen. People cannot blend so easily as to form a harmonious friendship or group, even if they are Questers. Yet many beginners in their enthusiasm try to create such friendships and have to learn their lesson when the friendship falls apart. It is better to let people find their affinity and form their companionships in a natural way. There is no duty laid upon anyone, whether teacher or taught, to give introductions unless a direct, intuitive bidding points to that duty.

50

Even where an organization is not actually obstructive or misleading, it is often cumbersome and unnecessary.

51

Can the inquiring and aspiring person find no better refuge anywhere than some rigid church or ashram? Must he join some institution and have the rest of his life laid out for him by others even if it does violence to his own finer feelings and best reasonings? Must he join a crowd of other aspirants or attach himself to some persuasive leader? It is a fact that many if not most do this, which shows the lack of strength in their minds and characters; but on the other hand a more popular way is easier and more comfortable.

52

Belonging to an elite group, whether or not it be real as self-claimed, allows its members to feel superior, to be condescending, and to denigrate others.

53

A movement may begin and seek to keep itself free from organization, administration, and authority, but it is unlikely to remain so. For human beings, fallible or ambitious, frail or emotional, will sooner or later seek to impose their ideas, will, or themselves on the others.

54

It was an old monk of the early Eastern Orthodox Church, Isikhi, who long ago witheringly remarked that if spiritual talk is too frequent and too prolonged, it becomes idle chatter.

55

Few are willing to sacrifice their desire for the gregarious support offered by joining an organization and therefore few see how this binds them to its dogmas, imprisons them in its practices or methods, and obstructs their free hearing of the intuitive voice of their own soul.

56

I am not enamoured overmuch of this modern habit, which forms a society at faint provocation. A man's own problem stares *him* alone in the face, and is not to be solved by any association of men. Every new society we join is a fresh temptation to waste time.

57

The great mistake of all spiritual organizations is to overlook the fact that progress or salvation is a highly individual matter. Each person has his unique attitude towards life; each must move forward by his own expanding comprehension and especially by his own personal effort.

58

There is a moment in the career of the seeker when he may have to face the problem of joining some special organization. Here we can deal only with the general question itself. For most beginners, association with such an organization may be quite helpful, but for most intermediates it will be less so, and for all proficients it will be definitely detrimental. Sooner or later the seeker will discover that in accepting the advantages of such association he has also to accept the disadvantages, and that the price of serving its interests is partnership in its evils. He discovers in time that the institution which was to help him reach a certain end, becomes itself that end. Thus the true goal is shut out of sight, and a false one is substituted for it. He can keep his membership in the organization only by giving up something of his individual wholeness of mind and personal integrity of character. The organization tends to tyrannize over his thoughts and conduct, to weaken his power of correct judgement, and to destroy a fresh, spontaneous inner life. He will come in time to refuse to take any organization at its own valuation for he will see that it is not the history behind it but the service it renders that really matters.

59

Their devotion to the guru, the cult, or the group is, in terms of real spiritual progress, both a help and a hindrance. As a sign, and insofar as it is a measure, of aspiration to rise toward a superior state of being, it is a help. But as another bar added to the cage in which they live, shutting out all those who are not co-followers or co-members, it increases partisanship and widens prejudice.

60

To tie oneself to a sectarian group and to its ideas is to form another attachment for the ego.

61

Group emotion is worked up until it becomes a substitute for personal inspiration. Either through ignorance of or inability to practise meditation, or both, the group members are happy to share, and are satisfied with, a common experience on the shallowest level. But nothing will replace individual work at self-development leading to deeper experience and higher knowledge.

62

When too much is made of an organization or institution and too little of the idea behind it, the leaders become tyrannical and the followers fanatical. That is, their character is corrupted.

63

Two of the grave and discriminative defects of the Indian methods of seeking Truth are the turning of men into Gods and the glorifying of imperfect institutions. While it is possible for the student to learn to some extent from these sources in the East and also in the West, he must keep in mind the fact that they are helpful only to beginners, and should exercise caution in joining any of their organizations. Our present times call for firsthand information, experience, and individual proof of the Truth, which the Quest alone offers. Institutions and organizations, on the other hand, offer nothing, demand much, and actually impede progress. There are a very few redeeming exceptions which justify their existence, but these are not generally known.

64

The assertion that spiritual chaos and anarchy are the alternatives to spiritual institutionalism and organization is absurd, for the contradictory claims and teachings of the various institutions themselves lead to a chaotic situation.

65

Only the uninformed can be deceived by the outside appearance of unity in these organized groups. The struggles and conflicts and factions which really exist inside them are a better indication of their moral grade than their tall talk in print or lecture.

66

Those who are distrustful of organization for religious purposes find good reasons in history for their attitude. The records betray its inner failure, how it really substitutes one kind of worldliness for another, how it merely offers ambition a different stage to play on, or how it replaces personal self-seeking by the corporate kind.

67

Why should many who are unable as individuals to lift themselves in meditation, devotion, or prayer be able to do so as a group? It is illogical to believe that they can, auto-suggestive to believe that they do.

68

The way of group organization is only a poor substitute for the way of individual inspiration.

69

I am quite chary of organizations, because I have seen too much in the West and the East of the evils which it quickly breeds, as I am quite unimpressed by centralization because I have seen how hard it is to eradicate the illusions to which it leads. Instead of organization, it is better to encourage individual effort; and instead of centralization, it is wiser to encourage individual deepening.

70

The biggest deceiver in religio-mystical life is the institutional establishment, the organizational group. For here the followers have the experience of being nourished when in actuality only the social need is being nourished. Here the truth and its virtue, beauty, strength, reality, and above all its transcendence, which is totally outside ordinary worldly experience, are imitated effectually and successfully. So the followers are satisfied and fall into complacence. The Quest is deserted and the copy which is substituted for it has the advantage of being much easier and pleasanter for all concerned.

71

The establishment of spiritual ashrams or communal colonies is an enterprise of which, we hope, we shall never be guilty. Such institutions usually find an enthusiastic response from persons who like to join cranky cults, indulge in endless tea-table talk, and worship leaders suffering from inflated egos. We however are working for those who have understood that it is better to worship God in solitude than in a public hall or church and who believed us when we constantly repeated that institutions invariably end as the greatest obstructions to the progress of genuine spirituality. Their material expansion is usually taken as a sign of the expansion of spiritual influence whereas actually it is a sign of the expansion of spiritual rot. Just as the League of Nations erected magnificent million-pound buildings as its headquarters only a short while prior to its total collapse, so these institutions flourish externally at the cost of their internal life. We ask those who have faith in our teaching to keep clear of spiritual organizations.

72

The history of Christianity in Nazi Germany illustrated the lack of spiritual vitality which is the lamentable state of organized religion, where the institution becomes more important than the teaching and the worldly strength of the man-made organization is preserved by the sacrifice of its moral strength. Philosophy has no room for organizations, foundations, institutions, and so on. Its teachers remain free.

73

Every form of organization which claims to be of spiritual service is, the more it grows, in danger of becoming a spiritual oppressor.

74

We establish institutions to uplift men. The institutions turn themselves by degrees into vested interests. The original purpose is then lost and a selfish purpose replaces it. The consequence is that men are both affected and infected by this moral deterioration of the institutions. They are no longer helped to rise, nor even prevented from falling.

75

It is unfortunate and regrettable, but all history bears out the fact that among religious believers and mystical followers, organization sooner or later leads to exploitation. It is more likely to happen, of course, after the prophet, teacher, guru has passed away, but in a number of recent cases it was by no means absent even during his lifetime.

76

There is no hint in Jesus' words that he wanted men to form themselves into an organized religion, to appoint a hierarchy, to create a liturgy. Was he himself not in protest against the Hebrew version of these things? Did not he suffer from its tyranny, and in the end die by it? Why should he want to set up a new institution, which would inevitably end in the same way?

77

As a spiritual organization grows in numbers, it grows also in the potentialities of internal dissension. The history of most organizations confirms this.

78

The service of an organization or a group association is that it may be able to point out the way to those who are just starting to travel the path. The disservice begins when it seeks to keep its own power over him and misguides him and misinterprets the truth under the sway of such selfish infatuation.

79

The struggle between a high original purpose and low personal ambition goes on within the organization.

80

Any organized sect which claims a monopoly on salvation, by that very act disproves its claim. For in the end we are saved by Grace alone, which comes from or through the Overself *within* us, whereas the sect is a man-made thing *outside* us.

81

It is not necessary for those who follow philosophy to enrol members or hold group meetings. They need collect no dues and seek no converts.

82

The answer to those who defend group work by quoting Jesus' single statement, "Where two or three are gathered together in my name, there am I, in the midst of them," is that it contradicts his repeated statement, "The Kingdom of Heaven is within you," and is more likely to be interpolated than authentic.

83

Within the exclusivity of a sect his power to think forcefully, creatively, and originally is lost. He is forced into a narrow area, deprived of the stimulating results of world-search. There is neither the wish nor the will to step outside the imposed borders of his own sect and measure other ideas, test other ideals, and benefit by other insights. There is a pathetic acceptance of mental captivity.

84

No organized church likes individual revelations to supplant its own authority.

85

All too soon an institution becomes a restricted, or even closed, system. Its ideas get frozen into dogmas, its members begin to suffer from intellectual paralysis, and its methods begin to savour of totalitarianism or tyranny.

86

The man who is captured by a particular religion, sect, group, or organization frequently builds a wall around it, sets up a barrier between himself and non-members, excludes every approach to God other than his own.

87

The independent seeker, who affiliates himself with no sectarian group, no fanatic organization, no narrowing cult, avoids the tensions and discards the prejudices which such affiliation usually brings with it. For those who are affiliated, contact with other denominations creates the need of defending the selfish interests and the given dogmas of their own, either directly or obliquely by attacking the others. In this way the tensions and prejudices arise and subsist. They cannot come to an end until this exclusiveness itself comes to an end. How many evils, hatreds, fights, and injustices come from it! How many unjust malignments of character does it lead to! How much blind bigotry does it cause, a bigotry which refuses to allow, and is unable to see, the good in cults other than its own!

88

As soon as they begin to organize a movement, the other things begin also to emerge—the narrow fanaticism, the limiting sectarianism, the intolerant attitude.

89

Every organization which perpetuates dogmas dares not admit new ideas which correct the error of those dogmas, for such ideas would affront the beliefs of its followers!

90

In all matters spiritual, mystical, and religious, humanity is bewitched both by the spell of the past and the prestige of the institution.

91

There are several systems, methods, groups, and organizations, but of acceptable ones there are only few.

92

Too often the clinging to a particular teacher, the membership of a particular group, leads at best to a naïve faith in the self-sufficiency of the tenets advocated, at worst to a new sectarianism.

93

Sectarianism, zealotry, and bigotry develop by stages in the minds of followers.

94

The bigger an organization becomes, the more likely are dissensions and quarrels to arise within it, despite all its professions of special sanctity or proclamations of brotherly love. The essential things get gradually lost, the accidental are made more of and treasured up. The Spirit is squeezed out, the superfluities brought in.

95

To quote in justification of group work or church gatherings Christ's words, "Wheresoever two or three are gathered together in my name, there am I in the midst of them," is no justification at all. For most groups are anything from ten to a hundred in number, most church gatherings range from twenty to a thousand in number. Christ did not say that he would be present with a dozen, a score, two or three hundred, he precisely stated the number should be two or three.

96

The belief that any institution or organization is divine has led to much superstition and unnecessary strife: the true belief that all such things are strictly human, and therefore fallible, as history repeatedly confirms, would have saved mankind much suffering.

97

All observation and experience suggests that when the things of the spirit are brought into organized forms, such as societies and sects, the harm done to members counterbalances the good.

98

Do not look for any group formation created by a philosopher, for you will find none. He is sponsored by no church, no sect, no cult, no organization of any kind, for he needs none. His credentials come from within, not from any outside source. He requires no one to flatter his personal importance. If, therefore, you hear of such a group be assured it is a religious or religio-mystical one, not a philosophic one.

99

An outward organization may be useful to those who are still on the religious and mystical levels but for the purposes of philosophic advancement it is unnecessary. Public societies are mere babels of dogmatic opinion and lead in the end to confusion. The correct history of many spiritual organizations is not an edifying one. No formal association or institution is of any real worth here. Every student must work hard on and for himself. Outside of that he may catch inspiration and receive help from an expert guide. The few who are able to walk together with him on this path will come along with time; the others would only be a drag. But if he wants to join with other really interested persons in studying the books together in an informal way, with no external bond, he may try it.

100

The seeker after Reality will be suspicious of professional spirituality, although the seeker after religion will be attracted by it. It is not necessary to advertise inner attainment. Lao Tzu pushed the same point to its farthest extreme when he wrote, "Those who know do not speak," to which we may add, "or proclaim themselves as adepts, form spiritual societies, and seek disciples."

101

Philosophy can maintain its non-sectarian nature only by maintaining its non-organizational and non-institutional character. Although certain societies and groups profess to be non-sectarian, their actual history shows plainly their inability to sustain this ideal. He who would be a true philosopher must turn to the only source of true philosophy—the fount within himself. That is, he must turn inward, not outward to a group.

102

Institutions tend to deaden inspirations.

103

Of all things Truth is the freest. So, if a man is to find it in all its genuineness, and not in its distortions, caricatures, or fragmentation, not in any substitute for it, then he must preserve his own freedom to search for it. But this is just what he cannot do so easily if he joins a sect.

104

If any teacher or organization asks you to swear ceremoniously that you will not reveal to others what you are taught, be sure that you will receive inferior occultism, not philosophic truth. For the truth hides itself from the unready: it does not have to be hidden from them.

105

Do not confuse the necessary secrecy of philosophic presentation with the portentous secrecy of charlatanic cults.

106

It is not necessary to call meetings or organize societies in order to propagate truth.

107

There is no crowd salvation, no communal redemption. The monasteries and ashrams, the organizations and societies, the institutions and temples have their place and use. But the one is very elementary and the other is very limited. Whatever is most worthwhile to, and in, a man must come forth from his own individual endeavour. Society improves only as, and when, its members improve. This is strikingly shown by the moral failure of Communist states and by the half-failure of established religions.

108

Most institutions and organizations have developed in time the fault of an egocentrism which causes them to lose sight of their original higher purpose, and so they join the list of additions to societies which have a mixed selfish and idealistic character.

109

Too many spiritual organizations exist mainly to serve those who create or staff them.

110

When those who direct the affairs of an institution become more concerned about the state of its revenue than about its state of spirituality, when they are more affected by its increasing financial returns than about its increasing materiality, it is time to pick up one's hat and stick and bid it farewell.

Relation to founder

111

A school should exist not only to teach but also to investigate, not to formulate prematurely a finalized system but to remain creative, to go on testing theories by applying them and validating ideas by experience.(P)

112

The formation of a society of seekers may have a social value but it has little instructional value, for it merely pools their common ignorance. The justification of a society educationally is its possession of a competent teacher—competent because his instruction possesses intellectual clarity and his knowledge possesses justifiable certitude.

113

Why should anyone who has come to show men the interior way proceed to delude them by pointing out an exterior one? In other words, if the kingdom of heaven is within us, what use will it be to set up an institution without us? The primary task of a man sent from God is not to found a church which will keep them still looking outward, and hence in the wrong direction, but to shed invisible grace. If he or his closer disciples do organize such a church, it is only as a secondary task and as a concession to human weakness.

114

Oscar Wilde gave some good advice about such matters when he said, "The only schools worth finding are schools without disciples."

115

The belief that a fully illumined master or religious prophet can be succeeded generation after generation by a chain of equally illumined leaders following the same tradition, is delusive. He cannot bequeath the fullness of his attainment to anyone, he can only give others an impetus toward it. He himself is irreplaceable. If churches and ashrams would only admit that they are led by faulty fallible men, liable to weakness and error, they would render better spiritual service than by continuing to maintain the partial imposture that they are not so led. If there were such public acknowledgment that their authority and inspiration were very limited, religious and mystical institutions would be more preoccupied with helping others than with themselves.

116

How can any institution, whether it be the family or the government or the church, be of better character than the persons who comprise it, and certainly those who rule or lead it?

117

To expect a Spiritual Master to repeat himself in the institution, organization, or order which gathers around him, is to expect what history tells us never happens. Shelley, Michelangelo, and Phidias did not found organizations to produce further Shelleys, Michelangelos, and Phidiases. New persons must arise to express their own inspirations. Why then found strangling institutions at all, why gather followers together into exclusive sects, why create still more monasteries and lamaseries, why make leader-worship a substitute for Spirit-and-truth worship?

118

Attachment to the group surrounding a master sheds a kind of prestige on them, and gives each one a borrowed light or strength, which may be real or false.

119

No association of spiritually minded persons can as such rise higher than the Personality who has inspired it, and in whose superior power and knowledge it has rested its roots. As Ralph Waldo Emerson pithily phrases the thought: "An institution is the lengthened shadow of one man." Europe and America, for instance, are dotted with groups working along routes of mental and semi-spiritual development, but in every such group you will find that it draws its real life from its Founder or from its Head. The point in development reached by the Head marks the limitation to which he can bring his followers, and he can take them no further.

120

In earlier centuries, the illumined man left his spiritual legacy in the hearts and minds of those who had felt his power, or been guided by his light, or known his peace. The institutions and organizations were usually the creation of disciples who lived later. But today there may be a legacy of printed books, recorded tapes, televised film.

121

The foundation of every effort to better human life is not an organized movement but the man who inspires it.

5

SELF-DEVELOPMENT

General description

"How am I to start upon this process of true self-knowledge?" The answer begins with this: first adopt the right attitude. *Believe* in the divinity of your deeper self. Stop looking elsewhere for light, stop wandering hither and thither for power. Your intelligence has become falsified through excessive attention to external living, hence you are not even aware in which direction to look when you seek for the real Truth. You are not even aware that all you need can be obtained by the power within, by the omnipotent, omnipresent, and omniscient Self. You have to change, first of all, the line of thought and faith which pleads helplessly: "I am a weak man; I am unlikely to rise any higher than my present level; I live in darkness and move amid opposing environments that overwhelm me." Rather should you engrave on your heart the high phrases: "I possess illimitable power *within* me; I *can* create a diviner life and truer vision than I now possess." Do this and then surrender your body, your heart and mind to the Infinite Power which sustains all. Strive to obey Its inward promptings and then declare your readiness to accept whatsoever lot it assigns you. This is your challenge to the gods and they will surely answer you. Your soul will be slowly or suddenly liberated; your body will be granted a freer pathway through conditions. You may have to be prepared for a few changes before the feet find rest, but always you shall find that the Power in which you have placed an abiding trust does not go into default.

2

Because he believes that self-improvement, the bettering of man's nature, is quite possible, he believes in the quest.

3

He who learns the essence of spiritual questing and the basic need in practical living, learns that he must come into command of himself.

4

Who is willing to work upon himself? Who even feels that he has any duty to do so? Yet this simple acknowledgment could lead to the discovery of God.

5

The student of true philosophy is more intent on growth than on study.

6

Each man should be himself, not represent and copy another man. But he should be his best self, not his worst, his lower, his lesser. This calls for growth, aspiration, effort, on his part. That is to say, it calls for a quest.

7

Out of his present self he is to evolve a better one and to actualize his higher possibilities.

8

The divine spirit is always there in man, has always been there; but until he cultivates his capacity to become aware of it, it might as well be non-existent for him.

9

The Overself is always there; it has never left us, but it has to be ardently, lovingly, and subtly searched for.

10

He must carry the idea of "I" to a deeper level of identification.

11

Why is it that despite all the visible and touchable counter-attractions, despite the innumerable failures and long years of fruitlessness, so many men have sought through so many ages in so many lands for God, for what is utterly intangible, unnameable, shapeless, unseen, and unheard? Because the simple but astonishing fact is that the Overself, which is the presence of God in them, is part of their nature as human beings! Mysticism is nothing more than the methodical attempt to wake up to this fact. The "soul" which metaphysics points to in reasoning, mysticism establishes in experience. We all need to feel the divine presence. Even the man who asserts that he does not is no exception. For he indirectly finds it just the same in spite of himself but under limited forms like aesthetic appreciation or Nature's inspiration. Even if all contemporary mystics were to die out, even if not a single living man were to be interested in mysticism, even if all mystical doctrines were to disappear from human memory and written record, the logic of evolution would bring back both the teaching and the practice. They are two of those historical necessities which are certain to be regained in the course of humanity's cultural progress.

12

Because the Overself is already there within him in all its immutable sublimity, man has not to develop it or perfect it. He has only to develop and perfect his ego until it becomes like a polished mirror, held up to and reflecting the sacred attributes of the Overself, and showing openly forth the divine qualities which had hitherto lain hidden behind itself.

13

The distinction between his lower self and his higher self will slowly become clear to him through inner experience and reflection thereon.

14

What, in a general way, is missing in his development as a human being moving on from animality to a higher Awareness must be supplied.

15

By such meditation and study the mind returns, like a circle, upon itself, with the result that when this movement is successfully completed, it knows itself in its deepest divinest phase.

16

That which appears as the spiritual seeker engaged on a Quest is itself the spiritual self that is being sought.

17

We have not to *become* divine for we *are* divine. We have, however, to think and do what is divine.

18

This identification with the best Self in us is the ideal set for all men, to be realized through long experience and much suffering or through ac- cepting instruction, following revelation, unfolding intuition, practising meditation, and living wisely. And this best Self is not the most virtuous part of our character—though it may be one of the sources of that virtue—but the deepest part of our being, underneath the thoughts which buzz like bees and the emotions which express our egotism. A sublime stillness reigns in it. There in that stillness, is our truest identity.

19

Each human being has a specific work to do—to express the uniqueness that is himself. It can be delegated to no one else. In doing it, if he uses the opportunity aright, he may be led to the great Uniqueness which is super- personal, beyond his ego and behind all egos.

20

As he develops more intelligence and subtler perceptions, he will wake up from being merely a conventional puppet and become a real person at last.

21

Even while he travels on this quest he should habitually remind himself of an easily forgotten truth—that what he travels to is inside himself, is the very essence of himself.

22

Beneath your everyday self lies a giant—an unsuspected self of infinite possibilities.

23

Within is mastery, within is colossal power—but you have not yet touched it. However little you have so far accomplished you can still do big things.

24

Our inmost being is a world of light, of joy, of power. To find it, and to hold ourselves in it, is to become blessed by these things. That this is a scientific fact valid everywhere on earth and not a debatable assumption, can be ascertained and proven if we will achieve the required personal fitness. Without such fitness, we must be content with belief in the theoretical statement or with passing glimpses.

25

Because there is something of God in me as the Overself, godlike qualities and capacities are in me. I am essentially wise, powerful, loving; but to the extent that I identify myself with the little ego, I obscure these grand qualities. I have the power to work creatively on my environment as well as on the body in which I am housed, just as the World-Mind, the Creative Spirit, works on the universe.

26

A man who wants to pursue this quest will have to become a different man—different from what he was in the past because the old innate tendencies have to be replaced by new ones, and different from other men because he must refuse to be led unresistingly into the thoughtlessness, the irreverence, and the coarseness which pervade them.

27

It is not only a moral change that is called for but also a mental one, not only a physical but also a metaphysical one.

28

There is no need to let go of his humanness in order to find his divine essence, but only of its littleness, its satisfaction with trivial aims.

29

Such a man cannot rest satisfied with the littleness that sees nothing beyond its own greed and desire. He will be haunted by higher ideals than the ordinary; he will want to be finer, cleaner, better, and nobler human material than the common one.

30

If in the end we have to walk this earth on our own feet, why not begin to do so now? Why continue to cultivate our weakness when we could cultivate our strength?

31

Where there is no attempt at self-improvement there is inevitable deterioration. Nature does not let us stand still.

32

The application of these ideals is hard, but let no one deceive himself into thinking that their nonapplication is much easier. Those who live without such life-purposes are subject to troubles that could have been avoided and to afflictions of their own making.

33

It is easy to drift, as so many others do, through a life of self-indulgence. It is hard to try continually to practise a life of self-control. Yet the deferred penalties of the first course are painful, the consequent rewards of the second course are satisfying.

34

The gaining of such flashes has been accidental. It should stimulate us to know that if we want to make it deliberate, there is a detailed technique, ready at hand for the purpose. Sages who know how and why these flashes come have formulated the technique for the benefit of those who want to elevate themselves.

35

From the first day that he began to tread this path, he automatically assumed the responsibility of growth. Henceforth there had to be continuity of effort, an ever-extending line of self-improvement.

36

"The prize will not be sent to you. You win it," says Emerson.

37

No one except the man himself can develop the needed qualities and practise them.

38

If he wishes to enter the portal of philosophy he will most likely begin with others, with what philosophers have thought and taught; but in the end he must make a second beginning—with himself. He will have to re-examine his own psyche, his own personality, but from a detached position, standing far to one side. He will have to decide each hour of each day how to apply the truth, gathered from books and teachers, to the events, duties, occasions, and thoughts of that day.

39

Effort at self-improvement and self-development, consciously and deliberately made, is an indispensable requirement. All talk of dispensing with it because one has surrendered to a master is self-deceiving. All avoidance of it is self-disappointing in the end.

40

He cannot shift the burden of responsibility from off his shoulders so easily as that. It remains inalienably his own by virtue of his membership in the human race.

41

He must begin to cease living at second hand, to help himself, to try his own powers, or he will never grow.

42

The responsibility for his spiritual development lies squarely upon his own shoulders. In trying to evade it, either by getting a master to carry it or by making a Short Path leap into enlightenment, he indulges in an illusion.

43

The truth cannot be had by muttering a mantram *ad infinitum* although that may yield a curious kind of transient relief from thoughts which chase one another. Nor may it be had by paying one week's income to a guru.

44

If a man is determined to succeed in this enterprise and optimistically believes that he will succeed, his efforts will increase and be strengthened, chances will be taken from which he would otherwise shrink; and even if he falls short of his hopes, the going is likely to be farther. What Ramana Maharshi said to me at our first meeting is apposite: "That is the surest way to handicap oneself," he exclaimed, "this burdening of one's mind with the fear of failure and the thought of one's failings. The greatest error of a man is to think that he is weak by nature. . . . One can and must conquer."

45

This is the ideal, but to translate it into the actual, to assert it in the midst and against the opposition of a grossly materialistic environment, calls for firmness and determination.

46

Let him not be satisfied with the amount of true knowledge he has got, nor with the quality of personal character which he has developed. Let him press forward to the more and better.

47

If, instead of merely daydreaming about it, or else attempting to obtain help from outer sources, the student would listen to and be guided by the promptings of his inner self, he would vastly hasten his progress on the Quest.

48

Social betterment is a good thing but it is not a substitute for self-betterment. Love of one's neighbour is an excellent virtue but it cannot displace the best of all virtues, love of the divine soul.

49

The man who is discontented with the world as he finds it and sets out to improve it, must begin with himself. There is authority for this statement in the life-giving ideas of Jesus as well as in the light-giving words of Gautama.

50

He has enough to do with the discovery and correction of his own deficiencies or weaknesses, not to meddle in criticism of other people's.

51

He can best use his critical faculties by turning them on himself rather than on others.

52

Progress in self-evolvement on the Quest must be due to the individual's own efforts. It can be encouraged or fostered only in proportion to the same individual's wishes and needs. Other people, who are not interested in an inner search, are, at present, fulfilling their own karmic need for a particular variety of experience; it is neither advisable nor feasible to urge them to follow this path.

53

It is a worthwhile cause, this, and does not require us to interfere with others, to propagandize them or to reform them. Rather does it ask us to do these things to ourselves.

54

Few know where really to look for the truth. Most go for it to other men, to books, or to churches. But the few who know the proper direction turn around and look in that place where the truth is not only a living dynamic thing but is their own. And that is deep, deep within themselves.

55

It is logical to assert that if every individual in a group is made better, the group of which he is a part will be made better. And what is human society but such a group? The best way to help it is to start with the individual who is under one's actual control—oneself—and better him. Do that, and it will then be possible to apply oneself to the task of bettering the other members of society, not only more easily but with less failure.

56

The Holy Land, flowing with milk and honey, is within us but the wilderness that we have to cross before reaching it, is within us too.

57

The great sources of wisdom and truth, of virtue and serenity, are still within ourselves as they ever have been. Mysticism is simply the art of turning inwards in order to find them. Will, thought, and feeling are withdrawn from their habitual extroverted activities and directed inwards in this subtle search.

58

If you are looking for truth, it is not enough to look only at your own country's, your own religion's statement of it, nor just this century's. You need also to look elsewhere, to heed the wiser voices of other centuries and to feel free to move East and West or into B.C. as well as A.D. But above all these things you must look into the mystery of your own consciousness. Uncover its layer after layer until you meet the Overself. All this is included in the Quest.

59

Nowhere in the New Testament does Jesus ask his followers to enter into a church but he does ask them, by implication, to enter within themselves.

60

To the extent that they stop looking outside themselves for the help and support and guidance they correctly feel they need, they will start looking inside and doing the needful inner work to come into conscious awareness of the power waiting there, the divine Overself. They themselves are inlets to it, never disconnected from it.

61

Why did Jesus warn men not to look for the Christ-self in the deserts or the mountain caves? It was for the same reasons that he constantly told them to look for it within themselves, and that he counselled them to be in the world but not of it.

62

Do not expect to find more truth and meaning in the world outside than you can find inside yourself.

63

Although the Infinite Spirit exists everywhere and anywhere, the paradox is that It cannot be found in that way before It has first been found in one's own heart. Yet it is also true that to find It in its fullness in the self inside, we have to understand the nature of the world outside.

64

He must start by believing that concealed somewhere within his mind there is the intuition of truth.

65

The only man you need for this great work is yourself. Stop looking outside and look within, for there is not only the material to work upon but also the god within to guide you.

66

We must find in our own inner resources the way to the blessed life.

67

The man of the world drinks and dances; the mystic thinks and trances.

68

Many men cannot find the higher truth because they insist on looking for it where it is not. They will not look within, hence they get someone else's idea of the truth. The other person may be correct but since this is to be known only by *being* it, the discovery must be made *inside* themselves.

69

He cannot know anyone else so well as himself. Why then try to know so many people so superficially when he can know only himself so deeply and truly?

70

The goal can be reached by using the resources in his own soul.

71

He should create from within himself and by his own efforts the strength, the wisdom, and the inspiration he needs.

72

The student must remember that success does not only come to him, it also comes from him. The plan of the road to achievement and the driving power to propel him along it must be found within himself.

73

Usually, it is by one's own efforts alone—but not excluding the possibility of Grace, however—that one develops the needed objectivity with which to correctly study himself and cultivate awareness.

74

The truth will be given us: we shall not be left to starve for it. But it will be given according to our capacity to receive it.

75

Ideally, we learn the wisdom of life best, easiest, and most from teachers, from instruction by those who know the Way in its beginning and end. Actually, we *have* to learn it by ourselves, by our own experience, by self-expression, all necessary and valuable, suffering as well as joy.

76

Only when all of the mind—unconsciously evolved through the mineral, plant, animal, and lower human kingdoms—enters on the quest, does it *consciously* enter upon the development of its own consciousness.

77

This intellectual preparation and emotional purification is a task that strains man's faculties to the extreme. Nobody therefore need expect it to be other than a lifetime's task. Few even succeed in finishing it in a single lifetime—a whole series is required in most cases. Nature has taken a very long time to bring man to his present state, so she is in no hurry to complete his development in any particular reincarnation. Yet such is the mystery of grace, that this is always a grand possibility, always the sublime X-factor in every case. But the individual aspirant cannot afford to gamble with this chance, which, after all, is a rare one. He must rely on his personal efforts, on his own strivings, more than anything else, to bring him nearer to the desired goal.

78

The egoism which falsifies our true sense of being and the materialism which distorts our true sense of reality are maladies which can hardly be cured by our own efforts. Only by calling, in trust and love, on a higher power, whether it be embodied in another man or in ourself, can their mesmeric spell ultimately be broken. Yet it is our own efforts which first must initiate the cure.

79

Turning inward upon himself might be retiring to a fool's paradise or into a real one.

80

To make progress inwardly is ultimately all that matters, everything else passes except the fruit of our spiritual efforts.

81

Mysticism is the theory and practice of a technique whereby man seeks to establish direct personal contact with spiritual being.

What exactly is the goal?

82

The ideal here is not set at becoming a sinless saint but at becoming an enlightened and balanced human being.

83

The ultimate point to be attained is *full* humanity. He alone who has developed on all sides in this way is fully human.

84

The aspirant's decision to aim for the highest Goal is the governing factor: if he sticks to this decision, he is bound to succeed sooner or later.

The question now arises: What is this Goal? It is the fulfilment of the Real Purpose of life, as apart from the lower purposes of earning a livelihood, rearing a family, and so forth. The aspirant will become fully Self-conscious—as aware of the divine Overself as he now is of his earthly body. And this achievement will be perpetual, not just a matter of occasional glimpses or fleeting intuitions. Even though the Quest has become more difficult under modern conditions, it has not become impossible. The timeworn means to this end must simply be brought up to date.

What are the means? They are thought, feeling, will, and intuition used in a special way. This constitutes the fourfold path, or Quest.

85

He has chosen a path to which he has been led both by instinct and by experience. As he tries to follow it, he will meet with all kinds of difficulties but he should not turn back. Because the interrelation of outward karma to inner character is so close, he should understand that these difficulties are linked up with his inner state, and that he begins to solve them by removing the imperfection of that inner state. He must understand that, although this goal is not easy to obtain, he must refuse to give up hope. The path is right by itself, and in allying himself with it, he is allying himself with what is, after all, the greatest force in the world.

86

How often have I heard, in talk or writing, that the philosophic requirements are set too high and are beyond average human compliance. My answer is that time and patience and work keep on pushing back the measure of what is possible to a man, that grace may fitfully bless him if he sustains effort and aspiration or recognizes opportunity and inspiration, and that these requirements are not set for immediate attainment but as an ultimate goal to be striven for little by little and to give correct direction to his life. "Hope on and hold on," I told Rom Landau at an outwardly dark and mentally depressed moment of his life. He did!—and later found himself, his own peace, and became in turn through his lectures and books a help to many fellow Christians.

87

The achievements of such personal self-sufficiency, of such detachment from the world of agitations and desires, is, he will say, something entirely superhuman. "Why ask frail mortals to look at such unclimbable peaks, such unattainable summits?" Philosophy answers, "Yes, the peaks are high, the summits do cause us to strain our necks upwards. But it is wrong to say that they are unclimbable. There is a way of climbing them, little by little, under competent guidance, and that way is called the Quest. True, it involves certain disciplines, but then, what is there in life worth getting which can be got without paying some price in self-discipline for it? The aim of these disciplines is to secure a better-controlled mind, a more virtuous life, and a more reverent fundamental mood."

88

Why is it that on the path we seem to meet students and aspirants only, not real teachers or genuine adepts? Why is it that so few ever seem to realize their spiritual selves? The answer is that the way is long and the game is hard, that the animal self is too strong and the human ego too foolish, and that the struggle against our innate bestiality and ignorance is too long-drawn and too beset with failures. This is what observation tells us. It may be saddening but by being realistic we at least know what to expect, what is the nature of the path we are undertaking, and what a tremendous patience we must bring to it.

89

He has come to a clearer knowledge of what the Quest means and what it will demand of him. The Quest of the divine soul has become his pole star. It was natural for him to feel repelled at first by the idea of overcoming the ego but now he sees its desirability. This will not mean giving it up in practical life however; for while he is in the flesh the ideal is to find a proper balance between egoism and altruism because he needs both. But because the individual's egoism is apt to be too big already and his altruism too small, religious teachers have usually deliberately over-emphasized subduing the ego. That is the moral side. On the philosophical side it is simply a matter of finding the Overself and letting it rule the ego thenceforth. Thus the ego is not killed but put back in its lower place. But first he has to become conscious of the Overself, he has to feel it as a living presence, and he has to do this throughout the day and night, awake or asleep. That is the goal. It is not really as hard as it sounds. For the divine self is always there within him, it is never absent from him, not even for a second. It is the unfailing witness of all his efforts and aspirations. When he has tried hard enough and long enough it will suddenly shed all its Grace upon him.

90
It is not wrong to aspire toward happiness but, on the contrary, our human duty. Those who, in the name of Spirituality, would turn life into a gloomy affair are entitled to their opinion but they cannot justly be called philosophers.

91
Every man will be forced to realize his own sacredness in the end: then only will his search for happiness find fulfilment.

92
Swami Vivekananda's works can be recommended as being authentic fruits of realization that come close to the doctrine here discussed, albeit his path was not the same. The Quest follows a double line of development: mind-stilling plus mind-stimulating, each in its proper place. And the ultimate goal is to discover that there is but one reality, of which all are but a part, that the separateness of the personal ego is but superficial, and that *Truth* is evidenced by the consciousness of unity. The first fruit of such discovery is necessarily the dedication of life to the service of all creatures, to incessant service for universal welfare. Hence, in this light, the yogi who has withdrawn into cave or forest is on a lower plane—good for him as a phase of his personal development but useless to those who must live truth, the truth of unity.

93
To forget self but to remember Overself—it is as simple as that, and also as hard as that.

94
Not to find the Energy of the Spirit but the Spirit itself is the ultimate goal. Not its powers or effects or qualities or attributes but the actuality of pure being. The aspirant is not to stop short with any of these but to push on.

95
He has to seek for the mysterious essence of himself, which is something he touches at rare, blessed, and unforgettable moments. It allures because it is also the Perfect, ever sought but never found in the world outside.

96

It is not the knowing *of* the Overself that he is to get so much as the knowing that *is* the Overself.

97

He comes at last to full consciousness of his inner being, his soul—in the correct sense of a word that is not often understood and which is used by people without knowing what they really mean.

98

If the distant goal of this quest is the discovery of true being, this does not exclude and ought not to exclude the fullest growth of the human being, the widest realization of his best capacities, making patent what is latent.

99

It is a prime purpose of the Quest to create a true individuality where, at present, there is only a pseudo one. For those who are at the mercy of their automatic responses of attraction or repulsion by environment, whose minds are molded by external influences and educational suggestions, are not individuals in any real sense.

100

The lotus, that lovely Oriental flower, is much used as a symbol of the goal we have to gain. It grows in mud but is not even spotted by it. It rests on water but is never even stained by it. Its colour is pure white in striking contrast to the dirty surroundings which are its home. So the disciple's inner life must be undefiled, unstained, and pure even though his outer life is perforce carried on under the most materialistic surroundings or among the most sensual people.

101

That which few men value and few men find is nevertheless the most worthwhile thing for which to search. What is it? It is what once found cannot be lost, once seen must be loved, and once felt awakens all that is best in a man.

102

The thirst for perfection is certainly present within us. This thirst is a pointer to its eventual slaking. But there is no necessary implication that this will be attained whilst we are in the flesh and on a level of existence where everything is doomed, as Buddha points out, to decay and death. It is more likely to be done on a higher level where such limitations could not exist. The perfection we seek and the immortality we hope for are more likely to be mental rather than physical achievements. For all mystics are at least agreed that there is such a level of untainted, purely spiritual being.

103

The fundamental task of man is first to free himself of animalist and egotist tyrannies, and second, to evolve into awareness of his spiritual self.

104

The goal is to free himself from meshes and fetters, to bring all the forces of his being under mastery.

105

The aim is to emancipate himself from earthly bondage, to redeem himself from animal enslavement.

106

His quest can come to an end only when the unveiled Truth is seen, not in momentary glimpses, but for the rest of his lifetime without a break.

107

We have to bring this awareness of the Overself as a permanent and perpetual feature into active life.

108

It is perpetual abidance in the divine that is to be sought.

109

Many are satisfied if they can attain just a glimpse of the Overself. But a few are not. They seek permanent abidance in the Overself, and that in the greatest possible degree.

110

But the main object of the quest is, after all, not these secondary betterments in bodily health, nerve, character, self-control—welcome as they are—but the discovery of truth and the living within the presence of the divine.

111

There is no such thing as an ever-receding goal on the Ultimate Path because there are not ten or twenty ultimate truths. There is only a single, final truth. This is the objective on this path and once he knows it he has attained the goal.

112

We must reflect in mind and act the true being of man.

113

If they think the goal of all this endeavour is merely to become frozen into a passivity which never expresses itself and a contentment which never sees the miseries, the disasters, or the tragedies of life, they are mistaken.

114

He seeks to fulfil a steady purpose which remains and is not an emotional froth which abates and later vanishes.

115

There are two paths laid out for the attainment, according to the teaching of Sri Krishna in the *Bhagavad Gita*. The first path is union with the Higher Self—not, as some believe, with the Logos. But because the Higher Self is a ray from the Logos, it is as near as a human being can get to it anyway. The second path has its ultimate goal in the Absolute, or as I have named it in my last book, the Great Void. But neither path contradicts the other, for the way to the second path lies through the first one. Therefore, there is no cleavage in the practices. Both goals are equally desirable because both bring man into touch with Reality. It would be quite proper for anyone to stop with the first one if he wishes; but for those who appreciate the philosophic point of view, the second goal, because it includes the first, is more desirable.(P)

116

What he chooses at the beginning of his quest will predetermine what he will become at its end. And the choice is between self-centered escape and selfless activity. Both paths will give him a great peace. Both will permit him to remain true to his inner call. But the harder one will give something to suffering humanity also. A merely personal salvation will not satisfy the philosophical aspirant.

117

Spiritual experiences that occur during adolescence are indications that he has possibilities of travelling on the spiritual quest. But he must decide whether he prefers abnormal occult experiences or the less dramatic, slower growth in the cultivation of his divine soul. A beginner cannot mix the two goals safely. And he can expect to have the help of an advanced mystic only if he seeks the higher goal.

118

He would be a rash man who promised everyone who embarked upon this quest definite experiences of a mystical, occult, extraordinary, ecstatic, supernatural, or any such kind. Such results sometimes come, sometimes not; but the persons who follow the regimes or endure the disciplines chiefly in expectation of them may well be disappointed, may even end in distrust in their teachers and teachings. A wiser type of aspirant will not insist on such experiences but will understand that there are more important and *more lasting* things.

119

In *The Secret Path* I presented the quest as shorter and easier than most people found it to be; in *The Spiritual Crisis of Man* I presented it as harder and longer, in an effort to redress the balance.

120

Now, in middle-age, the errors of my published work have become discernible. Among others, I have made the quest's goal far too near, its achievement far too easy, and the quest itself far too short. The conception of that goal which I have formulated is true enough, the reminder of a divine existence which I have given humanity is something to flatter oneself about, but the way of realization calls for efforts so superhuman that few people would ever have turned to it if my literary picture had been more faithfully drawn.

121

To improve and purify the ordinary self, to reach and realize the higher self, are clearly the most difficult of tasks. To govern passions, quieten feelings, control thoughts and develop intuitions, to direct tendencies, to remove complexes, and to remain steadfast in sticking to the chosen path—is not all this a Herculean task?

122

The Art of Self-Revelation is no tea-table philosophy, shaped and polished to beguile the tedium of the idle. Not many have attempted this path and fewer have completed it. For few find the going easy. The fleshly world with its snares waits for us all, and the escape is only for the starred ones.

123

It is to grow slowly into the discovery and realization of what he really is deep, deep inside. Coming to know it is hard enough but impregnating the moment-to-moment daily life with this knowledge is harder still.

124

The aspirant of today may be the adept of tomorrow, but the course is interminably long, the goal reached only through innumerable experiences and efforts.

125

After the optimists have had their say and the Advaitins have preached, the hard fact will be echoed back by experience: the goal is set so far, his powers so limited, that he has to call on the quality of patience and make it his own.

126

So far as history tells us, full enlightenment cannot be got in the span of a single lifetime, except among the notable few. Yet history has too many undiscovered secrets, and enlightenment is too subtle a matter to pass correct judgement upon.

127

The attainment of realization of the Overself is extremely rare, and the aspirant should not expect to do so in one limited lifetime. However, since its Grace is unpredictable, no one can say that it is impossible in a particular case.

128

If the recent scientific computation of the earth's age as four thousand million years be correct, we get some idea how long it takes to make a man. How much longer then to make a superman?

129

That which is cheaply bought is often lightly esteemed. We shall rate Truth more highly when we pay a high price for it.

130

Even a lifetime is not too long a period to devote toward gaining such a great objective. What we give must be commensurate with what we want to receive. Moreover the effort required, being worthy in itself and necessary to attain the full development of manhood, is its own reward whether there is any other or not. Why then should anyone relax his efforts or fall into despair because he has been able to make only little or limited progress toward the goal?

131

The illumination is possible for all men because they are incarnate in human and not animal forms. But all men are not willing to pay its price in mental control and emotional subjugation.

132

If the reader finds such a task too fatiguing he should remember that the reward is nothing less than enlightenment.

133

How few are those who have realized their aspiration to merge into the higher self. How rare an event it is.

134

It is obvious from the rarity of its historic realization that this ideal was always too ice-mantled a peak of perfection to be climbable by most men. Nevertheless we gain nothing by ignoring it, and it is at least well to know towards what goal mankind is so slowly and so unconsciously moving.

135

This truth may seem unsympathetic to natural human feelings, far too impersonal. It is not for the multitude who demand from religion satisfaction of desires, consolation and comfort, answers to prayers.

136

These adepts seems so immeasurably aloof from us, their attainments so superhuman, that we may well ask of what use to most men is the offering of such a quest.

137

He feels intuitively that there is, or ought to be, some elusive element, principle, purpose, or Deity behind all life and all Nature—but is it possible for a human being to become acquainted with IT?

138

Such a goal may be unappealing to many, held by their attachments as they are; but it is fascinating and alluring to a few, "old souls," much experienced after a long series of earthly lives, whose values have been altered, whose glamours and illusions have been eliminated. They feel like wanderers returning home.

139

The goal set up by this teaching may seem too foolish and perhaps even too fatuous for persons who pride themselves on their reasonability and practicality. This judgement may be the result of a slight acquaintance with the subject; it could not be the result of a full and satisfactory knowledge of it.

140

If men tell you that the path is a mere figment of the imagination, they are welcome to their belief. I, who have seen many men enter it and a few finish it, declare that the difference between the beginning and the end of the path is the difference between a slave and a master.

141

If the quest is presented as too difficult for everyone but the superman, an inferiority complex is created and those who could get some help from some of its practices are frightened away.

142

Jesus said that the way to eternal life is straight and narrow. He could have added that it is also long and difficult. Yet the beginner should not let these things discourage him. There is help within and without.

143

If the standard is set too high, love for it may not be strong enough to assist its attainment.

144

If the ideal is too rigorous, its would-be followers will be too few.

145

The achievement may seem too hard but it is not impossible. The best guarantee of that is the ever-presence within him of the divine soul itself.

146

We must take care not to fall into the depressing belief that this is to be attained by masters only and that we cannot attain it.

147

It is unhelpful to put this goal on some Everest-like peak far beyond human climbing. If many are called but few are chosen, it is their own weakness which defers the time of being chosen. In the end, and with much patience, they too will find the way beyond the struggle into peace.

148

It is not enough to find an ideal to help one's course in life: it should also be based on truth, not fancy or falsity.

149

The aspiration must not only be a desirable one, it must also be attainable.

150

There is always a valid reason for disparity between the sought-for objective and the actual performance. Those who begin hopefully and enthusiastically but find themselves disappointed and without result, ought to look first to their understanding of the Quest and correct it, to their picture of the Goal and redraw it.

151

If you want to find out why so many fail to reach the Quest's objective and so few succeed in doing so, first find out what the Quest really is. Then you will understand that the failures are not failures at all; that so large a project to change human nature and human consciousness cannot be finished in a little time.

152

It is only of limited help to the modern man, living under very different conditions as he is, to offer him the saint as a type to imitate or to quote the yogi as an example to follow.

153

He will not waste time in seeking the unattainable or striving for the impossible. For truth, not self-deception, is his goal; humility, not arrogance, is his guide.

154

That the Overself not only *is*, but is attainable, is the premise and promise of true philosophy.

155

If the goal is really unattainable, then the Quest is futile. If it is no more than approachable then surely the Quest is well worthwhile. But in fact the goal is both attainable and approachable.

156

Every man may awaken to the presence of Christ-consciousness within himself and thus step out of the merely animal and nominally human existence. It will then be a divinely human one.

157

That wonderful time when he can look straight into himself, through ego to Overself, awaits his endeavours.

158

The goal is far-off, it is true; but nevertheless it is reachable by those who will make the requisite effort to overcome self.

159

Despite all setbacks, the outcome of this endeavour can be only the fulfilment of hope. For that is God's will.

160

Even if the goal seems too far off, the attainment too high up for their limited capacities, even if it seems that one would have to be far better than ordinary to have any chance at all, that does not mean they should not embark on this quest. For even if they are able to travel only a modest part of the way the efforts involved are still well worthwhile.

161

What if the goal seems too distant or the climb too steep? Do as much or as little as you can to advance. If you lack the strength to go all the way, then go some of the way. Your spiritual longings and labours will influence the nature of your *next* body and the conditions of your next incarnation. Nothing will be lost. Higher capacities and more favourable circumstances will then be yours if you have deserved them. Every virtue deliberately cultivated leads to a pleasanter rebirth. Every weakness remedied leads to the cancellation of an unpleasant one.

162

If the fullest degree of perfection seems so far off as to depress him, the first degree is often so near that it should cheer him.

163

Few imagine their capacity extends to such a lofty attainment and so few seek it. Most of those who engage on this quest have a modest desire—to get somewhere along the way where they have more control over their mind and life than their unsatisfactory present condition affords.

164

If he knew at the beginning that it was so far and so long, and so troubled a journey, would he have embarked on the quest at all? That depends on the nature of the man himself, on the nature of his impelling motive, and on the strength behind it.

165

What man will set out on a task which he can never hope to accomplish? It is too much to expect the average seeker to become a mahatma. We portray the nature of this quest not because we hold such a vain expectation but because we believe in the value of right direction and in the creative power of the Ideal. The general direction of his thoughts and deeds—rather than those thoughts and deeds themselves—as well as the ideal he most habitually contemplates, is what is most important and most significant in his life.

166

His first need is to choose a general goal, not necessarily an exact point but enough to orient himself, to give him a direction.

167

An ideal helps to hold a man back from his weaknesses, a standard gives him indirectly a kind of support as well as, directly, guidance.

168

Let us not pretend to the Perfect or the hope of its attainment. But we can have the Ideal and follow it.

169

It is a truth which he must bring to life by his own personal experience.

170

If there were no possibility of finding one's way from this body-prisoned, time-encased condition, then no one would ever have become self-realized, and all preaching of religion and teaching of philosophy would have been futile. But we know from history and biography that such achievement has been experienced in all parts of the world and in all centuries, so that no one should give up hope.

171

Are the quest's goals worth what he has to pay for them? Is it even worth embarking on if he remembers how few seem to reach those goals? Time alone can show him that no price is too high and that right direction is itself sufficient reward.

172

The ultimate goal is for us to live from the Overself not from the ego.

173

Thinking which is fact-grounded, experience-based, and correct; living which is wise, balanced, and good; meditation which goes deeper and deeper—these are some of our basic needs.

174

Peace of mind can be enjoyed in this world: there is no need to wait for passage to the next one.

175

Different terms can be used to label this unique attainment. It is insight, awakening, enlightenment. It is Being, Truth, Consciousness. It is Discrimination between the Seer and the Seen. It is awareness of That Which Is. It is the Practice of the Presence of God. It is the Discovery of Timelessness. All these words tell us something but they all fall short and do not tell us enough. In fact they are only hints for farther they cannot go: it is not on their level at all since it is the Touch of the Untouchable. But never mind; just play with such ideas if you care too. Ruminate and move among them. Put your heart as well as head into the game. Who knows one day what may happen? Perhaps if you become still enough you too may *know*—as the Bible suggests.

176

The impossibility of realizing the Bodhisattva ideal alone shows it was not meant to be taken literally. For not only would the Bodhisattva have to wait until the two billion inhabitants presently occupying this planet had been saved, but what of the others who would have been added to this number by that time? The Bodhisattva ideal is supposedly set up in contrast with that of the Pratyeka Buddha, who is alleged to seek his own welfare alone.

177

That life will reach some higher end and thus justify all the fret and toil is more than a comforting belief: it is also an offering of the highest Reason, the revelation of highest experience.

178

A surgeon we know once wrote to us that the goal seemed so distant, the way so long, the labour so arduous, that he felt inclined to abandon the quest altogether as something beyond ordinary human reach. Our reply to him was that because a position could not be captured in its entirety that was no reason for hesitating to make a start to capture some of it.

Unique person: unique path

179

In every individual there is an original, mysterious, and incalculable element, because his past history and his prenatal ancestry in other lives on earth have inevitably been different at certain points from those of other individuals. His world-outlook may seem the same as theirs, but there will always be subtle variations. There is no single path which can be presented to suit the multitudinous members of the human species. There is no one unalterable approach to this experience for all men. Each has to find his own way, to travel forward by the guidance of his own present understanding and past experience—and each in the end really does so despite all appearances to the contrary. For each man passes through a different set of life-experiences. His past history and present circumstances have constituted an individual being who is unique, who possesses something entirely his own. It is partly through the lessons, reflections, intuitions, traits, characteristics, and capacities engendered by such experiences that he is able to find his way to truth. Therefore he is forced not only to work out his own salvation but also to work it out in his own unique way. Every description of a mystical path must consequently be understood in a general sense. If its expounder delimits it to constitute a precise path for all alike, he exaggerates. Although there is so much in life which the aspirant shares with other beings, there is always a residue which imparts a stamp of individuality that is different from and unshareable with the individualities of all others. Consequently, the inner path which he must follow cannot be precisely the same as theirs. In the end, after profiting by all the help which he may gain from advanced guides and fellow-pilgrims, after all his attempts to imitate or follow them, he is forced to find or make a way for himself, a way which will be peculiarly his own. In the end he must work out his own unique means to salvation and depend on himself for further enlightenment and strength. Taught by his own intelligence and instructed by his own intuition, he must find his own unique path toward enlightenment.

Each case is different, because each person has a different heredity, temperament, character, environment, and living habits. Therefore these general principles must be adapted to, and fitted in with, that person's particular condition.

180

Just as there is not a single radius only from the centre of a circle to its circumference but countless ones, so there is not a single path only from man to God but as many paths as there are men. Each has to find the way most appropriate to him, to the meaning and experience of truth.

181

There are as many ways to union with the Overself as there are human beings. The orthodox, the conventional, and the traditional ways can claim exclusiveness or monopoly only by imperilling truth.

182

It is an unnecessary self-limitation to believe that there is only a single path to enlightenment, only a single teaching worth following. Persons who believe or feel themselves to be unable to understand subtle metaphysics can turn to a simple devotional path.

183

There is no one particular type of aspirant to mystical or philosophical enlightenment. Taken as a whole, aspirants are a mixed and varied lot in their starting points, personalities, motives, and allegiances. They vary in individuality very widely, have different needs, circumstances, opportunities, outlooks, and possibilities.

184

We are all built by Nature in different ways: no two palms, no two thumbprints, no two persons are exactly alike.

185

The seekers are to be found at different levels and are attracted by different approaches according to their different intellectual development, emotional temperaments, moral capacities, and intuitional sensitivity.

186

The uniqueness of each person is emphasized by the differences which separate him from his fellows.

187

In one's search for Truth he may have progressed through orthodox Christianity, Christian Science, and Spiritualism—but, eventually, the Quest will lead him away from limited, organized public approaches, and bring him to the unrestricted freedom of the Presence of the Overself. Other movements, such as those mentioned, may be useful to beginners; but when some progress has been made, the path necessarily opens onto the Quest where it becomes unlimited, individual, and private.

188

All of us have to travel in the same broad direction if we would rise from the lower to the higher grades of being. But the way in which we shall travel the Way is essentially a personal one. All of us must obey its general rules, but no two seekers can apply them precisely alike.

189

Again and again one observes that the technique, exercise, method, or rule which brings good results for one person fails to do so for another. It is absurd to make a single uniform prescription and expect all persons to get a single uniform result from it. What has been done here is to give some of the best ones and let each reader find out what suits him most, not what suits his friend or another reader most.

190

Each man is unique so each quest must be unique too. Everyone must find, in the end, his own path through his own life. All attempts to copy someone else, however reputed, will fail to lead him to self-realization although they may advance him to a certain point.

191

Each seeker must find out his own path, his own technique for himself. Who else has the right or the capacity to do it for him?

192

We prefer to follow the creative rather than the compulsive way, to help men find their own way rather than force them to travel our way. And this can only be done by starting with the roots, with the ideas they hold, and the attitudes which dominate them.

193

There are too many differences in individual aspirants to allow a broad general technique to suit them all. A guide who can give a personal prescription is helpful, but even in his absence the aspirant can intelligently put together the fragments which will best help him.

194

Let him walk forward slowly or quickly, as suits him best, and also in his own way, again as suits his individuality which he has fashioned through the reincarnations to its present image and from which he has to begin and proceed farther.

195

There are not only widely different stages of evolutionary growth for every human being but also widely different types of human beings within each stage. Hence a single technique cannot possibly cover the spiritual needs of all humanity. The seeker should find the one that suits his natural aptitude as he should find the teacher who is most in inward affinity with him.

196

Let him take up whatever path is most convenient to his personal circumstances and individual character and not force himself into one utterly unsuited to both, merely because it has proven right for other people.

197

There is no single universal rule for all men: their outer circumstances and inner conditions, their historical background and geographical locality, their karmic destiny and evolutionary need, their differences in competence, render it unwise, unfair, and impracticable to write a single prescription for them.

198

The philosophic approach does not limit the seeker rigidly to a single specific technique. While it asks him to follow the basic path and fulfil the fundamental requirements which all beginners must follow, it also points out that this is only a general preparation. A point will be reached when he is ready for more advanced work, and when the personal characteristics and circumstances which are particularly his own must be brought in for adjustment if he is to receive the greatest benefit. No two seekers and the surrounding conditions are ever exactly alike and, at a certain stage, what is helpful to one will be time-wasting to another.

199

It is a common error, among the pious and even among the mystics, to believe that one path alone—theirs—is the best. This may be quite correct in the case of each person, but it may not necessarily be correct for others, and even then it is only correct for a period or at most a number of lifetimes. How often have men outgrown their former selves and taken to new paths? And how different are the intellectual moral and temperamental equipments of different persons? It is in practice, as in theory, not possible to tie everyone down to a single specific path and certainly not advisable.

200

Men are differently constituted. There are a dozen main types and innumerable subdivisions within each type. It is not possible for a single spiritual approach to suit them all.

201

No one reaches the world of truth through any other path than his own, the one which his individual nature fits him for. Someone else's help can at best improve his condition and prepare his mind but cannot take him into truth. Those cases which seem to contradict this statement are cases either of self-deception or of illusion. Too often time spent on these chalked-out paths is time wasted.

202

Each man's path is his own unique one, with its own experiences. Some are shared in common with all other seekers but others are not; they remain peculiar to himself. Therefore a part—whether large or small—of what he has to do cannot be prescribed by another person, be he guru or not. In the groups, organizations, schools, there is too much rigidity in the instruction, the rules, and the expectancy aroused of what should happen at each stage. This is too tight a program. It brings confusion and frustration and does not correspond to the actual situation which an independent observer finds among these circles.

203

The human being will bring about its own redemption, if only we would allow it to do so. But instead we hypnotize the mind with ideas that may suit other persons but are unsuited to us, we practise techniques that warp our proper development, we follow leaders who know only the way they have themselves walked and who insist on crowding all seekers on it regardless of suitability, and we join groups which obstruct our special line of natural growth.

204

It would be an error to try to make his own any spiritual path which, or teacher who, was not so in fact. Such an attempt might maintain itself for a time but could not escape being brought to an end when the false position to which it would lead became intolerable.

205

The individual uniqueness of each aspirant cries out to have its special needs attended to, but suggestion from outside or mesmerism from authority causes him to approach the Quest with fixed opinions as to what should be done. Others are being allowed to mold him instead of letting the inner voice do so, using their contributions solely to carry out or to supplement its guidance.

206

Every man's individual life-path is unique. It may not be to his best interests to conform to a technique imposed upon him by another man or to confine his efforts to a pattern which has suited others. What may be right for another man who is at a different stage of development may be wrong for the aspirant.

207

To deny his individuality is to destroy his creative mind.

208

The *Bhagavad Gita* not only emphasizes the need of solitude for practising yoga but also warns us that the duty, the path, the way of life of other men may be full of danger to us. Thus it also preaches the need of individualism.

209

There is no single path to enlightenment. Yoga has no monopoly. Life itself is the great enlightener. I met a man once who, after the shock of hearing his wife tell him that she had ceased to love him, that she had for some time had a secret lover, and that she requested a divorce so as to be able to marry him, felt a collapse of all his hitherto confidently held values and beliefs. For some days he was so affected that he could not eat. But his mind by then had become so extraordinarily lucid concerning these matters and himself, that he experienced moments of truth. Through them he came into a great peace and understanding, an inner change. What was the morning sun which awakened him? He did no yogic exercises, entered no churches, was too intent on his worldly business to read spiritual books. This brings me back to the theme: do not submit to the pressure of those who say there is only a single way to salvation (the way they follow or teach), do not let the mind be trammelled or narrowed. The truth is that the ways are many, are spread out in all directions, are individual.

210
From the clues, hints, and indications which search and experience give us, we learn in the end what is the true way to the God within us.

211
The quest is too individual a matter to fit everyone in the same way, like a ready-made suit of clothes. Each man has his own life-problems to consider and surmount. In trying to do so wisely nobly and honestly he does precisely what the quest calls for from him at the time.

212
Each quest thus has its own character and its own personality. This it shapes by the act of dedicating itself to the incorruptible integrity of the higher life.

213
Arnold Toynbee found his spiritual path in his study and work in history. It revealed to him, he says, the presence of God as others have found it through prayer and religion. The inner characteristics of men are various and so are the forms which the quest takes for them.

214
The course of each quester is not necessarily invariable nor are his experiences always inevitable.

215
The journey from anticipation to realization is a long one. On this Quest the curiosity to know what lies ahead can never be satisfied with perfect correctness because it must necessarily differ with different individuals.

216
Changes of circumstances which bring uncertainty of the future will not frighten him. They will interest him. He will seek to discover if they point the way to an incoming of new forces of experience necessary for his further development.

217
All human beings differ in some respects and in mind as well as in body. Each is unique. Each needs to find his own individual path. For in each aspirant there exists a certain direction, tendency, capacity, attribute, or gift along which line the possibility of his spiritual development can open up more quickly, freely, and easily than along any other. It is on this line that he should concentrate more effort and so take advantage of what Nature has given him. But to detect and recognize what is his best potentiality requires exploration and search, not only by his ordinary faculties but also and especially by his more sensitive and intuitive ones. It will not be found all at once but only after much groping around and feeling his way. Time is needed because this hidden possibility does not exist at the surface level. The earth which surrounds this gem obscures its whereabouts. If he is in a hurry and insists on a premature discovery instead of keeping up the search, he will identify the wrong stone. Once having found it let him stay with it as often and as long as he can.

218
There is a way suited to the particular individuality of each separate person, which will bring out all his spiritual possibilities as no other way could.

219
The purpose of all paths being to bring the traveller to the same single destination—union with God—any path which either fulfils this purpose or partially helps to do so, is acceptable.

220
He may work toward enlightenment and inner freedom, to the aspiration which draws him most.

221
Whatever helps consciousness come nearer to high moods is a useful spiritual path to someone.

222
He should take any approach which appeals to him, if it is morally worthy, and try to use what he can of it.

223
Several different methods of spiritual development have been offered to humanity. Some have more merit than others and some are more effective than others. But so much depends on the particular needs and status of each person, that the value of a method cannot be generalized with fairness.

224

It is misleading to pick out any one way to the Overself and label it the best, or worse still, the only way. It is unfair to compare the merits of different ways. For the truth is that firstly each has a contribution to make, and finally each individual aspirant has his own special way.

225

The claims that these simpler paths like devotion or repeating a declaration can lead to the goal, are neither true nor untrue. For they lead to the philosophic path which, in its own turn, leads directly to the goal.

226

Is there a single teacher, prophet, messenger, or saint who has been universally acclaimed and universally followed? For that to be, all mankind would need the same outer background and inner status.

227

Great or small there are certain differences between all persons. They cannot all pursue the same ways, therefore we should let others take a different view in religion from ourselves. They vary so widely that it is an adventure for society if there exists as great a diversity of approaches as possible—they are thus better able to suit particular needs. Why should anyone be afraid of diversity in religious views, of variety in religious practices? Let heresies multiply! Let the sects flourish! For out of all this free competition, the seeker has a better chance to find truth.

228

The modern seeker is fortunate in this: that he has a wealth of teachings to choose from—or by which to be bewildered.

229

We must not only acknowledge the differences between men but respect them. Consequently we must accept the fact of variations in responsive capacity and not demand that all should think alike, believe alike, behave alike.

230

What is too much for one individual is too little for another. No universally applicable prescription can be given to suit everyone alike.

231

All these paths should converge towards one another, as all must merge in the central point in the end.

232

However different personal reactions will necessarily be with every individual seeker, there will still remain certain experiences, requirements, and conditions—and these are the most important ones—along his path which must be the same for every other seeker too.

233

Each man's approach must inevitably be individualistic yet each will also share in common all the essentials which constitute the Quest.

234

Whether a man is a Zionist or a Zennist, whether he seeks the Christian Salvation or the Japanese Satori, the fundamental approach is more or less the same.

235

There is no cut and dried system or method which can be guaranteed to work successfully in every case. But there are suggestions, hints, ideas, which have been culled from the personal experiences of a widely varied, world-spread number of masters and aspirants.

236

Since each man's path is peculiarly an individual one, no book can guide all his steps. A book may help him through some situations, inform him about the general course of inner development, and warn him against the probable mistakes and chief pitfalls.

237

Each man has to strive for this higher consciousness in his own way. Each path to it is unique. But at the same time he may profitably avail himself of the general instruction contained in writings like the present one.

Knowing and working within one's limitations

238

One responds to the inner call according to one's capacity and history, one's circumstances and perspective.

239

It is fair for him to ask himself, "What do I bring to the quest: what equipment, qualities, and virtues to entitle me to ask for the results I seek?"

240

When the sublime light of the Ideal shines down upon him and he has the courage to look at his own image by it, he will doubtless make some humiliating discoveries about himself. He will find that he is worse than he believed and not so wise as he thought himself to be. But such discoveries are all to the good. For only then can he know what he is called upon to do and set to work following their pointers in self-improvement.(P)

241

However deep his commitment to the quest may be, he will have to reckon with his own frailties and his environmental pressures.

242

The great man knows he has limitations, he knows his defects and faults—but he is not afraid of them. "Paint me as I am, warts and all," said Oliver Cromwell to the artist who had, thinking to please him, omitted a mole on his face.

243

All do not start with equal capacities for the quest. Each is qualified to go only a certain distance upon it. Those who exaggerate their capacities harm themselves by their presumption. Those who underrate them practise a false modesty. It is an error either to deceive oneself about one's aspirations or to deter oneself unduly.

244

Hope is good for man: it confers endurance, spurs positive attitudes, and urges endeavour upon him. But if its base is ungrounded fancy and extravagant wishes, he is hurt rather than benefited by it.

245

Begin by admitting that you know really little or nothing about your deeper mind. That is better than learned tall talk.

246

It is much easier to set himself a discipline than to keep it.

247

We cannot all be Buddhas. We may not all have the strength to live like Christ. Only one in a million may be even a Himalayan yogi living alone and above us in his cave high up on the rugged mountain. But something worthwhile is within reach of all of us. Let us therefore aim at the immediately practicable, which in its turn will lead to something more. It is foolish to waste time and strength unavailingly grasping for what is out of reach.

248

There is a point at which man's mind must fall back baffled by the great mystery which surrounds him. Reflect and reason, search and probe as much as he can, he can go no farther. But this does not mean that his life is meaningless or that the universe is meaningless. Only a being superior to man might possibly penetrate this mystery. Therefore let him work within his own inescapable limits. It is futile to nurture wild ambitions which he is not qualified to realize. In short, let him know himself. He may then have a key to better knowledge of other things, especially of the meaning of his own life.

249

It is only the few, after all, who have the inborn inclination to sacrifice everything if needs be in the hope of attaining truth. What of the lesser souls who have no such passport, whose temperament, environment, family, or position forbids them from aspiring heroically to the highest goal? Can we hold no hope for them? Is it to be a case of all or nothing?

The answer is that nobody is asked to undertake more than lies within his strength or circumstances. There is room here for those with humble aims who do not feel equal to more than the slightest philosophic effort. Let them study these doctrines just a little where possible, but where even this is not possible let them accept these teachings on simple faith alone. Let them absorb a few leading tenets which make special appeal to them or which are more easily understandable by them than others. Let them practise a few minutes' meditation only once or twice weekly, if they do not find the time or tendency to practise more. Let them keep in only occasional touch by letter or otherwise with someone who represents in himself a definite personal attainment which, although beyond their own reach, is not beyond their own veneration. Thus they take the first step to establish right tendencies. If however they are unable to do any of these things, let them not despair. There still remains the path of occasional service. Let them give from time to time, as suits their capacity or convenience, a little help in kind or toil or coin to those who are themselves struggling against great odds to enlighten a world sorrow-struck through ignorance. For thus they will *earn* a gift of glad remembrance and internal notice whose unique value will be out of all proportion to what is offered. The karmic benefit of such offering will return to them, and even if it be long deferred they will have the intangible satisfaction which comes from all service placed on the Overself's altar.

250

If he is unable to gather enough strength to seek the Truth, then let him seek it for the sake of the services it can render to him.

251

Although hardly any seeker can perfect himself in the quest's varied requirements, all seekers can develop something of each needed quality.

252

The change in thinking and living habits must theoretically be a total one if the regeneration sought is to be that also. But the compulsions of earning a livelihood, fitting into the local community, and adjusting to family opposition make this impossible in all but exceptional cases. Men who have to take these actualities into their consideration in practice attempt to compromise with hard necessity and present environment. This does not mean that they discard the truth—they must indeed keep it loyally as the Ideal—but that they relate it to the prevailing conditions and somehow arrive at some kind of a reconciliation between the two. Nor does it mean that the teaching is impractical, for the few exceptions already mentioned are able to put it into practice a hundred percent simply because they are willing and able to pay the heavy price of isolation for doing so. It means that although the teaching is adequate to all circumstances, its devotees are unwilling to court the extra suffering and struggle involved in fighting the insanity and tension of those existing circumstances. The latter tend to promote materialism and are best suited to a materialistic way of thinking and living. Those who, while reading its true character aright, submit to it and refuse to withdraw from it, are entitled to do so—if at the same time they have the clear understanding that the higher illuminations, as well as the permanent one, will have to remain inaccessible to them. Is there not enough to do in climbing to the lesser ones, and are they not sufficiently glorious and rewarding?

253

There are many who are not seeking for the quickest attainment of the highest goal. They feel, quite pardonably, that the demands of training for it are too great for their modest equipment. But they are seeking for occasional inspiration and they would be content with just a few glimpses during their lifetime. Although these people are not fully committed to the Quest, they are in general sympathetic with it.

254

If he feels that rising to a higher level of consciousness would be too much for him, then he could simply try to become a better man.

255

It is some kind of a victory over self for a man to be willing to live without distress if he has to live within his limitations.

256

Those who feel that there are too many evils in the contemporary ways of living and of earning a livelihood, who sincerely deplore these evils, nevertheless often feel also that there is little or nothing they can do about it until society as a whole develops new and better ways. But this is only a first look at their situation; it reveals the appearance of it but not the reality. Do they really need to wait until the unlikely event of a wholesale and voluntary amendment takes place all around them? For the challenge today, as will be made clear in this book's later course, is *not* a social but an individual one. More men are free to take the first steps towards their own liberation from these evils than they usually realize. When their caution becomes excessive, it also becomes a vice. It may prevent them from making mistakes, but it also prevents them from doing anything at all—leading, in fact, to a kind of inertia. Even if they cannot do more, they can make a start to apply new ideals and then see what happens.

257

Is the Quest nothing but an endless adventure and never to become a final achievement? Are its goals too high for frail humans, its exercises too difficult for feeble ones? The historic fact that men have lived who have turned its adventure into its achievement puts an end to such pessimism. If, knowing and accepting our limitations, we object that this cannot possibly be done in a single lifetime, the answer is, "Then do what you can in the present lifetime, and there will be that much less to be done in the next lifetime."

258

When a man has the right stuff in him, all he needs is just opportunity, and nothing else. If he possesses a sufficient degree of talent plus the determination to succeed, there is no stage so humble that it cannot be made a jumping-off ground to better things.

259

The disciple's quest must begin with his own simple specific needs, not with complicated generalities.

260

He must begin with what he is and where he is: that's the starting point. After looking at the goal, and the direction leading to it, he looks for the next step.

261

Do not let the past hold you down. Do not let dust-laden memories keep you down. Make today a fresh day, a new beginning.

262

He can begin this inner work with whatever capacities he has now, from wherever he is now on life's road. There is no time that is not the right time, no place that is not the right place, no circumstances which cannot be put to use in some way. For there are lessons to be learnt everywhere, meanings to be gleaned in all experiences; spiritual tests and opportunities of the most varied kinds can be found in the most unlikely situations, the most unspiritual environments.

263

Time is needed to bring maturity to his development; the years must pass before his understanding is complete enough to stand on its own supports.

264

We must recognize what is not always recognized, that the growth of mind and character takes time, just as the growth of trunk and limb takes time. A man does not begin to mature and become what he is likely to be until he is past thirty.

265

The young man who has the wisdom to devote some of his abundant energies to this quest will one day be the envy of the old man who would devote only his slackened forces and shortened days to it.

266

It is entirely for the seeker to set his own rate of progress. Even the man who is interested only in theoretical discussion thereby, and to that extent, promotes his own good. If through inclination or circumstances he prefers to let his aspirations remain only at the level of reading and discussion, that at least is better than being entirely uninterested in them. It will be for him to decide whether to endeavour to obtain the fullest realization of his aspirations in practical life. There is room for both classes on this Quest.

267

He should not be discouraged because others have gone ahead on the path more quickly than he, any more than he should be gratified because some have gone ahead more slowly than he, for the fact is that the goal he seeks is already within his grasp. He is the Overself that he seeks to unite with, and the time it seems to take to realize this is itself an illusion of the mind. Let him, therefore, go forward at his own rate and within the limits of his own strength, leaving the result in the hands of God.

268

If they impose on themselves an impossible ideal, an unattainable standard, they must expect the sense of frustration that will overtake them later.

269

It is better that an aspirant should know his limitations now than that, failing to do so, he should know tragic disappointments and unutterable despair *later*. It is better in such a case that he should realize that he is engaged on a long search whose end he cannot reach in this incarnation.

270

How can the naïve inexperienced beginner fail to commit errors and neglect precautions; how can he not be deceived by his own imaginations or puzzled by the contradictions and paradoxes which beset this path?

271

The newly awakened aspirant should search for clues without losing his balance or overreaching new enthusiasm.

272
Of what use is it to reproach himself again and again for being what he
is? How could he have been otherwise, given his heredity, environment,
and history?

273
The quest says he is not so helpless as he thinks he is. Why give himself
up so unresistingly to the tendencies he finds in his heart, to the thoughts
he finds in his mind, to the inward dominion of his possessions and
passions? Why be so soft-willed as to refrain from making any effort at all
on the plea that he *must* accept himself as he finds himself?

274
What he cannot do in the beginning, he may be able to do in the middle
of his journey. He should not let misgivings about his capacity to travel far
stop him from travelling at all.

275
Those who already possess a flair for mysticism will naturally advance
more easily and more quickly than those who do not. But that is no reason
for the unmystical to adopt a defeatist attitude and negate the quest
altogether.

276
His weaknesses may come in the way of his seeking, yet he still remains
an authentic seeker.

277
The quest would have to be entered with a realization of all its complex-
ity and with a comprehension that his good intentions could be frustrated
by adverse circumstances if he lets his thoughts about them become
negative.

278
A man needs to know his limitations and to accept them. But he need
not accept them as absolutes. There is always the mysterious X-factor, the
second wind, the untapped unpredictable resources.

279
He should fit his aspiration to his estimated capacity but, in order not to
miss unknown possibilities which might yet emerge to the surface, he
should do so loosely and not rigidly.

280
It is true that enlightenment is to be found wherever it is earnestly
sought, and not in any special place such as India. However, one's own
desires and needs will provide him with a source of direction; and it may
be that these will indicate that one's individual progress may be hastened
or better served by a journey to some particular location.

281

No matter what the personal circumstances of a man may be, no matter whether he be rich or poor, well or ill, old or young, educated or illiterate, there is no point in his life where some part at least of the quest may not be introduced.

282

Would they have done better to have stayed at home, rather than to have gone off looking for gurus in the East? The answer must vary from seeker to seeker.

283

From a long-range point of view, is anyone really "lost"? It is sometimes consoling to remember that we have Eternity before us, and we can only do what we are capable of at a given time.

284

Why do seeking souls run off to India, and now to Japan, as they ran off to Europe in Emerson's time? If they had a less confused conception of the Overself, a clearer idea of what they sought, none of them would feel that he *had* to go to this or that country, place, person. But the tendencies inherited from former births and pushing him one way or pulling him toward somewhere else, set up this urge to move away and meet new experience, new people, perhaps new masters. In particular, they draw him back to the scene of previous lives which powerfully affected his spiritual seeking. This is attractive to him, perhaps even emotionally romantic, but it gives him nothing really that he has not in fact had before.

285

For many years I was enthralled with the spiritual glamour of India. The need to go there became a strong one, and in the end I surrendered to it. I learnt what the grasshopping tourist never learns; saw what the professional observer rarely sees; for both tourist and journalist usually lack the aspiration, the patience, and the preparations required to search for and discover what is really the best in any Oriental country.

I found much in that country that was of great interest and greater value, but I did not find the fulfilment of my Quest. That did not come to me until I was back again in the other hemisphere. Indeed, the Cosmic Vision, which revealed the Presence of Infinite Intelligence throughout life, throughout the universe and throughout history, which explained so many of the Higher Laws to me, came incongruously enough while I was sitting in a hotel room in Chicago. With this humbling insight, the need to go to India disappeared. And I then saw that it was really an ancient complex—a kind of auto-suggestion—inherited from my own far, reincarnatory past. Indeed, I found out that if I had remained loyal to the inward direction I had originally travelled, I need never have gone to India at all, nor to those other Asiatic countries where I sought for Truth. What I needed could be very well found within myself. But, I had accepted the suggestions out of my past as well as out of the lips and writings of other persons. And so I deviated from the inward way. The shortcut, which the journeys to Asia offered, turned out to be a long way, for I wandered over other men's roads, and, in the end, had to return, as we all have, to my own road. Indeed, there was nowhere else to go, and my Quest ended there.

The other ways were not without their usefulness and helpfulness, of course, but they lost that value the moment they were turned into substitutes for the interior way, which is unique and without a second because each one of us is unique. Each gets his own special experience of life, makes his own special set of contacts with other persons, and meets his own particular destiny. In his reactions to and dealings with all this, he is really reacting to and dealing with himself. He is showing quarrelsomeness, or trying to conquer it; he is losing himself in the day's activity, or saving himself from it in a half-hour retreat. He is letting negative thoughts or feelings stay in his heart, or trying to drive them out of it. He is practising a larger relationship and a kindlier attitude toward those he encounters in his day-to-day business, or he is failing to recognize why they—and not others who are quite different—have been put into his path by the Infinite Intelligence. His environment is really a testing-place and a disciplinary school.

And so I come back to the statement that going to India, or going to any other place, in quest of spiritual enlightenment is not so important as going inside one's self, and discovering Who one is. Moreover, if some have gone to India to look for an incarnate Master, others have gone to Palestine to look for a disincarnate one. There they lingered at the holy places, the sacred monuments, the historic ground where Jesus walked and talked. But, the attempts of both kinds of seekers bear real fruit only as and when they lead to the Seeking Within, for the indwelling Master, in the one case, or the indwelling Christ in the other. Yet, this final search the seeker could have begun anyway without leaving home. Indeed, Ramana Maharshi himself once said aloud: "Had I known how easy it was, I would never have gone away from home."

286

The question of how far he would be prepared to travel in this quest has no geographical reference. It is a metaphorical one and refers only to the time he can give each day to the exercises, studies, and devotions, as well as to the moral ideals he can bring himself to pursue. He is not asked for more than he feels he can humanly give under his present circumstances and responsibilities. As for going to India or elsewhere, that is unnecessary and even inadvisable. One of the greatest Western mystics I ever knew spent every day in the city of London, where he had a business to manage. He did his job and made a success of it, stuck to his ideals and became spiritually "aware." He was indeed an adept at meditation but he had never set foot in the Orient. The seeker has indeed not very far to travel. Four hundred years ago Sebastian Franck, a German who had attained the full spiritual realization, wrote: "We do not need to cross the sea to find Him—the Word is nigh thee, is *in thy heart*."

287

The belief that we have to travel to far places for the light of Truth is not really true but our own feebleness may have to make it true. As soon as we settle down in hope and confidence to discover the deeper forces within ourselves they begin to become active.

288

We delude ourselves with the dream that we are travelling to Italy or to Austria; it is not we who are travelling, but the ship and the train. *We* only travel when our souls move out of their narrow encasements and seek a larger life. And that can happen anywhere: it might be at our own familiar fireside at the bidding of an illumined book; it might come, of course, with our first view of the Himalaya Mountains. But merely to move our bodies from one place to a distant one, without a corresponding movement of the soul, is not travel; it is dissipation.

289

How many, of late years, have travelled on "the ashram circuit"! How much have I, and some friends, contributed toward this result! Yet in the end, to what does it all add up? Let an earlier president of the respected Ramakrishna Mission, head of the Ramakrishna Order of Monks, and abbot of Belur Monastery answer, in the warning which he gave an American lady who was enthusiastically going from one Hindu ashram to another, spending a few days at each during a six-week visit to India. Said Swami Saradananda with a large smile: "Remember, what is within you is everywhere. What is not, is nowhere." Do not these words admonish his visitor that there is nothing free in the universe, that she cannot get something for nothing, that no "guru" can give her what she herself must work for and provide, and that no seeker will be able to bring into close inner relationship with himself any spiritual master who is too far from, or too high above, his own range of development? When an Indian of such authority and experience makes this statement to such seekers, his words ought to be well weighed against those which have been written, pronounced, or circulated by those who do not know better.

290

Where should a man go in order to start on this Quest? Should he travel to the Orient? Can it be followed only in the Near East, the Middle East, or the Far East? The answer is that such a journey is quite unnecessary. Let him start in the land where he is living, where destiny has put him. But if he need not move from one country to another for the purposes of the Quest he may find it helpful to move for the purposes of a single department of the Quest—that is, meditation—from the noise and bustle of city life to the quiet and calmness of country life.

291

To those who want to travel to India or elsewhere in search of salvation, or of a master who shall lead them to it, the question must be asked, "Can you not see that if you take yourself there you will still have to cope with your ego there as here? Look deeper into your own heart, for that is where what you seek really is."

292

If a man has to go to India to find peace of mind, then he may lose it again when he leaves India. The same is just as true if he has to stay around a guru for the same purpose.

293

There is nothing wrong with the urge to visit India, for then he may learn more about this world of ours and the people in it, and especially about Indian spiritual traditions. The wrong sets in when he believes that just by displacing himself in space in this way he is likely to have enlightenment handed over to him by some other man, called a guru, on a platter. This cannot be, whatever wishful thinking on the one side and fanatical narrowness on the other may say. At the moment the fad is more Indonesia than India but the point of the matter is still the same. For enlightenment involves liberation from his ego, its captivity and deceitfulness.

294

The hidden teaching is unknown to almost all the yogis and swamis in India. It exists, however, and can be got without going to these people.

295

One man may go to the Orient and gain nothing. It is not emotional exuberance which produces a high spiritual result, nor visits to many ashrams, but the depth and concentration with which the truth is seen.

Stages of development

296

Many an old fable is a perfect allegory of this quest. The temptations and perils, the toils and adventures of its hero are faithful references to what the aspirant has always encountered in the past and will encounter in our own day.

297

The stages of the Quest pass by degrees from the disciplining of the ego to the opening of consciousness to the Overself.

298

On this journey there are stages of ascent, stations of understanding, lights of peace, and shadows of despair.

299

The Quest must traverse the three levels of body, mind, and spirit.

300

There is an Indian formula covering three progressive stages of the quest: Hearing, Reflection, Enlightenment. It means: Receiving instruction (from guru or text), Thinking constantly over the teachings until they are thoroughly assimilated, Experiencing glimpses of a mystical nature. With the end of this third phase, the aspirant has not only to repeat and prolong the glimpses until his whole life is permeated by the wisdom and peace which is their fruit, but also to receive and apply the highest and final philosophic doctrine. With this, his enlightenment becomes "natural," effortless, unbroken. It is unified with his activity, established whether he is busy in the world or seated in meditation.

301

According to the Hindu teaching, man passes through three stages of development from the Inert through the Passional to the Harmonious.

302

In the course of his life the student will pass from one phase of development to another, thus gradually enriching and expanding his whole character.

303

To start on the quest is the first step. To continue on it is the second, and possibly harder. Thoroughly to finish the quest is the hardest step of all.

304

It is true that he is only at the beginning of his quest, that its fulfilment may be far far away, but everything must have a beginning.

305
It is a progressive training which continues throughout one's lifetime.

306
There are times to intensify the quest, to hasten its tempo and stiffen its disciplines.

307
With growth of outlook, development of mind, correct instruction from text or teacher, correct interpretation of his own and others' experiences, he moves out of narrow sectarianism into a new universal level.

308
The attitude of faith in another person is undoubtedly helpful to beginners, provided the faith is justified. But it is a stage necessarily inferior to the attitude of faith in one's own soul. To turn inwards rather than outwards, to overcome the tendency towards externality, is to ascend to a higher stage.

309
Negative transference, positive transference, balanced orientation, *all* are stages of *external* adjustment and deserve no higher evaluation than that. On the internal level alone is the surest equilibrium attainable.

310
This creative changing of circumstances is a twofold process, practised both in the outer world where those circumstances belong and in the inner world of the spirit, where they are absent.

311
If he continues the inner work he will pass through various stages of development. It would be a mistake to believe that he has reached a final attitude or a fixed set of values.

312
Between the beginner and the adept is this difference: that the state of being which the one looks up to with awe-struck wonder seems entirely natural to the other.

313
The last lap necessarily brings him into the Silence of THAT which transcends intellect, but it is a silence that is rich with freedom and serenity. Here alone he may hear the wordless voice of God and, once heard, he can well afford to disregard all other voices.

314
Although the movement towards enlightenment goes forward by stages, the actual moment of enlightenment comes abruptly with a sudden transcendence of the darkness in which men ordinarily live.

315

The time will come, if he perseveres, when his mind will naturally orient itself toward the spiritual pole of being. And this will happen by itself, without any urging on his part. No outer activity will be able to stop the process, for to make it possible his mind will apparently double its activity. In the foreground, it will attend to the outer world, but in the background it will attend to the Overself.

316

He may stop in one or other of these cults for a time but, if he is seeking truth, he will not remain there. In the end, and after sufficient sampling and discarding over a number of years, his search will lead him to philosophy.

317

The ascending degrees of initiation into higher understanding of truth and large capacity to receive contemplative awareness open themselves to him one by one as he passes each successive test leading to it. These tests consist, in the lower grades, of willingness to submit physical habits, passions, and desires to discipline and, in higher grades, willingness to submit thoughts and feelings to it. In all, they lead to a progressive detachment from the animal and the ego.

318

When the disciple reaches the end of the phase through which he is travelling, his attention is diverted towards a new one. Uncertainty and chaos descend upon him with reference to it. He cannot clearly see his further way into it or easily get right direction through it.

319

There are tests, dangers, and pitfalls at various stages of this Quest.

320

This momentary glimpse of the Overself provides the real beginning of his quest. The uninterrupted realization of it provides the final ending.

321

When he begins to sense the inner peace and exaltation which is a perfume, as it were, upon the threshold of the Overself, he may understand how real this inner life is and paradoxically how unintelligible, indescribable, and immaterial from the ordinary standpoint. It is something, and yet not something which can be put into shape or form graspable by the five senses. Anyway it is there and it is the Immortal Soul.

322

It is inevitable that a seeking mind—as differentiated from a stodgy one—should pass through various progressive phases of thinking.

323

The personal man needs to grow and develop adequately as *man*. Only after this does he reach the stage when it is safe, and not premature, to undo the ego, and destroy its rule. For after this point the latter becomes a tyranny when the task now is to make it a subserviency.

324

From error at one end to truth at the other, the journey is long and tedious.

325

Let him take from different teachings what suits his mind and purpose: the study of comparative religion and mysticism may assist him here. But this is for a beginning; later he will need to specialize each period to its needed idea.

326

It is good as a beginning to believe in God. It is admirable as the next step to try to come closer to God by worship—but it is not enough. It is a fulfilment of a still higher duty to try to know that in us which is the link with God, which in contrast to man is of a godlike nature.

327

The order of progress is from belief to knowledge, and thence to love of that which is known.

328

If a man comes to this quest by thought or by suffering or by fate, he will end by love if he remains with it, love of that which shines forth during his first glimpse, love of the Overself. It is like the child losing, then finding, its parent.

329

First, he has a vague feeling of being attracted towards the Overself. Then he bestows more attention upon it, thinks of it frequently; at length attention grows into concentration and this, in turn, culminates in absorption. In the end, he can say, with al Hallaj: "I live not in myself, only in Thee. Last night I loved. This morning I am Love."

330

The stages in philosophic training usually begin with gaining a theoretical knowledge of the teachings. When this is well established, it grows in time into an aspiration for self-improvement and into an effort to mold character and conduct in conformity with the philosophic ideal. Such a maturation period is often a long and difficult one. In the third stage the "glimpse" of enlightenment begins to be experienced. The first glimpse has a far-reaching effect and is likely to be associated with the first contact with an inspired spiritual guide, or with the writings of such a man. In the case of some persons there is a different series of steps. The glimpse comes first, the theoretical study next, striving to express through living comes last.

331

The seeker will pass through three periods successively before he can enter the sublime land of realization. First he must experiment with and exhaust the external possibilities of religion; then he must practise the internal rite of meditation; lastly he must, with sharpened intelligence, pursue the subtlest of all philosophies.

332

That a higher existence is possible for mankind may be a strong intuitive feeling or a strong religious belief. It can develop through experience of a mystical glimpse into personal realization or more lastingly, more truthfully, through experience of philosophic insight.

333

The aspiration or yearning comes first on the Quest, the repentance and cleansing come next; study, prayer, and meditation will then naturally follow these preparations. He must first make himself ready for the illumination, then only will he get it. As a consequence of all these efforts and aspirations, he will begin to grow out of himself. Wisdom comes with the end of a long probation.

334

The third part of the quest is a moral and social praxis.

335

The higher stage is pure philosophy, for it re-educates his outlook and hence his consciousness. It demands close, concentrated study, however, and therefore few care for it. It is based on reasoning, not on mystic intuitions, and will be the logical development of modern science if it keeps on probing as men like Eddington, Planck, and others like them have done. Unfortunately the West has not carried reasoning to the bitter end, as the ancient Rishees did, for it has omitted consideration of the dream and deep sleep states from its data, as well as other important matters. Reason is not to be confused with logic, either; the latter is limited and cannot yield truth.

336

But the mystical experience is not sufficiently common to be made the foundation for popular instruction in the modes of obtaining it. Humanity in its present stage is not even mystical by nature, let alone philosophical, but it could become so by education and training. For mysticism always follows religion as a further stage in the individual's journey. The mystical consciousness is an inevitable stage of human evolution. Every man will attain it with the efflux of time. But he will not do so by a smooth mechanical clocklike progress. His ascent will be uneven erratic and zig-zag. Yet he will necessarily attain it. The few who want to anticipate the human evolutionary process must take to mysticism or philosophy.

337

First stage: This is attained by those who study metaphysics alone or practise mysticism alone. It is the withdrawal from the senses and their objects. It is negative. It leads to a perception that the external world is unsatisfactory. It is the great turning away from things of sense. It is an ascetic stage; it is accompanied by thoughts; it is a recognition that matter is not ultimately real. It is marked by moral change. It is the discovery through a glimpse of his spiritual nature which is an ecstatic sense of union with a superior immaterial being. He feels on occasions that he is divine.

Second stage: It affirms the unique positive ultimate reality. It yields the vision of mystic light of the Logos; it is attained by mysticism alone. It is entry into the Void; it is the discovery of Spirit; it is trance. It is thought-free, delights in solitude. This realization of God in the *heart* marks the Witness-stage of ultramystic experience. The man feels utterly detached from his own or the world's activities, so much so that he is ascetically tempted to withdraw into a retreat from life. If, however, fate forces him to continue in the world he will feel all the time curiously like a spectator at a cinema show; but this cannot constitute an ultimate human goal.

Third stage: It is in the world, but not of it. It is the return to the external sense-world and the discovery that it too is God-born. It never loses sight of its unity with life, but insists on its connection with action. Instead of becoming a refuge for dreamers, talkers, and escapists, it becomes an inspiring dynamic. It is the realization of All in himself and himself in All. With this attainment he throws himself incessantly into the service of mankind.

Only whole person finds whole truth

338

Whilst there are parts of our nature which remain still undeveloped, we are not complete men.

339

It is the wholeness of his bodily, mental, and spiritual being that man must develop.

340

Results will best prove the soundness of the integrated path, the effectiveness of the integrated personality. Man is a many-sided being. His development must accordingly be correlated with this fact.

341

The whole psyche of man must get into this task of self-spiritualization. Feeling alone cannot do it, will alone cannot do it, thinking alone cannot do it, and intuiting alone cannot do it. Every element must contribute to it and be shaped by it.

342

Can these competing tendencies, the extroverting and the introverting, be brought together in a single life? Philosophy not only answers that they can, but also that they must be integrated if the mystical life is to reach its fullest bloom. It wisely mingles the two ideals without despoiling either. Here, it not only co-operates with human nature but also imitates the rhythmic pattern of Nature. It is in harmony with Tao, "the way the universe goes."

343

It is not enough to develop any one of these parts of our being alone. It is a much more stupendous task to develop all three at the same time. Yet this is what philosophy asks for.

344

Work completely done, the body effectively used, the mind capably directed—such a roundly developed personality is the ideal.

345

If the whole truth is to be discovered, the whole being must be brought to its quest. If this is done, philosophy will be lived as well as known, felt as well as understood, experienced as well as intuited.

346

Man as a whole must enter on the Quest and then the complete organism will benefit when truth is found. If isolated functions alone enter on it then they alone will benefit by the truth.

347

So long as he is an incomplete person, so long will he never be able to find more than an incomplete truth.

348

It is not just one part of man which is to follow the quest but all parts of him. The whole truth can come only to the whole man.

349
Other experiences and other goals demand the strength and activity of only a part of his being from him but this search for a higher life demands his all.

350
He follows the quest somewhat hesitantly, discontinuously and cautiously, wary lest it demands more from him than he is prepared to give. There is no objection: he may set his own pace but in the end, of course, he must come into this quest with all of himself.

351
Why should he not be a human being as well as a yogi? Why should he not bring all of his nature to this co-operative venture that is Life?

352
The quest may become his central interest but this is no excuse for him to become unbalanced or disequilibriated.

353
If he comes to the quest with his whole being, turning every side of it to the quest's light and discipline, he may confidently expect the full insight, the full transformation and not a partial, incomplete result.

Attainments

354
The first reward is truth realized in every part of his being, the lower self becoming the instrument of the Soul. The second reward is peace, intensely satisfying and joyous. A keen and constant longing after the Soul's consciousness, a willingness to surrender all to it *inwardly*, are however necessary prerequisites.

355
The acceptance of these ideas can only benefit, and not harm, humanity.

356
If he will consciously put himself into line with this higher purpose of human living, he will not only become a better and wiser man but also a happier one.

357
The pursuit of Mammon is an uncertain adventure, but the pursuit of Truth is full of certainty. It rewards its own, even in apparent defeat.

358
Out of the Quest will come a yearning for what is the best in life and the highest in Truth.

359

With every year of growing experience and continued application, he will find more and more the truth of these teachings. He will in consequence be unable not to love them more and more.

360

Out of the medley of mystical researches and peculiar experiments, religious studies and metaphysical contemplations which have taken up so large a part of the Quest, there will emerge a few irrefragable certitudes.

361

When this truth is at last seen, that heaven is not a place in space but a condition of being, and that therefore it can to a certain extent be realized even before death, a feeling of joy and a sense of adventure are felt. The joy arises because we are no longer restricted by time, and the adventuresomeness arises because a vista of the quest's possibilities opens up.

362

A serenity which never leaves him and an integrity which always stamps him, are only two of the fruits of matured philosophic discipline.

363

If there were nothing more—no exciting or dramatic inner experience—possible than this ameliorating peace, this extra-deep feeling of stillness, it would be enough to make the time and care given to it worthwhile. But there *is* more for those who want also to know something of its source, its workings and connections. Beyond that little measure of knowledge, be content, for the Great Mystery swallows all who find it. Yet there is nothing to fear.

364

He whose resort is solely the personal ego is constantly subject to its limitations and narrowness and, consequently, is afflicted with strains and anxieties. He who lets it go and opens himself up, whose resort is to his Higher Self, finds it infinite and boundless and, consequently, is filled with inward peace.

365

The quest often begins with a great sadness but always ends with a great happiness. Its course may flow through both dark and bright moods at times, but its terminus will be unbelievably serene.

366

The Quest gives him the chance to achieve inner peace and find inner happiness; it does not give peace and happiness. If this does not seem to justify its labours and disciplines, remember that ordinary man lacks even this chance.

367

Therefore it is that, grey with wandering from his ancient goal, the aspirant turns tired feet across the threshold of immortal thought and dwells for a soft white hour upon the couch of unutterable peace. The words he has heard with his mortal ears have proved only of momentary worth to him, but the words he hears when he turns away from the world and listens with the inner ear will walk by his side until the end of Time.

368

When he has brought the host of conflicting emotions to rest, when he has trained the thoughts to obedience, when he has fought and beaten the ego itself, he comes to a state of peace.

369

To enter into the presence of a high inspiration, feel its ennoblement, and understand its message, brings a deeply satisfying joy.

370

The man who fails to find joy in his Quest has not understood the Quest.

371

There is no need for aspirants to engage in the cult of morbid suffering. There is no reason why they should not be happy. If the Quest is to bring them nearer to their essential self, it will also bring them nearer to its happiness.

372

When a man feels the presence of a diviner self within his breast, when he believes that its power protects and provides for him, when he views past errors and future troubles alike with perfect equanimity, he has a better capacity to enjoy life and a truer expression of happiness than those who delight only in ephemeral pleasures and sense satisfactions. For it will endure into times of adversity and last through hours of calamity, where the other will crumble and vanish.

373

Wisdom may or may not come with the years of old age: it is more likely to come with the labours in self-rule and the deepenings of study, concentration, and reflection, with the humbling religious veneration of the higher Power. It is, they say, its own reward but it is a bringer of gifts, of which inner peace is the most prominent and a kindly smile the most permanent.

374

He who has won wisdom as the reward of his quest wins virtue as its natural accompaniment too.

375

The student who has diligently applied himself to the primary tasks of self-improvement, and who has accompanied his efforts with honest and rigid self-analysis, will discover that many questions which formerly baffled him have been solved by the workings of his own intuition.

376

Nobody can earnestly work through a course in the higher philosophy without finding himself a better and wiser man at the end than he was at the beginning. And this result will come to him almost unconsciously, little by little, through the creative power of right thinking.

377

His judgements turn out to be misjudgements, and his caution to be indecision. Often this may be so, alas! But this is the kind of wisdom which comes with failure or defeat; it embodies the hindsight which, too late to be of possible use except in the future, is the consequence after the event. How precious then would be the acquirement of two values to which the Quest may lead a man—calmness and intuition.

378

Here on the quest, it is not only possible for him to meet the profoundest thoughts of the human mind but also its highest experiences.

379

He who finds the Overself, loses the burdens, the miseries, and the fears of the ego.

380

How does the quest remove his fears? By providing him sooner or later with firm assurance that the Overself's gracious power is not only illuminative but also protective.

381

Slowly, as he strives onward with this inner work, his faults and frailties will fall away and this ever-shining better self hidden behind them will begin to be revealed.

382

Even if his quest ends in total failure (which it cannot do) the ideals and ideas it involves will have left some impress on his character, for they are faint reverberations of whispers from his higher being.

383

The aspirant is not unreasonable in asking that some reward, if not an adequate reward, should become visible in time for all his struggles. If he is told to acquire the virtue of patience, he is not told to acquire the quality of hopelessness. There are signs and tokens, experiences and glimpses to hearten him on the way.

384

His meditations tend to make him sensitive and his studies sympathetic; the two qualities combine well so that others notice how kindly he is in personal relations.

385

It is essential to make clear that none should take to this Quest in order to follow or depend on some particular man, or to gain certain mystic experiences, for if he is disappointed in the man or frustrated in reaching the experiences, he will be inclined to abandon the Quest. No!—he should take to it for its own sake, because it is immeasurably worthwhile and because its rewards in improved character and developed understanding are sufficient in themselves to pay for his effort. If the Quest helps him to become aware of, and to eradicate, bad faults in himself, in his outlook on life and in his approach to others, it has justified itself. Even if the mystical consciousness fails to show itself, or to show itself often enough to please him, he has still had his money's worth.

386

The time will come when values will change, when ambitions, powers, possessions, and acquisitions will all be put back into their proper places, when their tyranny over the will and the feelings will be put to an end.

387

He who seeks his inner being, and finds it, finds also his inner good.

388

Those who will take the trouble to comprehend what all this means, and who will do what they can to practise the requisite exercises, will find with increasing joy that new life opening up to them.

389

When this inner work is sufficiently advanced, certain traits of character will either advance in strength or appear for the first time. Among them are patience, goodwill, stability, self-control, peacefulness, and equableness.

390

Those who are willing to practise the philosophic discipline may realize their spiritual nature for themselves and not have to depend upon hearsay for the knowledge of its existence.

391

It can be shown that the disciplines of philosophy offer much in return, that to the person who seriously feels his life needs not mere amendment but raising to a finer level there are encouraging experiences and beautiful intuitions awaiting him.

392

It is a new and different, a superior and fuller, a self-fulfilling kind of experience.

393

A life so full of exalted purpose, so inspired by a tremendous ideal, cannot be a dull or unhappy one.

394

The toil of the quest is hard and long. If it deters anyone from starting on it, let him remember that the rewards along the way, even apart from the grand one at the end, are sufficiently worthwhile to repay him for all he is likely to do.

395

The reward of all the years of long arduous striving will be their happy justification; the rich blessing of an infinite strength within him will pay off the failures and weaknesses of a past self which had to be fought and conquered.

396

During times of war and suffering, the spiritual Quest demonstrates its value by the inner support which it gives and the unquenchable faith it bestows. The forces of evil will be checked; the good will triumph in the end, as always. God's love for all remains what it ever shall be—the best thing in life.

397

No man may free himself from every form of outward suffering but all men may free themselves from inward suffering.

398

How weak, how helpless is the man who is himself alone. How strong, how supported is the man who is both himself and more than himself. In the one, there is only the petty little ego as the motor force; in the other there is also the infinite universal being.

399

Any man may detect the presence of divinity within himself, if he will patiently work through the course prescribed by authoritative books or a competent guide. It is not the prerogative of spiritual genius alone to detect it.

400

It is only in the rational balanced growth of the mind and the sympathetic heart, the disciplined body and the tranquillized nerves, the philosophic reflectiveness, mystic peace, and ultramystic insight, that a man arrives at last at maturity and normality and thus becomes really sane.

401

If the quest does nothing more than save him in his darkest hours from total submergence in the all-prevalent worldliness, it will have done enough.

402

The quest can give stability to the feelings, support to the mind, defense against the pettiness and the evil in the world.

403

The transformations effected by this inner work seem, when stabilized, to be a natural maturity.

404

Is all this too good to be true, too beautiful to be factual? Is it only a theory without grounds, a personal belief without evidence? No!—it is quite demonstrable to anyone who will undertake the work upon himself.

405

The rewards of this quest are not primarily material ones, although these may come. The only reward that can be guaranteed to the successful aspirant is that he will emerge out of the unregenerate state and come closer to the Overself's consciousness, that is to say, to the kingdom of heaven. Whoever looks for more may be disappointed. But to the man who through reflection or suffering, intuition or instruction, has got his values right, this will be enough.

406

From the first momentary glimpse of the soul till the final rest in it, he is being led to accept the truth that the love which he wants and hopes to find outside himself must be found within himself. The true beloved is not a person but a presence. When genuine love in its most intense form utterly overwhelms him, he will find that its physical form is a mere caricature of it and that its human form is a pale reflection from it. Instead of having to beg some woman or some man for crumbs of affection from their table, he will find a veritable fountain of everflowing love deep within his heart, and therefore ever available to him in the fullest measure. This is the one beloved who can never desert him, the unique soul-mate who will forever remain with him, the only twin soul he can seek with the absolute certainty that it is truly his own.

407

At the least there will be more outer harmony and less outer friction in day-to-day living, more inner peace and less inner anxiety.

408

It leads to amity in human relationships and dissolves enmity.

409

The more a man becomes acquainted with the true sources of his inner life—both in its good and bad sides—the better it will be for his outer life.

410

He will expand the meaning of his own habitual life-experience as he expands the awareness of the divine in himself.

411

Practical wisdom in overcoming the most difficult situations and perfect skill in managing the most delicate ones, are qualities which should emerge from the balanced training given by this quest.

412

It becomes the background, unknown to other persons, of all his activities. This is a considerable achievement, a consequence of *applying* to them what he perceived in meditation, learnt in study, and understood in reflection.

413

It is a teaching whose conceptions give the mind a reasonable understanding of life and whose practice gives the heart repose.

414

It is a gross mistake to believe that this is a path to worldly misery and material destitution. Says an ancient Sanskrit text, *Ratna Karanda Sravakachara*: "Whoever turns himself into a jewel-case of philosophic wisdom, perfect devotion, and faultless conduct, to him comes success in all his enterprises, like a woman eager to return to her husband." Note particularly that the promise is made to those who have travelled the *threefold* path and have also travelled it to its end.

415

He who is sufficiently ready to recognize the Higher Purpose of Life, and who has the courage to change and improve his way of thinking, thereby replacing negative thoughts by positive ones, will certainly be rewarded by improved circumstances and greater happiness than he may already enjoy.

416

No one who feels that his inner weakness or outer circumstances prevent him from applying this teaching should therefore refrain from studying it. That would not only be a mistake but also a loss on his part. For as the *Bhagavad Gita* truly says, "A little of this knowledge saves from much danger." Even a few years' study of philosophy will bring definite benefit into the life of a student. It will help him in all sorts of ways, unconsciously, here on earth and it will help him very definitely after death during his life in the next world of being.(P)

417

Although its promises and experiences may not appear glamorous in a worldly sense, the Quest reveals itself to be the best of all possible ways of living.

418

If it exacts the highest possible price in human satisfactions it gives in return the highest possible spiritual satisfactions.

419

The aspirant may have already discovered for himself some of the inner benefits of the Quest. Once the Overself has been experienced as a felt, living presence in the heart, it loosens the grip of egoistic desires—together with their emotional changes of mood—on one's consciousness and lifts it to a higher level, where he will soon become aware of a wonderful inner satisfaction which remains calm and unruffled despite outward circumstances to the contrary.

Ultimately, the aspirant has to rise into that pure atmosphere whence he can survey his personal life as a thing apart. Still more difficult is it for one to live on that level while expressing the wisdom and goodness known to him. It is, however, almost beyond human strength to achieve the second part of such a program. Therefore, he has first to establish the connection with the Overself so that its strength and understanding will then rule him effortlessly. The moment this connection is established, the aspirant will become aware of results from the descent of Divine Grace upon his personality. Such a moment is unpredictable, but, for the individual who sticks to the Quest, its arrival is sure.

420

Out of these intense struggles with his thoughts and emotions, these repeated meditations and altruistic actions, these constant self-analyses and ardent yearnings, he will eventually get something which words can hardly describe. It will be a new sense of sacredness, an enlightened awareness of a deeper self, a blessed loving serenity.

421

In meditation practice, metaphysical study, and right conduct we have the triune path which brings satisfaction, peace, wisdom, and true prosperity. Jesus taught us all this long ago but unfortunately his message has been largely misunderstood, distorted, and even falsified. However he also taught that we are all the children of God. It is a Father's business to look after his children. Despite the tragedy and horror of our times, those who have eyes to see can still see the divine arms enfolding us. Despite the presence of monstrosities in the world, there is also the presence of the Overself—beautiful, radiant, benign, and indestructible.

422

Intelligence exercised constantly in musing upon the nature of life, the movements of the universe, the psychology of man, and the mystery of God—if exercised in calmness, intuitive balance, and depth—leads to the opening up of the soul.

423

If he lets this purpose penetrate his entire life, he will soon joyously feel that he is part of the eternal structure of the universe, that he fits into the Idea of it at some point, and that with such a high relationship all things must work together for his ultimate good.

Dangers

424

Those who are frightened away from the Quest by these notes of its dangers are better separated from it.

425

The aspirant who lacks balance is liable to take a misstep at more than one point of his path.

426

If an unbalanced dreamer is not brought to actuality and reality by experience, he had better leave the quest alone. This is not to say that he cannot get mystical experiences in plenty, but that they will have little true worth for insight.

427

The uncertainties of the Quest may lead, especially in the neurotic temperament, to a variety of unhappy moods and unhealthy emotions as the years pass by. The student may at such times turn against himself in morbid masochism, or against the teaching he has been following, or against the personal instructor if he has one.

428

The novice too often lives under the delusion that he is following the Quest when he has yet to find the entrance to it.

429

The importance of right direction is such that if the angle of deflection covers a long period, the area of error stretches a wide distance.

430

A self-protective need of the quester is to find and keep both an apparent and a real sanity. The first is needed in defense against the world, the second against himself.

431

When yoga is improperly or over-practised, one of the harmful results will be a gradual slackening of interest in the common activities of mankind. The unfortunate practitioner develops a blurred and vague character. He becomes increasingly unfit to fulfil social obligations or business duties, and tends to become bored with responsibilities. He treats the fate of others with indifference. He does what is inescapable, but he does it in a casual, detached, and uninterested manner. In short, he becomes unfit for everyday practical life.

432

Keep away from psychic practices and occult explorations. They are filled with dangers and pitfalls. First devote your energies to the foundational work of learning philosophy, improving character, disciplining emotion, and cultivating calmness. Only after this work has been well advanced will it ever be safe for you to take up occultism, for only then will you be properly equipped to do so.

433

Once again must a warning be given against the dangers of falling into mere psychism and seeking for phenomena, visions, miracles, and other things which are still in the realm of a kind of subtle materialism and are always connected with the personal ego. The true spiritual experience is higher than that, purer than that, and will leave him absolutely calm, whereas the psychical phenomena leave him excited. Every kind of such phenomena involves thought or emotion, whereas the deepest spiritual experience goes beneath thought and emotion and especially beneath the personal ego. Only then does one come in contact with the Infinite life-power which is behind everything and which is the true goal of this Quest.

434

Those who imagine the Quest to be a spiritual joyride know only a limited phase of it. For along with the joys there are glooms, difficulties, struggles, conflicts, and vacillations.

435

That a proportion of those who are attracted to these subjects are psychopaths, is unfortunately true. They would be far better employed in getting proper treatment for their disordered minds, imaginations, and feelings. Mystical studies may easily exaggerate their condition and increase their imbalance. It is the serious duty of every responsible expounder to warn them off this field and to bid them engage in the quest of psychic and bodily health before attempting that of spiritual light!

436

When a man pays no heed to the warnings of prophets and the counsel of sages, and is still too ungrown to pick his steps correctly, he inevitably loses his way.

437

The awakening of inner forces ought not be attempted without an accompanying attempt to fortify character and guard against weakness.

438

In the case of mentally disturbed or emotionally unbalanced persons, trust in their own ego may easily be misread as trust in the Overself—with correspondingly lamentable results.

439

The danger is that he may get lost in the mazes of his own mind. Those who suffer from such psychic maladjustments cannot find truth but only its distortions. They have fallen into a mental quagmire.

440

Let him not deceive himself. Few have ever really entered that exquisite awareness and remained there. Others seem to have done so but the fact is that they merely touched its outermost fringe for a few moments and then passed into an egoistic conceited state which has trapped them.

441

Certain psychic experiences may arise, the pattern of which is familiar, having been observed in both the writer's own experience and numerous other cases. Between the ordinary state of undeveloped humanity and the truly spiritual state attained by highly advanced individuals, there is a psychic region conducive to mediumship and other pitfalls and dangers which has to be crossed. One is indeed fortunate to come through this safely.

442

From several different sources a variety of suggestive influences play upon the student's mind and habits, influences which may be all very well for others but which may be harmful to his own individuality at his particular stage of spiritual progress. This is true not only of the trivial affairs of everyday living but also of the loftier affairs of aspirational living. White truths and black falsehoods, cleverly combined half-truths and half-falsehoods are continually being presented to his consciousness. Not only his physical life, but also his mental life must become a process of careful acceptance and vigilant rejection. At a certain stage of this quest the seeker must be particularly careful to be on his guard against the skilfully suggested "truths" of others who mistake their own candle-glimmer for the sun's glory and the prejudices born of their own narrow experience for the wisdom born of insight. This caution is especially necessary in the sphere of mystical experience.

443

The wary seeker should be on his guard against those who offer pseudo-knowledge as well as those extremists who would lead him off balance.

444

Those who take to this quest for the sake of satisfying personal ambition, will do better in the end to leave it alone.

445

Travelling on this quest can be only another way of inflating their egos, increasing their pride, and renewing their sectarianism.

446

It is not easy, this quest. Some stumble along it and somehow manage to advance a little way, but others give up.

447

A longtime personal disciple of Professor Jung told P.B., "My friend and teacher Jung was not opposed to yoga: it was only that most of the people who came to see him were patients who suffered from psychosis. He thought this should be cured first, or yoga would be perilous."

448

Teachers have sometimes tried to discourage people from entering on the Quest, for, by their own experience, they know what a long and painful road it is.

449

Beginners come to this quest with little knowledge and much indoctrination, so that sectarian attitudes soon appear again, although clothed in a different jargon.

450

Too many beginners form too many misconceptions about this subject, too often got from miscellaneous cursory reading of mixed quality.

451

There is not only danger in dabbling in meditation but also in experimenting in it too long without adequate safeguards or qualified supervision.

452

Extravagant assertions and erroneous ideas constitute another peril which besets the developing beginner.

453

Good intent or sincere motive cannot by itself be enough to protect the fool against his own gullibility, the uncritical against his own stupidity, and the uninformed against his own ignorance. All this is as true of the quest itself as of that part of its practice called meditation.

454

Seductive activities, phenomena, ideas, or "guides" may try to lure him from this straight course into time-wasting sideshows or dangerous directions. Reform, psychism, politics, perverted teachings or counterfeit ones may call but must not be heeded. He has a long way to go yet and must take care to keep on the right road.

455

There is an evil quest too, whose disciples seek to serve their lower nature rather than to conquer it, and whose masters show themselves by action or teaching to be monsters.

456

Warnings must be given against possible pitfalls on the quester's way. Yes, meditation may lead to hallucinations, spiritual self-development may lead to spiritual vanity, and self-purification may lead to ascetic crankiness.

6

STUDENT-TEACHER

General notes

The few who have a broad experience of life, whose reason is sufficiently alive to judge both fruits and roots correctly and whose intuition is sufficiently active to recognize nobility when meeting it, who want the *whole* truth and nothing less, will find a friend (for he will not wish to be anything more) who will decline to permit others to hold a fanciful vision of an earthly perfection which is non-existent; who will be humble, sane, and balanced above all things, and yet prove with time—if they themselves prove loyal—to be also a sure and benevolent guide in this dark forest where so many wander bewildered, deceived, or self-deceived. Excessive unreflective saint-worship raises exaggerated and even false hopes. It has historically often ended with exploitation of the worshipper. But even where it does not, it is still incompatible with healthy self-development; an affectionate respect is wiser and safer. Let us not ask a teacher to be a god, because thereby we are liable to deceive and endanger ourselves, but let us ask him to be competent and illumined, truthful and helpful and compassionate.

2

Not by our own exertions alone, and not by the gift or grace of an external being alone, can we be brought to final realization, but by both.

3

Those who can let themselves be uplifted by some inspired or enlightened person should understand that he is capable of lifting them to the point of touching their best self, the divinity within them. Some may even gain a glimpse of it, a memorable unforgettable experience. But will they let it happen?

4

We are not left to find out for ourselves what the truth is. Now and then messengers appear among us, each bearing his own personal communication about the existence of a higher power and the need of a higher life.

5

We may help the Overself in drawing us to the goal by surrendering to the guidance of a competent spiritual adviser or we may obstruct it by clinging to the ego's. But an incompetent adviser will also obstruct it, and in fact become a channel for the ego's truth-obscuring tactics.

6

The difficulty of the task of self-improvement is not to be underrated and it is because of this as well as for other reasons that seekers since ancient times have been advised to obtain the help of a guru. From him they can get inspiration, guidance, and a certain telepathically transferred strengthening power which is called Grace.

It is not necessary to be living always near a guru in a monastery as so many seem to think. What is really necessary is to meet him on this physical plane once only, even if it be just for five minutes. After that his help can be received inwardly and mentally by telepathy without any further physical meeting. This is because the real guru is not the body, but his inner being, the Mind behind the body, and it is that inner being with which the seeker must try to come into relation. Such a relation he builds up himself by his own mental attitude, by his faith devotion and obedience to the way that is shown.

7

Wherever there is instruction to be got there is an ashram. And whenever you go there you will get instruction from the experiences of life. Therefore the whole world is an ashram to a discerning student. Much the same applies to the question of a teacher. Says a Bengali verse: "Wouldst thou make obeisance to thy master, my heart? He is there at every step, on each side of thy path. The welcome offered thee is thy master, the agony inflicted on thee is thy master. Every wrench at thy heartstrings that maketh the tears flow is thy master."

8

Any book or person seen or art production which reminds a man of his diviner self, is to that extent his teacher. Any happening or event or experience which alienates him from such remembrance, whether it be regarded by the world as good or as evil, likewise is his teacher. Even his own unworthy actions will, because of the consequences to which they must infallibly lead, also be his teachers.

9

Those whose inner development or outer circumstances or personal karma have prepared them for the truth will come to it anyway: they may need a little prodding or a lot of reflection, but in the end they will recognize it for what it is. But they confound this recognition with the relation of discipleship to some guru. The two things need to be separated if they are to be correctly understood.

10

Teaching is always available in some way or some form, for Life, through varied situations, takes care of its own; but a Teacher in his physical form may not be available just at the necessary point in time. In that case, one may be met through his writings. If this does not happen, he may come into the mental life during a great anguish or an enforced inactivity or an unusual relaxation or, finally, through or during meditation.

11

(Mira Bai) "On the way I found two guides: the spiritual preceptors and God. To the preceptors I make my bow. But God I keep in my heart."

The need for a teacher

12

Happiness depends on our understanding of life, understanding depends upon the penetration of insight, insight depends upon right instructions received from a competent teacher.

13

The inspirational and moral, the intellectual and meditational helps which a competent guide can give to a worthy disciple are valuable. If such a worthy, honourable, selfless, experienced, and expert guide can be found—and this may be counted exceptionally good fortune—the disciple should certainly submit to his tutelage and surrender to his influence.

14

The need of a saviour arises from the fact that the ego cannot lift itself by its own bootstraps, cannot rise out of its own dimension into a higher one, and will not willingly encompass its own destruction. Yet its spiritual career arrives eventually at a point where it finds and sees that it has done what it could, that further efforts are futile, and that only some power outside itself can bring about the next forward move. However, it may not without self-deception declare this point to be reached when in fact it ought to continue with its strivings; it may not cease prematurely from its struggles. If it does so, then it would be equally futile to seek a master's grace.

15

Those who refuse to admit that a Master is essential to the neophyte will at least grant that his aid is advisable. Only a man severely handicapped or a fool would undertake the study and practice of medicine, or building, or of any other art without a teacher, an expert who has himself mastered the subject. How then can anyone take up the art of soul-unfoldment, subtle and recondite as it is, without realizing the usefulness of a Master?

16

Heaven lies within and without us, it is true. But in most cases, only by the intervention of some authentic spiritual genius do we seem able to translate this into actuality for ourselves.

17

Life is teaching us all the time but its voice needs a human being as a more direct medium, its lessons need human speech or writing to gain clearer utterance.

18

Nature herself is forever silently voicing these majestic truths and if we are unable to receive them from her lips, as we usually are, then we must receive them from a teacher's lips.

19

We know that the mere reading of books and journals is not enough, and our essential conviction (as also the acknowledgment of the Orient since time immemorial) is that a personal guide who can instruct and inspire one to travel through the twilit jungle land which lies between ignorance and truth is indispensable.

20

The missing element in many quests is the spiritual guide.

21

One of the greatest helps to convert our timid thoughts and our trembling wishes into deeds is the inspiration received from a superior mind.

22

Most men find they need a concrete symbol to receive their devotion and concentrate their aspiration. In short, they find they need a Spiritual Leader, be he historical and of the past, or contemporary and of the present.

23

It is said that wisdom comes with experience. But the sages who offer to impart it, whether in person or in writing, may save us some of the effort and suffering which accompany experience.

24

Every generation has to find its own way through these mysteries and to these truths anew, despite the heavy freight of recorded teachings and revelations which it receives from all the previous ones. This is why new prophets have always been needed to provide the old, old clues.

25

Something or someone is needed to draw us from the ego to the Overself behind it.

26

When he finds out that all his efforts at self-improvement are movements around a circle, that the ego does not really intend to give itself up in surrender to the Overself and therefore only pretends to do so, he realizes that left to himself he cannot succeed in really changing his inner centre of gravity. Help is needed from some outside source if he is to free himself from such a hopeless position.

27

The purposes of human evolution require the presence at all times through human history of some spiritually fulfilled individuals to act as guides or teachers. At no period has the race been left entirely without them, no matter how bleak, how savage, or how materialistic the period has been.

28

While the dream is still continuing, he cannot help taking its scenes and figures as being quite real. But if someone rings a bell until he awakens from the dreaming state, he will then see that both scenes and figures were mere figments of his own imagination. In a sense, the teacher of philosophy acts as this awakener did, except that he directs his efforts to the sense-deceived consciousness of everyday life.

29

It is not enough to set up a spiritual ideal for him to attain. He needs also the psychological help, the emotional and mental re-education which can remove large obstructions to that attainment.

30

No seeker is so wise, so informed, so perfect, or so balanced as not to need the constructive criticism and expert counsel of a true spiritual guide.

31

Such is the world today, with its tensions and greeds, its confusions and wrongs, its ignorance and evil-doing, that if anyone has a store of virtue and an awareness of divinity, people have need of them and hence of him. There is too little of the one and hardly any of the other among us.

32

A man needs comfort and support in these times more than in ordinary times. Where can he best find them? By sitting humbly in intellectual discipleship under those who have been blessed by the higher power with the revelation of its own existence. He can absorb from them a certitude that the world is still ruled by higher laws and its history by higher purposes.

33

If someone knows what I do not yet know, if he has trodden farther on this path, then it is well to learn from him if he will teach me.

34

The instruction and criticism of a qualified living guide are worth having. But owing to the rarity of such guides, many seekers are unable to find one.

35

He should appreciate the value of finding a master worthy of being followed. The inner demand of the one will attract in time the outer meeting with the other.

36

No maniac can cure himself. We dare not leave the treatment of human-ity's mania entirely to the humanity themselves. The help of sane outsiders is needed. But it should be given indirectly and unobtrusively.

37

If the more mature, older, and more experienced nightingales find it necessary to give lessons in singing to the younger ones, why not the same situation among human beings?

38

It is the greatest irony of man's existence that in the end he will be saved from his meanness and misery not by those who shout the loudest but by the quietest, the most silent of his fellows. For the power and knowledge which he will gain from discipleship with them will be what he needs above all else—power over the baseness in himself and knowledge of the divine World-Idea.

39

In the single matter of learning meditation alone one will encounter all sorts of obstacles within oneself and difficulties without. They will be much more easily and quickly overcome if one places oneself under the training of an expert preceptor whose long experience in this matter and natural gift for guiding others makes his advice mentally enlightening and practically useful.

40

The beginner cannot take his lessons from the skies. He has to find a teacher, even if only to impart the right atmosphere and inculcate the right ideas.

41

The use of a teacher is, firstly, suggestive. His influence is a definite aid to incline us to travel along the proper path. It is, secondly, protective, for under his constant guidance we learn to be wary of pitfalls.

42

Not only is the teacher helpful in pointing out the proper path to be followed and also in exposing the errors of the disciple but furthermore in bestowing upon him an impetus to the practice of meditation and the strength to obtain the concentration required for it. The impetus is needed because through long habit engendered over many reincarnations of the past, most people are unbalanced. That is, they are either too extroverted and overactive with outward matters or live in a state of continual mental restlessness through being too busy with their own thoughts. The strength is needed because keeping the attention along a single track and sustaining it for a certain period is an extremely difficult task. Once the inner contact has been properly established, quite often the mere thought of the master will be enough to inspire the disciple and thus give him both the impetus and the strength required to make his attempts at meditation more effectual.

43

Other results of associating with one who is more spiritually advanced are that it incites a student to excel himself, strengthens him in the resolve to pursue the quest, and fans the spark of longing for the Divine.

44

It is said in the Yogic and Sufi schools that the company of enlightened men tends to arouse those who dwell in darkness to seek light, as it tends to hasten the development of those who are already engaged in this search.

45

It is when one reaches the end of a particular phase and has first to find, then to begin a new one that help from outside is useful. The same is true when one reaches a difficult place on the Quest. This help may be found in a book, a lecture, a guru, a chance meeting, or in some other way.

46

The help of a master shows itself principally, and is chiefly important in, the course taken by the mind during meditation.

47

One of the chief benefits of meeting with an illumined book or an inspired man, is that such an encounter opens up the possibility of moving more swiftly from a lower to a higher standpoint. It opens up truths which would ordinarily be too far ahead to be noticed, thus acting like a spiritual telescope. It also brings us face to face with our own errors in thought and conduct. Such a movement might otherwise take several years or sometimes a whole lifetime. But it remains only a possibility. It is for us to recognize the true character of the opportunity and for us to grasp and take the fullest advantage of it.

48

It may be that he keeps the spiritual quest in the background of his mind only. If so he needs a quickening impulse. Such an impulse can be given him but only by a master. He imparts the necessary impetus which helps the student towards the realization of his finest aspirations.

49

Whoever seeks to raise his own consciousness to the Overself's, will get most help from seeking out an individual who has already accomplished that task. In the presence of someone whose own consciousness is in the Overself, he will receive the inward inspiration which can energize and lead his personal efforts in the same direction.

50

The entrance of a book of truth, or of a man bearing truth, into the aspirant's life will, at certain periods when he is ready and prepared for further development, be like turning on the light in a room to shut out the darkness.

51

The earnest seeker will get more from a single meeting with a truly inspired man than from attendance at a hundred sessions in an organized spiritual school or ashram. For the first will awaken his intuition whereas the second will merely add to his information. The first will really advance his progress whereas the second will only give the illusion of doing so. But such is the widespread ignorance and inexperience of these things, as well as the suggestive power of pomp and prestige, that the organized institution will always attract fifty followers where the lone illuminate will attract five.

52

A human channel is needed for the superhuman inspiration, grace, teaching, or revelation because the recipient minds are not sufficiently sensitive, pure, or prepared to receive it directly for themselves.

53

His own little experience may be too limited to comprehend mystical revelations aright. Consequently he may in parts or at times misinterpret them. A safeguard against this is first, to call in the experience of other seekers, which he may do through their books or speech, and second, to call on authority, which he may do through joining his inner life to a trustworthy teacher.

54

The beginning aspirant lacks the experience to judge himself aright and even the intermediate lacks the impersonal view to judge himself correctly.

55

Even a single meeting with a master is vastly important to the aspirant. He may never enter into any personal relation with the master but that meeting will alone suffice to do four fundamental things. It will vindicate the value of his aspirations and demonstrate their attainability; it will convince him that the Overself does exist and show him in what direction he is to seek it.

56

When he himself forgets it, man is reminded of his divine linkage by prophets, teachers, and sages.

57

One advantage of having a personal teacher is that, to some extent, you can watch his mind work.

58

The master can see the disciple's character and motives, hidden complexes and unrevealed weaknesses better than he can himself.

59

So long as experience and results have not established sufficient confidence in his intuitive guidance and sufficient trust in his philosophic knowledge, he needs to continue travelling with a teacher.

60

The master is the wonderful catalyst who makes possible a quickened development, an inspired renewal of the aspirant's inner life.

61

At a certain stage in the life of the aspirant it is of the utmost importance to him that he improve his character and karma. This, neither he nor anyone can hope to do so effectively alone as when studying under a genuine teacher. In the latter case, it is possible for him to accomplish within a relatively short time that which would ordinarily require many more years of floundering self-effort.

62

What the earnest mind is struggling to formulate to itself vaguely and uncertainly and unclearly, the teacher states decisively, assuredly, and definitely.

63

A phrase or two, coming from an inspired man, may set a subconscious process working in the mind of another and lead him in the end to acquire a new truth or a new view.

64

Those who come forward as gurus driven by the ego, the ambitions, and ulterior motives are not gurus at all. They are trespassers on a fine vocation. We must remember that those who work to earn a livelihood and come home tired have not the time or strength to think for themselves or to search for themselves. For them the ready-made support of established religion is indeed helpful, while the guidance of sincere, competent, and available teachers is even more sought for.

65

To follow one's own path, rejecting the idea of seeking the expert help, tested knowledge, and accumulated experience of a Master is to follow a haphazard course of trial and error. The determination to maintain such independence and to make one's way by one's own effort is not of much use. One will be far better off working under guidance than without it.

66

An aspirant is most fortunate if he has been led safely upwards past the delusory sidetracks and bypaths which detain so many other seekers. Only in this way can his consciousness arrive at what really constitutes the Highest Truth.

67

Teaching is necessary. How can those who do not know the true cause of their afflictions know the way out of them? Someone must warn them, someone must awaken them.

68

We do not go all the way with the Tibetan saying that "without the guru you cannot get liberation," but we do go part of the way.

69

The need of a guide and mentor is obvious but this is no reason to exaggerate it to the extent that so many have done.

70

Sri Ramakrishna once said: "A man who himself approaches God with deep longing for Him, and earnest prayer, will find Him even if he has no *guru*." When asked why a teacher was necessary at all, he replied, "Very few people have this deep yearning and therefore the *guru* is necessary for them." By this he meant that the teacher inspires and encourages seekers of God not to give up when the going is difficult, but to stick to the Quest, regardless of the many long years it inevitably takes.

71

It is always pleasant to learn that a seeker has found a good teacher. It may be puzzling then to hear that the teacher can no longer continue with his pupil. However, in such a case, the individual should not be unnecessarily distressed, because he can most certainly continue to make progress on the Quest irrespective of whether or not he has an outward teacher. All he needs to do is to pray humbly to God, whose love and forgiveness will accompany him always where a human teacher's cannot.

72

Is there then no real need of a master? The answer is "No!" for some men but "Yes!" for most men. He is needed to *wake up* the sleeper by telling him the highest truth *from the very first time*, and then descend by degrees to the stages while still holding on to the truth. The master serves only by showing a seeking person his real self, his Overself: or holding a mirror up to him. This can be called, also, giving him a "glimpse," or, more truthfully, being used by the higher power as a vehicle to do so.

73

He who is working under the guidance of a master is not exempt from making mistakes, but he will make fewer and expose them sooner and correct them quicker than he who is not.

74

I write all this in no sneering or disparaging manner, but rather as one who understands sympathetically the need of most beginners and many intermediates to find guidance outside themselves for the all-sufficient reason that they cannot find it inside. Indeed it is because I have been a disciple that I myself know why others become one, and can approve of their action. But that experience is also why I know the limitations and disservices of a discipleship.

75

To say that no teacher is necessary is to set oneself up as a teacher by that very statement.

76

Self-instruction cannot be as correct and efficacious as instruction by an expert, a specialist, or a fully experienced person who can also communicate adequately as a teacher.

77

The original Shankara, Adi Shankara, made it an absolute necessity that whoever sought to realize the spiritual Truth must seek out a guru. This injunction has hypnotized the Indians who came after him as it hypnotized those before his time because it was laid down in the *Mundaka Upanishad* long, long before. Shankara even warned his readers and hearers that even an expert student of the *Vedas* should not engage in such a search by himself. Yet there are several cases in Indian history where men have experienced this realization without any guru whatever.

78

We need to build up an intimate inner relationship with a being whose compassion is wide enough to understand us and whose power is developed enough to help us. It does not matter that he is dead.

79

Those who know only a single mode of living, that of the extrovert, or a single mode of thinking, that which is sense-based, need to expose themselves for sufficient time to the influence of a spiritual master before they can begin to become even dimly aware that they have a soul. But since a fully evolved master is hard to find, something else must act as his next best substitute. This must necessarily be an inspired writing produced by such a man.

80

The truth is that nearly all aspirants need the help of expert human guides and printed books when they are actively seeking the Spirit, and of printed books at least when they are merely beginning to seek.(P)

Books as teachers

81

It is not essential to find a teacher in the flesh—he may be in print. A book may become a quite effective teacher and guide.

82

In the absence of a sage's personal society, one may have recourse to the best substitute—a sage's printed writings.

83

Inspired texts, portions of scriptures, great men's writings and sayings offer guidance on the course of action to be followed, the ethical considerations to be heeded, the decisions to be made under certain pressures, crises, or confrontations—decisions whose consequences are often quite grave. Who can price the value of such readings at such times?

84
Books are most useful to those who, whether by necessity through lack of sincere competent instruction or by choice, to avoid narrow sectarianism, seek the goal by themselves.

85
Most students seeking inspiration have no other choice than recourse to the printed words.

86
The personal contact with a master does not necessarily require a face-to-face meeting. It can also be effected through a letter written by him—nay, to some degree, even through a book written by him. For his mind incarnates itself in these productions. Thus, those who are prevented by circumstances from meeting him physically, may meet him mentally and gain the same results.

87
The perspicacious student will cling steadfastly throughout his life to the writings of illumined masters, returning to them again and again. Their works are the truest of all, pure gold and not alloys.

88
There are men whose thought went deeper and understood more clearly than that of their fellows. Their record exists, their sayings and writings also. Their study is worthwhile, their precepts can be put to the test in practical everyday living.

89
In these books the voice of men who were spiritually illuminated long ago speaks to him. They are the only way in which it can speak to him today. Therefore he should respect and cherish them.

90
Those who have towered above all other men as Masters, who have left records of their path and of its attainment, can be good guides.

91
Why not make these great men your teachers through their preserved teachings? Why not be the disciple of Socrates, Buddha, Saint Paul, and dozens of others?

92
However distant a teacher may be, whether in country or century, by means of this written record he is able to help whoever is willing to lend his time and eyes.

93
If a book gives correct teaching about the quest and necessary warning about its pitfalls, it should be studied with proper care and respect.

94

A man can take from the printed word what he is unable to hear from the spoken word.

95

The truth-seeker will be wise to make use of such outward helps as appeal to him. They may be the written word, the printed book, the molded statuette, the pictorial representation, or the human photograph—always provided they are referable to a genuinely inspired source. He should study the words and works, the lives and examples of practising mystics, and follow in their footsteps.

96

Good books are not to be disdained, despite contemptuous references by fanatical mystics or ill-balanced ascetics. Negatively, they will warn him against misleading elements likely to cause a deviation from his correct course. Positively, they will guide him where no personal guide is available.

97

But he must beware of imagining that the pleasure he derives from spiritual reading is any sign that he is making progress in spiritual living. It is easier to read lofty thoughts than to think them out for oneself, and to live them is the most difficult of all.

98

Books, too, serve as guides if they are properly used, that is, if their limitations are recognized and if their authors' limitations are acknowledged. In the first case it is the intellect's own inability to transcend thought that stops it from realizing truth. In the second case it is the evolutionary status of the man's ego, and the accuracy of his attitudes—themselves victims or controllers of his emotions, passions—which matter. For if his mind cannot register the impact of truth, because of the blockage set up partially or even all around him, the author's work will reflect his ignorance. He cannot teach what he does not know; his own mental obscurity can lead only to the reader's obscurity. Yet such is the deceptiveness of thought, that a wrong or false idea may be received and held in the mind under the belief that it is a right or true one.

99

The writings of these Masters help both the moral nature and the intellectual mind of the responsive and sensitive, who are excited to the same endeavour, exhilarated to the same level, and urged to realize the same ideas. These stand out from all other writings because they contain vivid inspiration and true thought.

100

The very fine writings of philosophers and mystics of all times may bring into one's life some emotional inspirational and intellectual guidance, even, possibly, stimulating his power of will. Through the long, unavoidable years of struggle on the Quest, they can, to that extent, act the part of a teacher or guide. However, it must be remembered that some are infinitely more worthwhile than others, and it is essential for one to be able to discriminate between what is true and helpful and what is false and worthless.

101

These subjects are becoming more widely known and more studied than they were a half-century ago. There has been quite a flow of literature, original works, commentaries, and translations in our time making both mystical and philosophic ideas more available.

102

With the universal spread of elementary education, and the issue of cheaper paper-covered texts and translations, it is now possible for most earnest seekers living in the free countries to come into possession of the teaching.

103

If he cannot understand the more intellectual portions of these books he should not worry because they are written for different classes and those portions which he cannot follow are particularly addressed to highbrows and have to be expressed in a more complicated and scientific style.

104

If the literature on these subjects is so much larger today, the problem of choosing correctly what is most reliable is so much more difficult.

105

Book teaching is too general. It makes no allowance for individual differences, for the wide variation from one person to another. It is always necessary for the readers to adapt the teaching to their own sex, age, character, strength, and circumstances.

106

From these great writings, he will receive impulses of spiritual renewal. From these strong paragraphs and lovely words he will receive incitement to make himself better than he is. Their every page will carry a message to him; indeed, they will seem to be written for him.

107

Every book which stimulates aspiration and widens reflection does spiritual service and acts as a guru.

108

With such books he will feel for a while better than he is, wiser than he is.

109

One of the helps to kindle this spark into a flame is the reading of inspired literature, whether scripture or not—the mental association through books with men who have themselves been wholly possessed by this love.

110

A chance phrase in such an inspired writing may give a man the guidance for which he has long been waiting.

111

The words of inspired men are like a lighthouse to those seekers who are still groping in the dark.

112

Perhaps one prime value of a book is its power to remind students of fundamental principles and its ability to recall them to the leading points of this teaching, for these are easily lost or overlooked amid the press of daily business.

113

He will draw from such reading the incentive to keep on with his quest and the courage to set higher goals.

114

It may not be in the power of any piece of writing to guide a man all the way along this quest but it certainly is in its power to give him general direction and specific warning.

115

Let him study the literature of mystical and philosophic culture to become better informed about the Quest, about its nature and goal, and about himself.

116

By comparing what is described in the books with what he has so far experienced for himself, an aspirant may check and correct his course.

117

Those who were awakened by this reading could then look elsewhere for the personal guidance they seek.

118

Through a book help is given without involving the helper in the personal lives of the readers, but through a letter or a meeting involvement begins.

Issues in seeking a teacher

119
It is a man's own fault if, through his failure to seek spiritual guidance or understanding, none is vouchsafed to him. "Ask, and it shall be given unto you," said Jesus in this reference, which complements and is necessary to the assertion of the Chinese sage: "Those who know do not speak."

120
It is said, "When a pupil is ready, the Master appears." This means that such is the wonderful sensitivity of the mind, such is the reality of telepathic power, that when a man's search for truth has reached a crisis, he will meet the man who or the book which can best resolve that crisis. But the crisis itself must be filled with uncertainty and doubt, with helplessness and despair before the mysterious forces of the Overself will begin to move towards his relief. It should seem to him the most momentous consequence that it shall be brought to a satisfactory end, if life in the future is to have any meaning for him at all. There must be a sense of inner loneliness so acute that outer loneliness compares as nothing with it. There must be no voice within his world which can speak to his condition. This critical period must fill his mind with exaggeration of its own self-importance to such an extent as to blot out every other value from life. It will be at such an opportune moment, when his search for truth will be most intense and the required preparation for meeting its bearer most complete, that the bearer himself will arise and bring into his night the joyful tidings of dawn. The influence of such a man or his book at such a period is incalculable. Emerson gives its innermost meaning in his lines, "If we recall the rare hours when we encountered the best persons, we there found ourselves. . . . God's greatest gift is a Teacher." The seeker knows at last that even if he has not found the truth he is at least on the way to finding it. He has begun to find harmony with himself.

121
If the strong yearning for truth be absent, a man may meet a thousand masters of the quest but he will neither recognize them for what they are nor experience any exaltation in their presence. This yearning must indeed be as strong as the hunger of a starving man or the desperation of a traveller lost in the desert.

122
His desperate need drives him to go in search of help wherever he can find it.

123

In obedience to this inner urge he should take a path which will lead him to the friendship of the few sages living in his time and bring him to their feet.

124

The man who begins to feel this need in himself should seek out spiritual direction. He should find an authoritative source to instruct him in spiritual truth and to clear up his questions.

125

Contrary to common belief, the teacher is not found in the inner psychic life first and then the discovery reflected in the outer physical life later. He is met first in the flesh; but the discovery must eventually become a settled psychic fact before any real relationship can be established between the two. He must be found unshakeably established in the innermost depths of the heart as a presence and in the background of the mind as a picture.

126

There has arisen too much harm and exploitation from the teacher-seeking attitude of some. Firstly, the request for a teacher should arise from a deep, sustained, and urgent sense of needing such help—not merely for the sake of having one.

127

His Overself may lead him to seek and find another man who shall be its intermediary with him: its representative to him, its image for him.

128

A knowledge worth understanding is not less important than a teacher worth seeking.

129

If a seeker believes that he has achieved a certain extent of self-preparation and self-purification, if he is convinced of the desperate need of a master, and if he does not succeed in finding a worthy one, then let him pray for help in the matter.

130

It is not enough to try to follow the counsel given by prophets, mystics, and sages, to look within. It is necessary also to look deep enough and long enough to get really worthwhile results. This applies just as much to the search for help as to the search for truth.

131

The individual seeking a teacher must not be disappointed nor discouraged if he is not accepted as a pupil. Prayer and aspiration directed toward the Higher Self will bring the sought-for guidance from within. Moreover, he may have been given help of which he is as yet unaware and, eventually, this will come through into his conscious mind. He should not exaggerate the need for a teacher. Ultimately, his development will depend on principles rather than on personalities.

132

The seeker should resolve to appeal directly by constant aspiration and prayer to his own higher self, in the knowledge that it alone can help him if he is to work without a teacher. On the other hand, if his karma has decreed that he is to have a guide, his higher self will bring before him the mental image or intuitive thought of the Master. If this happens, he will not need to seek out the Master's physical person; the inner picture will bring results.

133

Although it is true that meeting with inspired men does arouse some persons for the first time to the need of a higher life, it is also true that deep probing would show to what a large extent previous events or reflections had already mentally led such persons to the verge of this need. The inspired teacher does not create it. He only indicates it. Fate brings him at the right moment into the other person's life to enable this to be done.

134

And somewhere, sometime, for every man who sincerely seeks there must come a Guide, merely because this personal opening of the gate is part of Nature's program.

135

At times it seems to him that the help promised him has not materialized. This is his opinion. But it may also be that his ego was so strong that the help could not reach him because the ego stood in the way too obstinately. In any case it should have been made clear to him in books and conversations that the advanced mystic is not a Master but only a fellow student. If he could not get the required help from such a one he must accept the fact that it simply was not meant to be.

136

Even when a teacher is found he may be a master of one path only and unable to guide aspirants properly along those with which they have individual affinity and for which they have the requisite mental or emotional or volitional capacity.

137

Another false idea is that the masters seek out disciples, make the advance towards them, whether "astrally" or physically. On the contrary, aspirants must take the first step themselves, must request acceptance.

138

With all my Western education and intellectual outlook, I am still simple enough to believe, with Eastern people, that it is worthwhile making a journey to get the blessing of a superior person.

139

But although philosophers do not engage in making proselytes or in starting crusades, the man who is attracted by any tenet of philosophy will sooner or later find someone who will be ready to explain or discuss it with him.

140

When it is said that the readiness of the seeker determines the appearance of the master, this applies to the first fundamental initiation of his spiritual life. It does not mean that a master will come into his town and seek him out, but that he will come into his life. And this may be brought about in various ways—as by the seeker himself being led, either by worldly circumstances or by his own seeking, out of his own town to the town or country where the master is living.

141

The location of his spiritual guide will in part be the accident of his own geographical situation, for he will obviously be limited in his selection to possibilities and reputations in his own country or nation or race. The sheer physical and financial difficulties of travelling throughout the world—not to mention the obstacles of personal circumstance, family obligations, and ignorance of where to search and whom to approach in foreign lands, combine to set this limitation upon his inquiry and hence upon his opportunity.

142

It is foolish to seek holiness geographically or holy men in particular places. I have found that one man may live in a Himalayan abode and be a scoundrel and another man may live in a Bowery slum and be a saint. Wherever they live, men always carry their own thoughts and their own selves with them. The Soul, which is the object of our quest, is within us. The Master, who is to guide us upon our quest, will appear whenever we are ready for him and wherever we happen to live—or else we will be led to him. There are men in the West, in Europe and America, not less wise and noble than any men in Tibet and India. If we have not met them, "the fault, Dear Brutus is . . . in ourselves, " primarily in our unworthiness, and secondarily in our incapacity to recognize what is beneath the surface.

143

It is not necessary in the modern West to follow the Oriental custom of living with or near the Teacher. However, it *is* advisable to try to arrange a meeting, even if only for a few minutes. When this is impossible, one substitute is to enter into a written correspondence with him—and to keep his photograph in a hallowed place where one's eyes fall frequently upon it and one is thus reminded many times a day of the need to work continuously at improving oneself and one's character.

144

The effect of the first meeting with a master fades off with time, like the effect of a mystical glimpse. When that happens it needs to be renewed by another meeting, and that again in turn still later by a third.

145

It is right and just that the ardent aspirations of a sincere candidate should eventually bring him a rewarding meeting in person with someone more advanced or in print with a qualified disciple. If he merits more, if he adds preparation to his aspirations, then a personal meeting with such a disciple may follow. But it is wrong and unjust for him to be too demanding. He should expect further meetings only as he works upon himself enough to be worthy of them, as well as only as the disciple has time to spare for them. And if he is so fortunate as to meet an adept, he should be satisfied with that single meeting.

146

Such a meeting always brings certain tests with it and usually leads either to a powerful enhancement of the relation or to an abrupt cancellation of it altogether. This is because the tests arise from the power of opposition.

147

The beginner who ventures out in quest of a teacher may have to stumble from charlatan to incompetent until he either finds the right one or abandons the effort as impossible.

148

In most of the other affairs of life we find it necessary to use the services of specialists. Just so, here. We surrender our body to the surgeon. We must surrender our mind to the spiritual guide. Both, if incompetent or unscrupulous, may maim us for life. It is of the greatest importance therefore to exercise right judgement in the choice of one or the other.

149

When Dillip Roy, a famous Bengali musician, first came to Sri Aurobindo for an interview, the latter said: "You must tell me clearly what it is exactly that you seek and why you want to do my yoga. Seekers approach yoga with diverse aims. Some want to get away from life. Others aspire after supreme bliss. Yet others want yoga power or knowledge or a poise impervious to the shocks of life. So you must first be definite as to what, precisely, you seek in yoga."

150

If he falls into the wrong hands, or if he lets himself be guided by an incompetent amateur instead of a wise and expert man, his way will be hindered and even the good he thinks he does get will turn out to be evil.

151

He should be determined to wait calmly for the assent of his whole being before he makes a decision which must necessarily and tremendously affect his whole future.

152

Most people react strongly to these gurus—either emphatic rejection straightway or infatuated acceptance superficially. A clear perception which is unaccompanied by sitting in judgement or rushing into acquiescence, which justly notes what *is*, unidealized yet unbiased evaluation, is rare.

153

The ordinary aspirant, whose intuition is not sufficiently developed, should test the man he proposes to accept as his master. This will require him to watch the other closely for a period of time. In some cases a week will give the answer, in others three months will be needed. In all cases, the aspirant ought not commit himself until he has had enough evidence that he is committing himself rightly.

154

Discrimination is of utmost importance in the selection of a spiritual path and Teacher. One must apply all his intelligence and intuition, caution and common sense to a decision of such consequence.

155

Those who lack the innate discernment or wide experience needed to detect the real character and true capacity of a master, should wait sufficiently long and seek outside advice before entrusting themselves to him.

156

The faith that the Overself is working through a particular man can be tested for its validity by watching, for a sufficient length of time, what happens to those who reject him utterly or respond to him ardently.

157

In their excessive eagerness to discover a master, they fail to practise discernment.

158

But to wait for the *true* master requires a certain patience and strength.

159

A true sage is hard to find. A false one, drooling his plagiarisms or his platitudes, is easy to find.

160

Just because a man happens to feel he has attained happiness or truth, is no sufficient ground for accepting that he has done so. He could get the same feeling out of the self-betraying attainment of the illusion of happiness and the illusion of truth. Hence we have not only to overcome the difficulty of finding honest and disinterested spiritual guidance but also the difficulty of finding competent undeceived guidance.

161

This problem of finding a master in what is almost a masterless world, is a difficult one. The only realistic suggestion which can be given is to select somebody in whom you have so far been able to place most confidence. But if such a person does not exist, then select the book which helps you most and make it your tutor.

162

The next best thing to studying under a teacher, if the latter is not available, is to associate with his mental image, where the latter is available through a previous meeting. If, however, even this is not possible then the seeker should study the teacher's writings. In this way the teacher takes the disciple by the hand through the medium of the printed word.

163

The seeker who is fumbling for the right direction to take should welcome the help of a competent guide. But where such a guide is not personally forthcoming, the best substitute is a personal disciple of his or, failing that, a book written by him.

164

The disciples' case-histories of a spiritual guide, like the patients' case-histories of a medical physician, are always instructive and significant.

165

As to the *public* teachers of the occult, there are none in the West really competent to lead people into truth, whatever their claims may be. The real teachers are so rare nowadays that it is almost impossible to find them. In these circumstances it is safer and wiser to confine oneself to the study of authoritative books rather than to associate with inferior sources of help.

166

The seeker who has gone unsatisfied from cult to cult for several years should waste no further time seeking God through such organizations or through self-named Masters but should strive earnestly to purify his heart of all lower feelings, such as anger, envy, irritability, fear, and depression, and work constantly on his character to improve it. After vigorously doing this for at least six months he may begin to pray daily for further guidance.

167

It is often said that when the pupil is ready the Master will appear. But I have not yet read anyone's additional statement—that he may be invisible and unhearable—that is, he may be entirely within you.

168

I do not say that finding the master internally in this manner is the best way, but that for many seekers it is the only way. Their own limitations combine with destiny to make it so.

169

If it is his destiny to find a master only in the mind and not in the body, if circumstances force him to search internally and not externally, then he will be wise to accept the leading and not rebel against it. For he will find that, faithfully followed, it will bring him to a vivid presence within, a voice that guides where there is seemingly none to guide.

170

In many matters it is needful to submit to the will of destiny. He should know, however, that by the right mental attitude, the inner contact and the inner meeting can be obtained even if the outer cannot. That inner meeting, after all, is the real one—more real than the physical. It is enough to have had a single physical meeting to receive ever afterwards the possibility of this inner contact.

171

The truth is that the Master may appear in three ways: first, inwardly alone for the whole lifetime; second, inwardly at first as "the Interior Word" and then later as the physically embodied human guide; third, as the embodied Master from the very beginning. The first two cases presuppose the practice of meditation and its development to a certain degree of intensity. The third case needs no prior meditation but it does require an attitude of search for truth, help, or guidance developed to as great an intensity as in the other cases.

172

All seeking and finding of spiritual instruction through a spiritual teacher becomes real, in the end, on a mental plane only. Therefore he should direct his efforts in that direction with complete faith.

173

The difficulty which you mention about finding a teacher need not be overrated. You have within yourself a ray of God, which is your own soul. If you pray to and beseech it constantly for guidance, it will surely lead you to all that you really need to know.

174

Those whose quest of the Overself through a master has failed them should take this very failure as instruction on the quest itself. Let them remember that God is everywhere present, that there is no spot where God is not. Therefore, God is in them too. This indwelling presence is the Soul. Let them turn to it directly, no longer seeking someone else to act as an intermediary, no longer running here and there in search of him. Just where they are now is precisely where they may establish contact with God through their own Soul. Let them pray to it alone, meditate on it, obey its intuitive behests, and they will not need any human agent. From this moment they should look to no one else, should follow the Buddha's advice to depend on their own forces. But since these are lying latent within and need to be aroused, the aspirants need to exert themselves through physical regimes that will provide the energies needed for this great effort.

175

If you can find someone whose person attracts you most, or whose teachings appeal to you more than those of others, or whose writings inspire you above all other men's writings, then make him your spiritual guide. You do not have to apply for his permission for it is to be done within the privacy of your own inner life. You are not dependent on his personal acceptance or rejection for the idea of him which you believe in and the image of him which you form to become alive and effectual. But, you will object, is not the whole process a self-deceptive one and does it not lead to worthless hallucination? We reply, it could become that if you misuse it and misinterpret its results, but it need not if you work it aright. For telepathy is a fact. Your faith in, and remembrance of, the other man lays a cable from your inner being to his own and there will flow back along it a response to your attitude.

176

Those who seek a teacher may be reminded that they may take anyone who appeals to or inspires them, and by their own mental attitude of faith in and devotion towards him, together with obedience to his published teachings, draw inner help and inspiration telepathically from him. Thus they create for themselves a mental relationship which, to that extent, is not different from what would have come into being as part of the regular teacher-disciple relationship. They need also to be reminded that even after a physical meeting, in all cases a teacher can be found only when they are sufficiently sensitive to have the capacity to feel his mental presence within themselves and when they are sufficiently developed to be ready for him. The most practical course for most seekers is to engage in the work of self-improvement.

177

What is the hope for those who are unable to enter the shrine of mysticism and have left the fold of religion? Are they to be abandoned to a bleak despair or a hard cynicism? Are they to become engulfed in the waters of moral wickedness? No, let them take the unseen hand of a personal saviour or spiritual guide, whether dead or alive—someone whom they believe to have attained adeptship in yoga, or sagehood in philosophy, and who has announced his intention to give his life to the enlightenment of mankind. Let him become their secret refuge. Let them ask and deserve his grace. The same help can be utilized by those who feel they cannot make the intellectual effort demanded by philosophy but wish to advance beyond the stage of ordinary mysticism in which they now rest.

178

The wise and good dead men who have left their examples for imitation or their words for germination, and any living men whom we have heard met or read about—all these are our spiritual guides; all these can become our masters if we only make them so. Why then should we narrow ourselves down to a single man with a single point of view?

179

If he cannot find entry into the society of a master, he can meditate upon the life stories of historic masters of the past. Let him take the significant situations and devotional attitudes of these great souls into his own thought and study, to analyse the one and imitate the other. Let him think often and long of their character and conduct. Let him also read and reread the written messages they have left us. In this way he will imbibe something of their quality.

180

Such is the rarity of qualified teachers that today it is no longer a question of selecting one who particularly or personally appeals to the seeker, but of finding one at all!

181

The search for a master is often fruitless and abortive. Why is this? The answer is first, that few such masters exist today and second, that few of the searchers are qualified to work with one.

182

Those who have this knowledge are not easily accessible nor, even when found, do they easily divulge it. They are exceedingly rare.

183

Not only are teachers more rare but the most sensitive seekers feel shyly inhibited from approaching them.

184

It is a claim at once irrational and unjust that no man is to be saved who does not approach a master in the flesh. For few men can find such a master nor, finding him, can they always know him except from a distance.

185

In ancient times there were few books to guide the aspirant and fewer still available to him. Consequently the need of a living guide was much greater than it is now. Even in ancient times such teachers were hard to find. "That Guru is rare who can bring riddance to his disciple from the sorrows which agitate his heart," says *Skanda Puranam.*

186

Men of the highest spiritual calibre are not necessarily waiting around for disciples to come to them. They know quite well that each man is his own teacher in the end.

187

If the aspirant is fortunate enough to meet a man or woman in person or writing who genuinely represents the true and real, no effort will be made to influence him; it will be left entirely to his own free choice whether he follow this light hidden behind a bushel or any will-o'-the-wisp masquerading as a light.

188

It is hard to establish human contact with a master, hard to get him interested in one's personal activities.

189

It is not the actual meeting with a master that constitutes its importance, but the *recognition* that he is a master.

190

There are men who come as ambassadors from heaven, and the writings or arts of men, which come as revelators. But unless the reaction includes recognition, the contact is fruitless, the meeting useless.

191

How shall he know who is really a master, and who is not? It is easy at a distance of a thousand years to put an estimate on those who have left the effect of their spiritual greatness on generation after generation, but it is hard to measure contemporaries who look like other ordinary mortals.

192

Sometimes an aspirant, a candidate, a neophyte, or a disciple will refuse the opportunity of personal contact with a master when it occurs, because he feels unworthy, shamefaced, or even guilty. It is a grave mistake for him to reject what a favourable destiny thus offers him. However sinful he be, there is also the fact that he aspires to rise above his sins, else he would not feel sorry for them. However pure the master himself be, there is also the fact that he blames no one, shrinks from no one, extends goodwill to the virtuous and the sinful alike. Of the master it may truly be said that the utter absence of pride or conceit leads to the utter absence of the thought that he is holier than another. The chance to meet him should be taken despite all personal fears of him or personal feelings of one's own lack of virtue.

193

Occasionally one feels he is not worthy enough to contact a spiritual teacher because he does not have a "clean heart." This is a wrong mental attitude. He needs assistance in getting this "clean heart" and there is nothing wrong in seeking such help.

194

You will walk a long time or visit many cities before you find another illuminate. Greet him well, therefore, and think of him well, that you may make something of this fortunate meeting.

195

It needs some humility and more discernment to approach such a man and ask him to give us the benefit of his knowledge, his insight, his experience, and his wisdom—all of which are unusual and rare.

196

If such a man's presence, face, bearing, and teaching show something godlike in him, we should not hesitate to give him the benefit of recognition as being inspired, even if we are not willing to give more.

197

Remember that the master is not likely to live as long as you are, since he is probably an older man. Take the best possible advantage therefore of his presence.

198

If he lets the chance slip by unused, it may not occur again.

199

He may secure valuable help from different sources that he meets on the way but he must above all find the teacher to whom he belongs by inner affinity and in whose school he feels most at home. Once found, he should stubbornly refuse to be drawn out of the teacher's orbit, for if he were to allow it to happen, he would lose precious years and encounter needless suffering, only to have to return in the end.

200

Do what he may, he will not be able to change teachers permanently. The spiritual guide allotted to him by destiny, as well as by affinity, is the one he has to accept in the end if not in the beginning. This is his real master, the one whose image will rise again and again in his mind's eye, obscuring or blotting out the images of all other guides to whom the seeker turned for needed temporary direction.

201

Among living mortals there is one with whom he may find this link, one whom he may never meet in the flesh but only through a photo, a work of art, a name uttered by someone, or perhaps through a piece of published writing. Among those who no longer live in the body, but with whom the link was made in former births, the echo will return and the *idea* itself will suffice.

202

What we can hope to find today is no longer a teacher to instruct our minds nor a master to guide our steps but an inspirer to set us aflame, to show us the world as the Overself sees it. There is for each seeker only one man in the whole world who can do that. He and he alone can work this miracle.

203

It is a strange mystery why destiny has decreed that these seekers after God should have to depend on this one man's lit mind and strong heart for the help they need more than on any other man's. Strange, because until they find him their search seems to have a great lack in it which almost brings them to anguish.

204

The attraction which makes a man select someone as his master and makes the master willing to help him is analogous to chemical affinity. It is not that they deliberately and consciously choose one another but that they cannot help doing so.

205

The master knows, automatically and immediately by his own intuition, whether a candidate for discipleship is in affinity with him or not, and hence whether to accept or reject the man or not.

206

If he is sensitive and aspiring, and if there is any real spiritual power in the other man, he will feel involuntarily an internal excitement and an intuitive expectancy almost from the first minute of their meeting. But if he is also at a sufficient degree of readiness and longing to learn, and if there is personal or prenatal affinity with this other man, then he will feel shaken to the depths of his being, captured in mind and heart. For he will feel the beginnings of discipleship.

207

With the meeting, the aspirant's supreme chance has come. When an aspirant comes into contact with an advanced soul, his own longing is like a magnet which itself spontaneously attracts spiritual force and thought from the other man. Thereupon he experiences an uplift and an enlightenment. If the meeting is a personal one this result is at its fullest. If through a book or letter written by the other man, it is still present but in a weaker degree.

208

Seeking the Master: Great possibilities attach themselves to the first interview between the student earnestly seeking direction, needing guidance, or requesting counsel, and the illuminate who has established communion with his own Overself. These possibilities do not depend upon the length of time it takes nor upon what is said during the actual conversation itself. They depend upon the attitude which a student silently brings with him and upon the power which the illuminate silently expresses. In other words, they depend upon invisible and telepathic factors.

209

Only when he is finally ready for a master will he find a true one. But to be ready the aspirant must bring his character to its highest possibility. When that is done then even at the first meeting the power of attraction will speak silently yet eloquently. Both will know, before that first meeting ends, that the other is the right one; there will be no doubts, no hesitations; they can exist only when judgement is wrong. He will know an affinity of soul that can and has previously been experienced with no one else. Affinity has its own clear language. It will put both men at perfect ease.

210

When a sensitive heart, a receptive mind, and a strong yearning for spiritual perfection meet a man who embodies such perfection to a large degree, there is or should be some recognition, some brief purification, some intellectual clarification, some emotional exaltation, amounting in all to a miniature mystical experience.

211

When the predestined disciple meets the master for the first time, he may feel either that he has known him before or else that he has known him always.

212

Sometimes we have the feeling on meeting a stranger for the first time, that we have known him long and known him well. The feeling on first meeting the destined master is much the same but greatly expanded and deeply intensified.

213

The feeling which is aroused on this contact—whether affinity or antipathy—must be his first guide to the choice of a master.

214

He may feel the force of a real attraction when first meeting his master, in most cases, but it is just possible he may not.

215

The man in whose presence your character rises to its best and your faith to its highest, is the man who can help you spiritually. Without this inward affinity it is of not much use to attach yourself to a guide, however reputed he may be.

216

The seeker whose preconceived picture of what constitutes a master is correct—but this is uncommon—will be able to recognize one at their first meeting. He will feel with positive certainty the inner greatness of the master. Yet it does not follow that this is *his* particular master. There must also be a feeling of personal affinity as well as an intellectual appeal of the doctrines taught.

217

Without this feeling of affinity, and the considerable satisfaction which derives from it, he would be prudent to look elsewhere and not accept this person as guru.

218

Take that man as your teacher whose character and mentality approach the ideal you have formed, and with whose doctrine and personality you feel in sympathy.

219

The meeting with a master is a rare opportunity which should not be missed but should be eagerly followed up. It may not recur again during one's own lifetime or during the master's lifetime. But it can be followed up only if the aspirant feels intuitively that there is a "ray of affinity" between them, through which the inner contact can be established.

220

Sometimes disciples attach themselves to a master with whom they have no basic affinity. They have been drawn to him by a partial self-deception about his nature or by a partial misconception concerning his teaching. After a period has elapsed when the harmony with him or his teaching has come to an end, and the usefulness of both is not sufficient to justify the connection, they usually leave and seek elsewhere for inspiration or help. But in those cases where, for some improper reason, they fail to do so, he may deliberately provoke an incident or arrange a circumstance which will prompt them to go away.

221

It often happens that seekers do not get the true master simply because they would not be attracted to him even when they met him. They naturally are drawn to one whose temperament, character, mentality, and actions are like their own. The unbalanced and the neurotic would be repelled by a sane and equable teacher, the hysterical by a disciplined one, the futile dreamers by an efficient and active one.

222

There is really no choice in the matter—only the illusion of a choice. That which draws him to a particular master is predestination. He may try again and again with someone else. He may not wish to come to this man, but in the end he *must* come. His head may argue itself out of the attraction but his heart will push him back into it.

223

It is said that a man will recognize in a moment the master with whom he has true affinity, when meeting his person or words. That is true, but the recognition may be so vague or partial or faint that a few years may pass before he will become aware of it, and hence before he takes any action about it.

224

It would be foolish for anyone to continue to follow a teaching for which he has no liking, or a teacher with whom he has no affinity. But it would also be foolish to judge either by merely personal and emotional reactions alone.

225

What is present in the surface consciousness as a mild interest may be present in the subconscious as a strong love. But, however long it may take, the disproportion will eventually be righted. When this happens, and as pertains to this particular matter, the man comes to know himself as he really is. This is why the meeting with an old Master or a new truth may not lead to immediate recognition, may indeed take some years to ripen.

226

A guru who is supposed to be an enlightened man but who awakens no feeling of kinship, awe, peace, reverence, or goodness in the person who approaches him may not be enlightened at all—or may not be the proper affinity for the seeker, who may take this as a signal to look elsewhere. But it would also be a signal to be patient, wait a little, look deeper, and really get to know what is in this man.

227

Something within seems to recognize the true teacher when he appears. This is not miraculous when one understands that the visible present has its root in the invisible past and that discipleship is a relation which reappears in birth after birth. However, the philosophic path does not depend only on faith or intuition but also on rational appeal and proved fact. Therefore, some time must elapse before one knows thoroughly that he has found the right path and the right teacher.

228

Another sign that you have found the right master is when you find that he is the one who inspires you to go more deeply into yourself during meditation than any other.

229

He will recognize his master not only by the feeling of affinity and the attraction of his teaching but also if, ever since the first physical meeting, the other man's face persistently keeps recurring to him.

230

He who has found his destined Master will know it well after a few months at most. For he will find that it is as hard to leave the Master as for helpless steel filings to leave a powerful magnet.

231

The blessing of peace or power which the seeker feels in such a man's presence, the fading away of all questions in his aura—these are indications of authenticity and spirituality.

232

Another thing to look for as a sign of the right master is that his way of thinking should be congenial to the seeker.

233

That person is best fitted to be a man's master with whom he is able to be his own best self.

234

Humility is required to recognize that here is a man whose wisdom is greater than one's own.

235

The kind of master he seeks will be a loving one—a master who is large-hearted enough to receive him, sins weaknesses foolishnesses and all.

236

Other things being equal, choose your teacher from among those approaching the end of life, or at least well into middle life. For they have the mature experience which younger people lack; they can give the tranquil counsel which comes from the acceptance of life, the adjustment to its situations, and the waning of physical desires.

237

The teacher is not to be measured only by his weaker disciples nor by his foolish ones. A juster measurement must take into reckoning the wiser and stronger ones also. What he has done for most of them has been done in spite of themselves, for the egos have thwarted or twisted his influence all too often. Nevertheless it is there and in twenty or thirty years it will still be there, inevitable and inescapable, awaiting the thinning down of the ego's resistance.

238

It is a discriminating seeker who responds only to what is wise and true and fine in a teacher, but rejects what is frail or fallible in him.

239

A student is often dismayed, anxious, or upset by the aura of apparent impersonality which surrounds the Teacher. Such reactions are natural but also must be checked—which can be done by learning to smile at oneself and be at peace.

240

Do not look for truth among the unbalanced, the ego-obsessed, the brainless, the hysterical and the unsensitive. Look for it among the modest, the serene, the intuitive, the deep-divers and those who honour the Overself to its uttermost.

241

Many take to an imperfect, half-competent or half-satisfactory teaching because no better one is available.

242

Incompetent instruction is undesirable but it may be helpful in some cases if it is stopped at the proper point.

243

The student may be certain that if there be competent guidance on this path there is no standing still. Either he must go forward and onward until he reaches the goal, or he must get rid of his guide.

244

How useless it is to go to a teacher who has only an intellectual—that is, a talking—knowledge of it, for help is clearly shown by an old Hindu story. Once upon a time a certain king developed a desire to obtain divine consciousness. He obtained a Brahmin pundit as his guide. For two months he received teaching but found that he gained nothing in the actual experience of divinity. He thereupon threatened the Brahmin with his royal displeasure. The pundit returned home in a sorrowful state of mind. He had done his best and did not know how to satisfy the king. His daughter, who was a girl of high intelligence, saw her father's distress and made him tell her the cause. The next day she appeared at the court and informed the king that she could throw light on his problem. She then asked him to order his soldiers to bind both herself and himself to separate pillars. This was done. Then the girl said, "O King, release me out of this bondage." "What!" answered the king, "You speak of an impossibility. I myself am in bondage and how can I release you?" The girl laughed and said, "O King, this is the explanation of your problem. My father is a prisoner of this world-illusion. How can he set you free? How can you gain divinity from him?"

245

If anyone who presents a world view really knows what he is talking about, there should be some noticeable vitality in his talk.

246

If a teacher empties the purse or wallet of his pupils, be sure he is a false one. If he demands servility from them, he is most likely a false one. If he makes no response to someone's approach yet has the stamp of authenticity, he may not be the particular one with whom that person can find affinity.

247

A weakness among these cultists is that they persist in seeing their leader with a kind of character and a height of consciousness which are not sustained by the facts. He is turned into an unerring superman or even deified as a living god. His virtues are either exaggerated or invented, his most commonplace words are pondered over as if they were oracles of prophecy or epigrams of wisdom. And if they do not gift him with cosmic omniscience and total prescience, he is gifted with something like it. The consequence is that the expectations of votaries, having been lifted too high, must fall too low when his personality is deflated and his shortcomings are exposed. Their disappointment inevitably follows. However, since not many spiritual seekers of the kind who join organizations are possessed of the qualities of discrimination and intelligence, the bulk of his followers cling to their idol. An honest and sincere leader would be alarmed at such exaggerated worship, and do his utmost in self-deprecation to bring it to an end. He knows that making a cult of a particular person will divert attention from the proper object of devotion.

248

We have seen a number of spiritual teachers either arise in the West or come here from the East and each one seems to find a certain number of adherents. These teachers and their teachings are of varying quality and may be helpful to many of those who join them. But it is necessary to give a measure of warning against exaggerations made by the teachers about themselves or, if not, made by their followers. It is easy for untrained and inexperienced seekers to be taken in by confident claims to the highest enlightenment. It is better to look for the signs of humility and impersonality.

249

The excessive importance given to the guru, the exaggerated devotion given to him, can only have value in the earlier stages of the quest. The point of view then present has so much ego in it that the aspirant would not be satisfied unless he had a guru. But it is still an attachment, this relationship, so it has to be let go later on.

250

This over-idealization of the guru, so widespread in India and so much copied now by Western seekers, could indicate an elementary stage.

251

We may extend great reverence to the person who is worthy of it—saint or sage—but we may bend the knee in worship only to the everlasting Spirit. No human being has the right to receive it, much less to demand it, and it is idolatry to give it.

252

He is a human being, after all, a person not a demigod. Worship of the man is not only irrelevant but also, in a sense, irreverent.

253

We may admire him for his fine qualities but that does not mean we have to agree with him in all his views.

254

"So many teachers come to us with their doctrines. Who of them is right and who is wrong?" Gautama was asked. "Not because you think, 'Our teacher is one to whom great deference is due,' should you accept a doctrine," was the answer.

255

A superficial emotional approach to truth is less concerned with the message than with the messenger, with the ideas taught than with their human origin.

256

Many Orientals suffer from the bad consequences of an exaggerated respect for their spiritual guides whereas the Europeans and Americans suffer from the consequences of an insufficient respect for them.

257

It is not necessary for disciples to indulge in fulsome panegyrics about their master. This helps no one, for it raises extravagant hopes in their hearers; it lowers their own capacity to receive truth; and it embarrasses the master himself. They need to learn that his greatness can be far more sincerely appreciated by restrained description, that the grandeur of his inner being is better pictured, and more readily believed, by dignified statement of the truth as it is. If others can be impressed only by fanciful embellishment or foolish exaggeration, they are not ready for him and should seek elsewhere among the cults which cater to the naïve.

258

In their overpraise of the guru, the disciples prevent the careful inquirer from learning the truth. In their refusal to see the plain facts of the guru's human weakness or imperfection because they are committed by their theory to see him only as God, they alienate such an inquirer and strengthen his involuntary feeling that to become anyone's disciple is to abandon that very search for truth which is supposed to be the motive for doing so.

259

All this exaggerated praise tends to put off cooler and clearer minds, so that what is deservedly laudable tends to get minimized.

260

Why do they arbitrarily try to make the illuminate into a perfect and superhuman creature and not let him remain the human being that he really is? Why do they remain quite unseeing to his shortcomings and find glib excuses for his failings? Is there not enough genius or greatness still left in him to be quite worthy of our deepest admiration? Why not give him his due without this unnecessary act of deification, which merely drags the sublime down to the absurd? It is because they inhabit a plane where emotion runs high and fanaticism runs deep, where discrimination is absent and imagination all too present. It is because they have not attained the attitudes of, nor felt the need for, philosophy.

261

The practice is all too common in the Orient of presenting a guru to the literary public in a most fulsome and adulatory manner. Those followers who write as if their spiritual guide is a faultless person, never blundering in any way and ever angelic in all ways, do their guide a disservice. They deprive him of his humanity and others of the hope of attaining his condition. His reliability and competence, his trustworthiness and holiness, as a guide, are not diminished if his limitations and faults as a human being are acknowledged.

262

Their followers put these men forward as being flawless demigods, not knowing that by doing so they render a disservice to the men themselves as much as to the cause of truth. What is worse, they throw confusion into the path of all aspirants, who form wrong ideas as to what lies ahead of them and what they ought to do or be.

263

The traditional attitude of an Oriental towards a guru attains fantastic degrees of utter materialism. We have observed disciples drinking water in which the guru's feet were washed, and kissing the tail of the horse on which he rode. They are in part the result of the poor teaching they have received. They mistake servitude to a guru for service to mankind.

264

I distrust the legends which are told about most gurus by the disciples. They all exaggerate. Why? Because *they have stopped seeking truth.*

265

When a man turns belief in the superior knowledge of the guide into belief in the virtual omniscience of the guide, it is dangerous.

266

After having charted all the merits and capacities of the enlightened man, his devotees and disciples easily fall into exaggerations and forget his limitations, or ignore the simple fact that he remains a man among men.

267

The disciples exaggerate the master. They create a new deity. If later some among them inevitably discover that he has his minor faults and makes his little mistakes, there is almost an emotional collapse, a nervous shock. Why, with all his wonderful attainments, can they not accept him as a human being?

268

It is inevitable that they will demand continuing individual attention and it is just as inevitable that he will be unable to give it. Disappointment will ensue and negative thoughts will start breeding.

269

They associate him with omnipotence, if not omniscience, but when time shows up the extravagance and the exaggeration of their idealized expectations, their faith falls to the ground, deflated.

270

Nearly every professional who helps people intimately or mentally has to undergo certain tests or temptations or ordeals. When he deals with a neurotic patient of the opposite sex, the psychoanalyst, the physician, or the schoolteacher may pass through the same experience as the spiritual guide. If she is too emotionally affectionate or too physically sensual, or if she is starved of affection or sensuality, she may naturally fall in love with him for a time. I say "for a time" advisedly because the succeeding phase—equally known to the spiritual guide—is to become antagonistic to him. Psychology has identified this first phase and calls it "transference."

271

The same disciple whose exaggerated enthusiasm caused him to regard the master as an archangel, now, by a curious process of transformation, regards him as an archdevil!

272

The guide is up against the fact that most aspirants expect too much from him. Even if he warns them at the start, his words are given little weight or else are soon forgotten. They expect him to use some trick, whose secret he alone knows, to turn them quickly into illumined mystics or even powerful adepts. Consequently they react emotionally against him in their later disappointment.

273

When the discrepancy between the real man and the preconceived mental image of him becomes too obvious and too large, they blame him instead of themselves.

274

It is because followers place him in such a unique and exalted position in their hearts that they do real psychic injury to themselves when they believe it necessary to throw him down from it.

275

The first and last illusion to go is that any perfect men exist anywhere. Not only is there no absolute perfection to be found, but not even does a moderate perfection exist among the most spiritual of human beings. Hence, the atmosphere of personal idolatry is not a healthy one. It is right that the impact of an unusually outstanding personality should produce an unforgettable intellectual or emotional experience. But it is wrong to believe him a god rather than a man, or to lead others to believe it, for that is an excess which can only lead to the reaction of disappointment in the end, as sooner or later he will be reduced by further knowledge to human proportions. To ask that a spiritual master or a loved mate shall be perfect in every respect is to ask the impossible and the non-existent. In the case of a seeker, it is likely to result in missing the very opportunity he is seeking. In the case of one who is already associated with a master or mate, experimental straying away is likely to result in disappointment and a retracing of steps. Let us not turn them into what they are not. They are human, they make mistakes; they are not gods.

276

This desire to deify their teachers, which is so common among Indian disciples, can have no place among philosophic ones. We look upon the teacher as a man, as one who incites us to seek the best and inspires us to self-improvement and guides us to the truth. But he is still a man to be respected, not a god to be worshipped. He has his imperfections.

277

How honest was that reputedly wise man Socrates in saying what so few gurus have ever said. He had just answered Xenophon's request for advice on a certain matter and concluded: "But my opinion is only that of a man."

278

It is not my business to make known matters that would only stir controversy about past history quite uselessly. But it would be a serious omission of duty not to utter a warning that human perfection does not exist; that famous figures in history, politics, warfare, government, literature, religion, mysticism, and art have committed grave errors of judgement, impression, or teaching; that these errors are known only to a few in each case, and will probably never be known to posterity at all. A man may be successful in leading his people through a war to final victory but, on the way, he may have made blunders that were heavily paid for by others. A teacher may be spiritually enlightened but personally inexperienced; his opinions on unfamiliar matters may not have much value.

279

So long as a man is turned into a god and is worshipped as such, so long as he is regarded Perfect and without defects, so long are those concerned—both the man and his followers—kept outside the philosophic goal by their own deficiencies.

280

The Master had his shortcomings or frailties just as we all have, but he also had what few of us have—a direct contact with the Overself.

281

Where is the man who is wise enough to give everyone else spiritual guidance, personal advice, marital counsel, and prediction of future? Who with a single look knows all about you as he already knows all about God and the universe? Let us not look for fantasies of wishful thinking but see humans as humans.

282

Let him not expect to find perfection in any mortal. Let him be satisfied to find someone who has so developed his spirituality that he is worthy to lead those who are still much in the rear.

283

There is no man without his defects: it is a dreamer's notion that the perfect human being exists on our planet. Hence the disciples who servilely copy their guru in all things may copy his defects too!

284

Where is such a master, such a faultless paragon of virtue wisdom strength and pity, to be found? Look where we will, every man falls short of the ideal, shows an imperfection or betrays a weakness. The ideal sage portrayed in philosophical (as distinct from mystical) books, has not come to life in our times however much he may have done so in ancient times.

285

Behind the majestic phrases of most of these spiritual teachers, we usually find in the end of a searching investigation based on living with them or on the historic facts of their lives, that there stand poor frail mortals. Hence those few who emerge as being one with, and not inferior to, their teachings stand out all the more as truly great men.

286

It is misleading to put such a man forward, as so many Indians put him forward, as being faultless. His consciousness of the Overself may be perfect, but his conduct as a human being may be not. Is there anywhere a faultless man?

287

He may be wise but he may not be wise all the time. For history shows lapses of judgement, impulsive actions, and other regrettable happenings due to karmic pressures even where least expected.

288

There are many ways to undermine the student-guru relationship: if the guru is put upon an unreachable pedestal, if he is turned into a god and his humanness is denied, or if the guru is believed to be perfection itself. The possibility for perfection in any man is a debatable point.

289

There are no Buddhas in our age, only would-be Buddhas. Let us face the fact, acknowledging man's limitations, and cease bluffing ourselves or permitting ourselves to be bluffed by the self-styled Masters.

290

Too many seekers create a supernatural halo around the master's personality. Too many wrap it in dramatic and romantic garb. Too many expect too much from the first meeting with him. The consequence of all this is often a tremendous emotional let-down, an unreasonable disappointment after the reality of an actual meeting, and they lose their balance altogether. It is inevitable that a close-up view of the master will not prove so striking as a long-range one seen through romantic glasses. From a distance it is easy to bestow admiration and feel awe for a man they have almost turned into a deity. But drawn into close contact with him it is just as easy to swing in the opposite direction and turn the master into a man. They do not notice how brief is their firsthand acquaintance with him, how few are the appearances that constitute the data for their conclusions, how conceited it is for spiritual pygmies to think they understand a spiritual titan. Because what they appear to have found does not correspond with the mental image they have previously conceived of him, he is judged to be no master at all. Nor are these the only reasons for such a failure. Equally important is the fact that such a meeting, or the period immediately following it, becomes the signal for opposition by adverse force. Evil spirits may find their opportunity just then to lead him astray, mischievous ones may try to bewilder his mind, or lying ones may give untrue suggestions to him. His own weaknesses of character and faultiness of judgement may become greatly magnified and foist an absurdly wrong estimate of the master upon him. He may even feel personal antagonism toward the master. All this is of course a test for him. If he thinks he is judging whether this man is fit to be his master, life in its turn is judging whether he is fit to have such as master. Here then are some of the answers to the question "Why, if we concede that the adepts have a right to hide from the multitude, do they also seem to hide from the earnest seeking few?" The adepts are confident that those individuals who are really ready for them will meet them when the right time comes. They know that this will happen not only under the direct working of karma, not only under the impulsions of the seeker's own higher self, but also under the wise laws which govern the quest itself. These are high and hard truths. But they are the realities of life, not dreams for those who like to be self-deluded. Whoever rejects them for such a reason does so at the risk of being harshly shocked into awakening one day.

291
They approach such a man with a kind of awe, if not of reverence. It may or may not be justifiable: that depends first, on the man's quality and second, on his mood.

292
It needs clear eyes to see the truth about these spiritual teachers, eyes such as both their ardent followers and intolerant critics do not possess.

293
Most people are simply not competent to select a guru properly; they are too governed by outer appearances, physical impressions, and emotional reactions.

294
The search for an ideal master may obstruct itself through an excessively critical attitude equally as through a sentimentally romantic one. For however divinely inspired he may be in his best moments, the master must still remain quite human in many ways most of the time.

295
Those who form romantic grandiose exotic or miraculous pictures of what a master is like and of what they seek in a man before they can accept him as a master, doom themselves to frustration and assure themselves of disappointment. For they do not yet understand what masterhood really is, hence they are still unfit for personal instruction by a master.

296
If he is not connected with any religious association or mystical tradition, any institution or monastery, he is looked upon askance. For who or what is there to validate the "correctness" of his teaching and the credentials of the man himself? They look for a doctrine that is "official" and a revelator certified by "authority."

297
The man who seeks a master to whose cosmological vision, expressed thought, and behaviour he hopes to give perfect acceptance, seeks the impossible. He does not want a teaching which is liable to disproof by scientific knowledge, yet he does not want to limit himself merely to that knowledge.

298
If his preconception of a master is wrong, as is likely because of the ludicrous caricature in the pictures drawn by popular cults and books, he may not be able to recognize a real master even when he meets one. There will be an inner struggle instead. He will suffer the agony of mental or moral indecision.

299
He may seem cold and unapproachable by the sentimental standards of those who mistakenly regard him as a glorified clergyman.

300
He sees an image which he has himself created, not the reality of the other man. Only by close association with him under one roof will it be possible to find out how different the image is from the person it is supposed to represent. The first is a perfect but impossible creature. The second is a human creature.

301
It is understandable and even pardonable that the weak, the neurotic, the unhappy or the undeveloped, the innocent or the inexperienced should look for a father image who will carry all their burdens, material as well as spiritual. They are entitled to do so. But they should seek him within religious or mystical circles, not within the philosophic circle.

302
The mistake so many seekers make in approaching such a man is to demand that he teach them on *their* terms, in *their* way, and not his own.

303
If he has not got the appearance they think he ought to have or they expect him to have, that is another cause for offense. The reality is blamed—and not themselves—for disappointing the fantasy.

304
You do not see the master when you see his body. You do not know him when you know what he looks like. You do not love him if you are attracted only by his handsome appearance. The real master is his mind.

305
A man's spiritual status does not reveal itself immediately to anyone who looks at his physical body. Not only so, but if the latter is ugly, deformed, and senile, repulsion may misread his inner nature completely.

306
Those who reject truth because of the external repulsiveness of the truth-bearer, do so for the right reasons, that is, they are not ready to receive it. Those who accept truth because of the external attractiveness of the truth bearer, do so for the wrong reasons, that is, they have not received it at all. For in both cases it is not the mind or the heart to which appeal has been made, but the senses. It is not reason or intuition, sufficient experience or sufficient authority which has judged the testimony for truth, but bodily sight hearing and touch.

307

The personal traits of the spiritual guide may repel the seeker. Yet if no one else is available who has the same knowledge, it is the seeker's duty to repress his repulsions and enter into the relationship of a pupil. If he does not, then he pays a heavy price for his surrender to personal emotion and sensual superficiality.

308

A master would not necessarily be recognized as such if he were walking in the street, not even by those who are looking for one and have read all the books about him.

309

That a man wearing quite ordinary clothes whose face was clean shaven, whose hair was of quite average length, could be an adept is much less likely to be thought by most persons, than one who was theatrical-looking and conspicuously dressed.

310

In the worldly life a successful man usually seeks to give others the impression of his success but in the spiritual life an unassuming man may be a great master.

311

The aspirant is not ordinarily in a position to judge what illumination really is, and who is a fully illuminated man. He can only form theories about the one and use his imagination about the other.

312

Many will speculate on the teacher's motives. That they could be pure and selfless, seeking only to bring men closer to awareness of the Overself and to knowledge of the higher laws, only a few will perceive. To the others he will be a man like themselves, actuated by selfish motives.

313

Those who reject a noble message and sneer at its messenger, who pronounce him to be a false prophet, a deceiver of men, thereby pronounce their own selves to be falsely led and self-deceived.

314

To many blasé and worldly people, the teacher will be classed with ambitious charlatans at worst or regarded as self-hypnotized at best. But even to those who do not question his sincerity, the goal he points to them must seem so utterly absurd and distant from the commonly accepted goals and the path to it so oddly eccentric that few persons are likely to be attracted to them.

315

Those of his followers who expect him to behave with impeccable propriety and are ready to leave and follow someone else if he does not, will either be victims of, or gainers by, their own judgement. If the teacher is really unified with his Overself, any judging of him done by external standards will be only partly applicable. There is a point where neither his character nor his motives can be correctly measured by such standards, and beyond which they may be quite misleading.

316

The mystical and cultist circles which talk much about these matters use the name "Master" to trail such an accumulation behind it of falsified facts, superstitious notions, and nonsensical thinking, that it is needful to be on guard for semantic definition whenever this term is heard.

317

The mistake that some followers make is to fail to see that their demigod is recognizably human. The mistake that most non-followers make is to fail to see that he is, in his best moments, superhuman.

318

The excessively critical attitude which seeks to find a flaw in a holy man and soon succeeds is as foolish as the excessively devout attitude which pronounces him perfect and continuously faultless. The hostility of the one leads to imbalance; the naïveté of the other leads to expectancy. The holy man is still a man subject to the limitations of his species.

319

The Theosophic teaching that the master takes on the karma of his pupil is often misunderstood. So many students think that the master hesitates to accept a pupil because of this heavy liability of accepting his karma. The measure of truth in this belief is that the master does have some moral responsibility for the self-injuring mistakes committed by the pupil as a direct consequence of special knowledge entrusted to him or for society-injuring misuse of special powers transferred to him or aroused into activity within him because of special instructions given by the teacher—in either case before he was sufficiently strong morally and pure in motive. But the general karma of the pupil is not accepted nor can it be accepted by any master. That is the pupil's making and he himself must work it out.

320

The student is mistaken if he thinks the teacher ever places obstacles or temptations in anyone's way. He does not have to do that; it is done by life itself, or, more precisely, by the karma arising from the individual character and its special needs. The teacher may note them and act accordingly, but he does not create them. In the end, the student himself creates his own obstacles and his own temptations by his thinking, by his character, and by his karma.

321

He is not only an instructor but is too often called upon to play the role of mentor, to be a wise counsellor at all times and a trusted friend in difficult times, to solve personal problems and guide personal decisions. This ideal person is yet to be found, alas! But the wish for one is strong enough to clothe lesser men in imagined perfection.

322

Those who regard him as an unreliable visionary are not less victims of prejudice than those who regard him as an omniscient prophet.

323

Even the man who talks from the Overself's inspiration can convince only those other men who are ready. Not all are sensitive to his spell.

324

They equate man's powers with God's powers, blandly refusing to see that he can *create* nothing but can only provide the conditions which make some creations possible. They exaggerate what is true, that he possesses, potentially, certain godlike attributes, into what is untrue, that he can do what God does.

325

It is a self-deception to believe that the master can interfere in all sorts of miraculous ways in the disciple's worldly life or intervene in all sorts of arbitrary ways in his spiritual life. The master's true function, the most important role he can play in the disciple's career, is to assist the latter's efforts to withdraw into his inner self, to guide, strengthen, and protect his endeavour to practise meditation.

326

There is a common Indian belief—picked up by and transferred to some Western cults—that without submission to a leader, master, guru whose guidance is to lead them and whose power is to lift them into Nirvana, they can never win access to this goal. It is an exaggerated belief when it refers to authentically enlightened men and a false one when it refers to all others. Blind acceptance of it has precipitated a nervous breakdown in some cases, and much feeling of morbid frustration in most cases where seekers have failed to find a guru or, finding, have become disappointed or disillusioned afterwards.

327

There is no celestial witch-doctor, no angelic magician coming to change their characters overnight.

328

Those who do not understand that true development is self-development will look for, even demand, a guru's "magic," as they believe it to be. This will lead them to frequent his vicinity or even live in it permanently, in order to be more or less constantly under his mesmeric influence. Thus they come to depend increasingly on an outside source—another person—and remain ungrown.

329

The disciples exert so much pressure and encouragement on the guru to do what he cannot do for them that they go on believing their own desires in the matter, that is, their ego, rather than him. They think he can give them total protection against risks, perils, and falls on the spiritual path. That is impossible, said Ramana Maharshi. The guru is not omniscient and not almighty. He is still a limited human being. Why force him into accepting a false position?

330

The idea of a master as being some sort of free perfect and infallible counsellor in all the domestic personal and professional perplexities of life is an appealing one. If it were true there would be many more disciples. But it is only a romantic piece of wishful thinking.

Qualifications, duties of a teacher

331

To place oneself under another's spiritual tutelage is an act which may be dangerous or may be auspicious. It depends on the other—on whether his mind is really irradiated with the divine effulgence or whether it is darkened by its own ego.

332

Spiritual help cannot be given indiscriminately and at the same time given wisely. It should be conditioned by readiness, worthiness, and willingness to receive it. It should be offered only by those who are properly equipped, suitably qualified, and purely motivated.

333

Dr. Osborne Mavor, a Scottish physician, said: "Building up personality is a job for Socrates, Christ, and Confucius working in the closest co-operation. I should not care to entrust my personality, such as it is, to any individual of a lower intellectual and moral standard than that." This critique is also applicable to spiritual teachers, as well as psychotherapists, against whom it was directed.

334

I divide all teachers into two classes: titular gurus and real gurus. The former are quite common, the gap between their doctrines and their behaviour being noticeable, whereas the latter are rare indeed for they have achieved a conquest over the ego which reveals itself in their conduct and reflects itself in their lives.

335

The demand for inspired teachers is always insistent but the supply is wholly insufficient. Unless the teacher is an inspired one he will be of little help to the would-be mystic. By inspired, we mean either in communion with his higher self or fully united with it.

336

Few are the teachers, guides, priests, and leaders of men who do not put into their work the false opinions and favoured prejudices that they themselves have been taught or have acquired. Few, also, are those who have scrupulously striven to become as free from these things as they possibly could be.

337

Such teachers are unable to free themselves from the relativity of their own position. Hence they give instructions which are pertinent only to those who wear the monk's cowl.

338

The appeal of a teacher will depend upon the depth of his own inspiration, and the appeal of his teaching will depend upon how well it fits in with the prevailing thought and the pressing need of his epoch.

339

The modern teacher should be a man of the world, not a man of the ashrams. He should be one who does not practise a fastidious asceticism, does not frown on human frailty. Such a man begins his teaching by making other men feel that wisdom is priceless and holiness is beautiful.

340

He must so manage the two tendencies that they balance each other. Insofar as he deals with the eternal verities, he can utter only the old, old truths. Insofar as he belongs to his period he must restate them in a contemporary way.

341

The possession of such power and influence, although it is directly limited to spiritual matters, is indirectly manifested in worldly matters too; for men have to live and act in the world. He will gain more esteem as a teacher, and certainly as a leader, who is known to be honourable, conscious of his responsibilities and obligations, whose character is well-balanced and whose promises are solid, whose statements are backed by facts and whose doctrines are worthy of trust.

342

He is a true messenger who seeks to keep his ego out of his work, who tries to bring God and man together without himself getting in between them.

343

Such a teacher would not claim to be an intermediary with God but rather a counsellor with man.

344

No master who is a true channel for the divine life will accept the adulation of others for himself. Their flattery will never be allowed to fool him. Instead, he will always transfer it where it belongs—to that life itself.

345

He will accept none of the homage for himself; he knows it is not due to him, but to the higher power which intermittently uses him.

346

He is not a leader anxious to appear infallible before the members of his cult.

347

He who has found authentic peace within himself is in a position to assist others who are still seekers, but he who has not yet transcended mere theories and erudite studies *about* peace can only give them some more thoughts to add to the burden they already carry.

348

The man who lets himself be warmed by sunshine will be able to radiate some of its effects to others. But they ought not to claim in consequence that he is the sun! He is not the originator of those effects but only their mediator.

349

"My son," said an old sage to me, "the ocean does not rise any higher when streams flow into it, so the true master does not swell with pride when many disciples attach themselves to him. He takes it as a matter of natural course; for he knows that they come to seek out the true Light, not merely his body."

350

Humility will not let a man teach others until he knows himself what he tries to teach them.

351

Patiently and perseveringly, the true teacher established himself in awareness of the truth before offering to lead others into it.

352

The guide under whom he studies, who watches both his progress and his lapses, can minister to him competently only if he himself is a liberated and inspired individual with an aptitude for such service.

353

He who is to act as a spiritual guide to others should himself have reached the goal toward which he proposes to lead them.

354

If the faith of such a man stimulates those who receive his message, they in turn stimulate his own. If they feel inspired by the contact with it, he feels awed and humbled by its power over them.

355

Only that man who has overcome the lower nature himself can help others to overcome it in their turn.

356

The capacity to receive truth is one thing; the power to communicate it to other men is another. Moreover, only he who has himself lived near to our own experience of the quest, our own falls and slips and tumbles, who himself remembers how he struggled step by step along it to reach his present height, can best help those he has left far behind him.

357

Only he who has securely established his own realization can safely guide others to theirs. Automatic progress on the quest can be guaranteed by nobody. Like all human enterprises it is subject to ups and downs.

358

He who is unhappy in himself, or whose home is discordant and unhappy, can show the way to happiness only out of intellect, not out of experience.

359

If his counsel is to be effective enough to help others, it must spring from a mind which has faced and resolved the same problems within itself. But it need not necessarily have done so in external conduct. It may have done so in imagination or in intellect only. The quality of the mind will measure the value of such a course.

360

The true teacher assists his disciples to find their own spiritual feet so that they can walk increasingly without leaning on him or anyone else. It is the duty of an honest disinterested spiritual guide to point out to his followers that their dependence on him is a weakness to be overcome, not a virtue to be cultivated. The false teacher, seeking to profit in some way by the situation, makes them utterly dependent on him.

361

The true teacher seeks to bring his disciples to learn how to guide themselves. So he patiently explains and willingly discusses his own counsel where the false teacher leaves it wrapped in obscurity and involvement. The true guide directs them continually toward that place where in the end they must realize the truth—within themselves—for there is its only source.

362

He is a proper guide who gives each disciple a chance to develop according to his own individuality and does not try to make him a copy of the guide. But such a tutor is rare, and would not even call anyone "my disciple."

363

Just as the ego-led teachers seek publicity so the egoless teachers seek anonymity.

364

A true teacher will practise the utmost self-abnegation and will seek and work for the day when his influence or interference are brought down to nothing.

365

The ordinary kind of guru points to himself, his necessity and importance; but the rare kind points *away* from himself, to the seeker's own higher self, its reality and availability.

366

It is only the half-baked, half-finished masters who have this craving for power over others, whose little egos need a following of adoring disciples. The fully developed ones—and they are quite rare—remain unaffected but not indifferent. For they recognize in each person who comes to them a heeding of the inner call, a response to the pulling power of their own divine Source.

367

He desires not to win disciples but to lose them! He wants them to seek find and follow not mortal man but the light that burns serenely within their own hearts.

368

The sincere teacher seeks to wean his disciples at the earliest possible moment. To succeed in doing so, he will promise nothing as a gift but will emphasize how necessary it is to apply the teaching to their personal lives honestly and continuously.

369

The Master Jalaluddin Rumi did not allow disciples to have constant contact with him. At a certain point he dismissed them. They had henceforth to work alone upon the foundations laid down. He was an original Teacher, and a successful one.

370

Every text and every guru must in the end, and better from the beginning also, point away from themselves. But this will happen only if full authentic enlightenment is present.

371

Such a teacher looks for no adoration but rather directs it toward the disciple's own Soul.

372

If the true master imposes no obligations toward himself on those he helps and demands no rewards from them, this is because he wishes to retain his freedom, his independence, his detachment as much as it is because he gives out of compassion and goodness.

373

Emerson conquered the most subtle temptation that can beset a man of his type. He was openly a teacher, and the teacher's natural tendency is the wish to be looked to for continual guidance. But Emerson was too pure a soul to show the teacher's egotism. He wished to set others firm on their own feet. Mr. Woodbury tells us how, finding himself differing from his revered master, he went and stated his case. Emerson deliberated, then, with his bright kindly look: "Well, I do not wish disciples." It was a shock, but a healthy one. It shook the pupil off from his support, but thereby he learned to walk alone.

374

The man who can sometimes make other men aware—however momentarily—of their divinity is a true master.

375

The guide will not only point out the way to spiritual maturity but also will encourage the pupil to follow it. He seeks no other recompense than your loyalty, no better payment than your faith, no superior satisfaction than your own spiritual progress.

376

The true mentor will possess a penetrating insight into his pupils' needs.

377

Such a guru seeks neither money nor personal power.

378

He will be able to perceive from what source a man draws his life, whether from the impulsion of the ego or from the inspiration of the Overself.

379

The instantaneous and adequate nature of his replies to all questions shows a deeper understanding than the merely intellectual, hence must be intuitive, inspirational, or realizational. On such a basis a man's fitness for guruship becomes more evident.

380

The role of spiritual guide involves a code of ethics, a special moral responsibility on the part of the guide.

381

The appellation of spiritual teacher should be given only to one who not only can communicate spiritual truth intellectually but who also *lives it* fully.

382

The teacher must not only provide instruction; he must also set an example of how to live and act in the world, and he must not only do both of these but he must also provide a profounder influence than other men by virtue of his own attainment, as telepathically revealed by his mere presence.

383

The perfect teacher is he who lives up to the teaching itself. The semi-perfect one tries to live up to the teaching. The imperfect one does not even try: avoid him.

384

Actions, deeds, are the final test of the spiritual man or guru. The life he leads must be a pattern.

385

The spiritual guide who asks his disciples to practise self-discipline and remodel their characters, will seem to them to be offering impossible counsels of perfection unless he himself is willing to do or has already done what he asks. However sound his theoretical guidance may be, it will fail in persuasive power to the extent that it is not at one with his own experience.

386

What the Hindus call a spiritual dispeller of darkness, what the Eastern Christian Church calls a Spiritual Father is not only holy himself but is also an experienced teacher of the way to holiness for others.

387

He who takes upon himself the task of guiding disciples should possess sure-footed experience gained by years of work with the most varied kinds of apprentices.

388

To be a guru is to accept a responsibility. For this, one needs the capacity in oneself and the mandate from the higher power.

389

Only when a man is permanently and consciously established in the higher self may these occult powers be safely acquired and these relations with disciples be safely entered into. Only when other planes of existence are accessible to him and higher beings from those planes are instructing him can he really know how properly to live down here and be able to competently instruct others to do so.

390

Nobody is entitled to wear the mantle of a master merely because he has received teaching from a master. He is at best only a transmitter of information and not the originator of it. For he may transmit knowledge which he does not himself understand, which is far over his head or which he is even capable of misunderstanding and therefore likely to lead others totally astray. How can such a person be called a qualified master? Let us therefore make a sharp differentiation between those who are competent to be called teachers and those who are merely transmitters of teaching.

391

It is all right for a teacher to have only a partial and limited knowledge of his subject so long as he recognizes it as such, and so long as it is not applied in cases where complete knowledge is essential.

392

So long as some of the truth—perhaps some vital aspects of it—remains hidden from him, so long must he be stern with himself and reject the temptation of setting up as a master.

393

He must live in freedom and not in dependence, whether outwardly or inwardly, on followers or disciples: therefore he keeps them at a distance that they in turn may find and experience the truth within themselves. His work ends at pointing the way.

394

A professional lawyer or surgeon accepting clients is expected to have certain qualifications before he undertakes to serve them. A spiritual prophet who sets out to guide others needs certain qualifications too. He needs the intellectual capacity to explain teach and clarify, the temperamental patience to put himself in their shoes, and the altruistic compassion to work for their benefit. Moreover, given the innate facility, it is easy to teach ethics to others and hard to live those teachings oneself. He needs the ability to set a right example for imitation in his own conduct.

395

It is quite wrong to conceive of a spiritual guide in a highly sentimental way. He would reveal his incompetence and bungle his work for you not less if he were to pamper as to nag you, not less if he were to be emotionally too solicitous about your personal life as too authoritarian. For he would make you more egoistic and less disciplined, more dependent and less self-reliant, more incapable of achieving real progress and less informed about the factors concerned in it. He would, indeed, make you a flabby parasite instead of an evolving entity.

396

He is a man whose perception goes farther, whose awareness goes deeper than the rest of his fellow men. It must go so far and so deep that it rests durably in the "I Am" of the Overself. Without this he does not possess the first, the most essential and most important of all the credentials needed for communicating to others the art of attaining the Overself. The second credential, and admittedly a lesser one, is the compassionate desire to effect this communication as much as possible. The third is that he have special power to teach others what he knows.

397

It is possible for one who has mastered his own mind to affect that of another person, whether the latter is in propinquity to him or is placed at a great distance from him. This fact becomes especially evident where there is an attempt to learn and practise meditation.

398

What the master can do for a disciple is limited. He can stimulate the latter's natural aspiration, guide his studies, and point out where the pitfalls are; but he can do little more. He cannot take on his own shoulders responsibilities which the disciple ought to take.

399

It is the will of a higher power that he, whose own inner eye is open, shall be instrumental in opening that eye for others wherein it is closed.

400

His help is provided by what he is—the power of example—and by what he teaches—the power of suggestion.

401

What a guide may be able to do in certain cases is to facilitate the awakening of higher consciousness and to make easier the entry of higher truths.

402

He understands the feeling of love which a disciple expresses and he accepts it on the level of the same feeling which he himself gives in turn to Those who are his leaders. The attraction is inevitable. But in the case of female disciples, it must be kept on a high level and never allowed to mix with lower emotions. It must be pure and, in a certain sense, even impersonal. The teacher walks the path of life outwardly alone and uninvolved with any "person" as such. The only way anyone can come closer to him is to approach the attainment of union with his own higher self. Do not expect the adept to behave as ordinary human beings, with their desires and emotions, behave. He has committed suicide in that direction. It was the price demanded of him for what little peace he has found.

403

The disciple who poses as a master is a fool. The master who poses as a disciple is a sage.

404

He cannot submit to the pressures and claims of a personal relation without falsifying his status and adulterating his service.

405

He has the power to awaken the Glimpse-experience in other men, but not in all other men. He can succeed with those only who are ready enough or sensitive enough.

406

It is usually quite impossible for the average aspirant to determine who is a fully qualified master. But it is sometimes quite possible to determine who is *not* a master. He may apply this negative test to the supposed master's personal conduct and public teaching.

407

If a man claims to have attained the fullness of his higher being, we may test his claim by the moral fruits he shows. For he ought constantly to exercise the qualities of compassion, self-restraint, nonattachment, and calmness on the positive side and freedom from malice, backbiting, greed, lust, and anger on the negative side.

408

He who takes up the vocation of spiritual service should do so only if he be sufficiently prepared for it morally—only if he be destitute of ambitions and greeds, detached from women and the thought of women, isolated from personal motivations, liberated from the lower emotions.

409

A master issues no command and requires no obedience. Others may do so but not he.

410

He will bear no grudge if his advice is rejected.

411

The guru who performs the Oriental potentate to his court of disciples may be unconsciously playing up to their desires or expectations but also playing down to his own desire for power. It may help to keep them in juvenile dependence on him but also keep him within the ego and thus reduce his capacity to serve them.

412

Even if he were not ethically more sensitive and hence more scrupulous than most people, his own spiritual dignity and personal self-respect would alone forbid his taking advantage of the credulous, the inexperienced, or the unbalanced.

413

The spiritual guide who is not himself free from passion is a dangerous guide for those who are still struggling in the grip of passion. The teacher who has not utterly subdued personal egoism is unfit to assist those who seek liberation from it. He should learn to solve his own problems before he can safely venture forth to help solve the problems of other people.

414

The true teacher identifies himself with his student and does not sit on a Himalayan height of self-esteem.

415

A guru who thinks of himself as having disciples has attachments. The ego is present in him. They are mentally held as possessions.

416

A man who is privileged to carry a message from the mountaintop down to his fellows should feel no envy of other messengers, no emotional disturbance at their success or his own failure. If he does, it means that the ego has inserted itself into his work and poisoned it. On the contrary, he ought to be glad that some more seekers have been helped to hear truths which they could not hear for themselves. He ought to rejoice at their blessing, otherwise he is still worshipping himself and not God. A true messenger will not look for followers but for those whom he can help.

417

Exposed to flattery and obsequiousness though he will be, he will nevertheless keep quite free from pomposity and vanity.

418

The teacher has to bear patiently with the defects and weaknesses of his students. He could not do this if his insight were too limited, his compassion too small, and his calmness too superficial.

419

The teacher whose own mind rests in the serenity of the Overself will feel no concern over the slow advance of any of his disciples. He has submitted this in advance to the care of the Overself, just as he submitted his own in earlier days. Yet this detachment will not in any way abate the constant flow of counsel, guidance, encouragement, and inspiration which will go forth from him to those disciples.

420

If the truly advanced mystic ever gives the impression that he frowns on any person who has erred, a totally false impression has been received. For he knows that it is through that small part of evolution which is devoted to free will that we learn and grow. He who has himself learnt and grown in this way never frowns at the mistakes of others, but, instead, forgives them.

421

Helping others to understand the art of proper living is itself an art. A man may be good and yet not a good teacher.

422

Wise teachers try to harmonize the contradictions. They use practical scientific ways along with mystical interior ones.

423

The man who is fluent and articulate makes a better teacher so far as communication is concerned; but the man who has had divine experience, who knows what he is talking about, is still the best teacher of all.

424

If he knows in experience as in theory, and if he possesses the ability to communicate this theory, then the impressions left will not be vague but quite distinct.

425

A teacher who gives a well-argued discourse about the Truth helps us, but so does the teacher who announces the Truth in non-discursive terms. Both are needful in their place.

426

The guru is one who not only knows the truth but can teach well what he knows—and not necessarily in words, for silence can also be used as an effective medium.

427

The spiritual guide must be someone to be trusted more than any man, to be looked to for guidance, knowledge, hope, inspiration, and warning.

428

He respects every confidence that is reposed in him and keeps all confessions in the hidden archives of memory.

429

Whatever confidence he receives during the interview, the other person may feel sure that it will not be betrayed.

430

The man who professes to guide others spiritually and to inspire them with higher ideals cannot escape being watched. If he resents the ordeal, his service to them will be impaired; but if he accepts it, he shows thereby that he is not looking for self-glory.

431

Contempt and slander will be the unequal reward some will pay him; miscomprehension and minification will be received from others. He will accept them all unconcernedly.

432

No true master will take money for his services.

433

Such a man could not charge others for his time, his counsel, or his trouble, could not commercialize his work, could not bring himself to make money out of truth-seeking wanderers. His service to them is a holy thing, unpriced and unpriceable. For it is done at the dictate of his higher self.

434

We must recognize a sharp, clear-cut distinction between spiritual teaching as a duty and spiritual teaching as a business. The one expresses his true relationship to the disciple, the other seeks financial return from him.

435

Spirituality is no commodity to be bought and sold in the marketplace. It must be worked for step by step and won by personal effort. This still remains true even though in the end it is conferred by Grace, for without such preparation the conferment is unlikely, nay almost impossible. This is not less true if the efforts may mostly be buried in the history of past lives.

If any religious organization or cult-leader even mentions a price, a fee, or even a contribution as a prerequisite to Grace, initiation, or higher consciousness, then the devotee is being deceived by imposture.

436

It is an ancient tradition that such instruction should be given free and that a teacher is degraded by receiving payment.

437

The Overself is costless. It is, as Jesus pointed out, as free as the wind which comes and goes. Whoever has realized it will gladly teach the way to anyone who is ripe and ready for his teaching. If any man puts a price on it and offers to sell it to you, be sure he is offering a false or shoddy imitation.

438

If he accepts gifts or contributions he will probably be asked for, or expected to allow, concessions of his time, attention, and even grace which others may not hope to receive. The intensity of devotion rather than the value of offerings must always govern the master's response.

439

A guru has an official position, which is accompanied by appropriate duties. They include: (1) taking a personal interest in the disciples' inner welfare and growth; (2) instructing them in the truth, and in the way to its attainment; (3) inspiring them telepathically with glimpses of the higher states; (4) encouraging them to persevere in travelling along the way; (5) warning them against the pitfalls and obstacles.

440

The teacher's duty is to give direction, provide knowledge, warn against pitfalls, correct errors. It is not his duty to save the pupil necessary efforts of will and thinking.

441

The master powerfully removes the sluggishness of the intellect of his disciple; clarifies his ideas about what is eternal and what is perishable, what is real and what is unreal, what is material and what is mental; and opens to him the realm of truth slowly but unmistakably by constant appeal to his reason.

442

The first service of the Master is to point out the way, both inwardly and outwardly, to the disciple. This shortens his journey by several lifetimes, which would otherwise have to be spent in wanderings, explorings, gropings, and searchings.

443

It is to expound truth and correct errors, to place an example before the others, and to purify them by his company that such a teacher appears in the outer world.

444

Another phase of his work is to stimulate the yearning for higher attainment where it exists, and to inculcate it where it does not.

445

It is his work to show them what they cannot see for themselves—their own higher possibilities.

446

His function is to interpret man—and more especially spiritual man—to himself.

447

His task is to make known to other men their godlike possibilities within themselves.

448

His mission is not to bring men pleasure, but to raise them to appreciate truth.

449

The teacher assists his students to attain a degree of concentration beyond that which they are able to achieve by themselves.

450

He detonates the higher potentialities of each disciple, breaks the closed circle of his senses, and leads him towards a moral and mystical regeneration.

451

The duty of any spiritual teacher is to lead the seeker to her own Higher Self, to find her own source of inner light and strength and thus not to lean on outside human beings.

452

A guru who is quite competent does help the learner: he shows the way, illuminates problems, untangles knots, dispels confusions, explains meanings, and encourages effort. Tutelage has its place.

453

He who directs anyone's wakening spiritual faith is that man's teacher.

454

If he guides us to notice hitherto unobserved truths, if he leads our thought and faith away from hitherto strongly held errors, then a teacher fulfils a useful function.

455

His services include the unveiling and exposing of psychic or mystic experiences which are merely self-suggested or mainly hallucinatory.

456

He cannot do more than help them find and fulfil their own ways to the goal, but it is enough.

457

The teacher has to be firm at some times, gentle at others.

458

A spiritual guide's duty to an erring man will not be fully carried out if he only arouses the man to recognition of the necessity of taking a new road.

459

It will not be enough to show them the path. He must also keep them steadfast on the path.

460

He who would appear publicly as a religious prophet or mystical teacher must deal with the people of his century as he finds them, must speak to them in a language which they can understand. But even though he thus tries to conform to the requirements of those he has come to help, he cannot give them the intuition, the sensitivity, and the intelligence needed to understand his message, nor the aspiration and reverence needed to appreciate it.

461

Some teachers do not have a single disciple—they merely help a few people in a friendly way.

462

He who teaches well, learns himself.

463

He who has dedicated his life to this kind of service will find before long that others come to him—perhaps a few at first, but later many more—to pile on his sturdy shoulders the burdens and sufferings, the perplexities and gropings which they find so difficult to deal with themselves.

464

There is a kind of guru active in East and West alike who hungers for followers, is eager to acquire disciples, plays the dictator to his little circle, and not infrequently tries to get money from them. His teaching may be quite plausible, his promises quite attractive. But he is self-appointed, not God-appointed.

465

When he lets his followers regard him as a demigod and will not accept the slightest criticism from anyone, it is a sign that his personal ego is active.

466

Certain teachers develop an unhealthy lust for power, imposing their personal will on hapless disciples.

467

Many seekers through following such self-styled teachers have either remained stationary or gone astray altogether.

468

If his following of the quest is wrong it may also be because he has chosen for guru a man with an enlarged ego making exaggerated claims.

469

The peril of incompetent guides is not lessened when, as so often happens, they are sincere. For they may be, and usually are, utterly ignorant of their own limitations.

470

The teacher whose motives get mixed up, whose desire to help and serve others twines around his desire to gain money, prestige, influence, or power is one who begins to teach before he is ready to do so. Both he and his disciples will have to pay the price for his premature activities.

471

When the heart has ardently cherished the wish for a master and the mind has consequently entered a highly suggestible state, the chance meeting between a would-be follower and an over-eager spiritual Fuehrer is foolishly regarded as a divinely ordained event!

472

It is better to have no teacher at all than to have one who has psychologized himself into the delusion that he has reached the God-realized state, who mistakes self-deception for self-realization.

473

The man who constantly tries to make other persons over into a copy of himself, who tries to change their living habits or thinking-ways into the same as his own, who seeks zealously to proselytize their religious beliefs, is too often merely asserting his own ego and practising a subtler, more self-deceptive form of egotism. If he really felt love for them, as he often professes, he would leave them their freedom to choose what suits them, not thrust himself and his own beliefs aggressively upon them.

474

The kind of spiritual guide that most people want is one who pats them encouragingly on the shoulder, flatters them constantly in speech or writing, and habituates them to refer all their personal problems to him for solution. The kind of guide they really need is one who will critically point out their faults and weaknesses and who will unhesitatingly throw them back on their own resources. It is better to encourage men in good conduct than to pamper their neurotic religiosity.

475

The aspirant comes to the philosophic teacher with a mind filled by error and ignorance. He comes to the philosophic life with a character filled by egoism and prejudice. Thus he is the largest stumbling block in his own path. He himself prevents the spiritual consciousness from approaching him. So the first duty of a teacher is to show him all this error, ignorance, egoism, and prejudice for the ugly things they are and make him aware and ashamed of them.

476

He must cast aside much of his carefully heaped-up pile of knowledge and begin afresh. To make a man teachable, you must first convince him of his own ignorance. And the master will show him that he really knows little of his own self.

477

It is an important part of his task to show men what their personal lives look like from an impersonal standpoint. Hence he points out the fallacy of their egotistic actions and the foolishness of their egotistic purposes.

478

Whatever he says or suggests to his disciples is said or suggested with a view to their ultimate good. Therefore he may sometimes recommend a course of action which brings immediate pain or self-denial or self-discipline.

479

He may gently chide one man for errors and shortcomings, or firmly warn another man against sins and lapses.

480

It is hard to bring a man from a wrong point of view to a right one, not only because he may not be intellectually or intuitively capable of making the transition, but also because he can make it only by losing some of his emotional egoistic self-esteem. This is true of general propaganda among the masses as it is of the preliminary correction of pupils by a master.

481

The first task of a genuine guide is not to flatter the seeker but to criticize him, not to let him remain ignorantly in the grip of his unrecognized weaknesses but to point them out relentlessly to him.

482

Let him not think the teacher brutal for pouncing on his faults.

483

One of the first duties of a spiritual guide is to correct the beginner, show where he has mistaken his way, and expose his fallacies of thought, feeling, and conduct. A competent guide will be quick to perceive and fearless to point out these matters however unpleasant a duty it be and however unpalatable to the pupil.

484

It is part of the task of a spiritual director to point out tactfully but firmly the faults and deficiencies of his disciples, to make them more aware of what is needed in their moral self-correction.

485

The spiritual director who is over-severe in his correction of the aspirant's faults, needs correcting himself.

486

The paternal spiritual guide who coddles his bleating disciples renders them a disservice.

487

It is a common experience with abbots of monasteries in the West and with gurus of ashrams in the East that attention given to one disciple may rouse the ego's conceit in him and the ego's envy in the others.

488

The guide who refuses to appease the ego of those who approach him, may nevertheless be eager to help them. Yet they will resent his counsel and feel rebuffed! They do not see that he is trying to help them in a wiser way by showing them how to help themselves. Only longer time and further experience may bring them to their senses and show them the logic of his advice and the prudence of his attitude.

489

The spiritual leader who is always soft and sentimental may help some of his pupils but he would help them more if, at the same time, he were also hard and firm. The first attitude will attract more to him, but without the second to balance it neither he nor they will get the proper view of life.

490

A true teacher must warn his followers against false expectations and irredeemable promises.

491

One of the first tasks of a philosophy teacher is to restrain the missionary fervour of his younger pupils and to impress upon them the need of caution, discrimination, and even secrecy in this matter.

492

It is not enough that he has the penetration to perceive the truth; he must also have the courage to tell it to his disciples, even though he knows it will shock them.

493

The guru whose ego still harbours vanity will find it flattered by every new disciple, will be endangered afresh by every widening of his personal influence.

494

He finds that the disciples come to him for their emotional comfort, they do not come for their ego's emotional quietus. They want to remain enclosed in its little circle, not to be taken completely out of it.

495

The kind of master needed and sought after by those who are on the religio-mystic-occult path is one who will take a keen interest in their personal life as well as spiritual welfare, one who is always willing to help them with any and every problem, one who by virtue of residence or correspondence is always and quickly available to them. The philosophic master is not like this but of a different kind.

496

He is not a missionary telling others that they *must* follow the Quest but an educator telling them that they may follow it if they so choose.

497

The title "leader" implies its corollary "follower." But a spiritual leader of the kind here described does not want a mass of followers trailing behind him in a partisan spirit. It is enough for him to give others a few inspirations, ideas, insights, and yet leave them free to work on the material as they wish, unobligated to join any movement.

498

It is needful for you to understand that a philosophic teacher never really wants anyone to follow him but only to follow Truth. Socrates humorously described himself as practising the same vocation as his mother who was a midwife—the only difference between them being that whereas she helped women to deliver themselves of infants, he helped men to deliver themselves of the true ideas with which their minds were in labour. His business, like that of all genuine teachers, was not to impart truth as something new and foreign but to assist the student to elicit it from within himself. Every genuine teacher tries in his work to lead the student's mind in such a way that his thinking gradually changes without his becoming conscious of the fact at the time, although he will recognize it in retrospect later. He makes students think for themselves; stimulates them to solve their own metaphysical, personal, and emotional problems; periodically gives an inner mystical impetus to their meditation practice; and points out the pitfalls and fallacies which lie in their life-path. Because his outlook is so disinterested, because his primary purpose is to liberate and not limit them, to give and not get, such a teacher's services can never be bought by anyone—although they may be claimed by those who are prepared to cast off the shoes of conventional prejudice at his door and who are willing to refrain loyally from imposing upon him their preconceived notions of what characteristics the teaching, the teacher, and the quest should possess. Thus if he will not shackle them, they in their turn must not shackle him. Such would-be disciples are rare, but such teachers who practise what they preach are rarer still.

499

The method of a philosophic teacher is not to make the decisions of the pupil for him but rather to lead him to make them for himself. The teacher will outline the process of arriving at the correct conclusion, but he will not deprive the pupil of the responsibility of trusting that process and accepting its outcome. The teacher may even make available information which will be helpful to the student in arriving at a decision, but beyond that he cannot go if the student is to arrive at independence and maturity. The relationship which we find in mystical or Oriental circles, which leaves the pupil completely or continuously dependent upon his guide and causes him to come constantly running to and fro for advice as to what he should do next, will only increase the helplessness of the pupil. The philosophic way is to help him develop his own ability to dispose of problems and confront situations effectively. The philosophic method is to lead the pupil to the point where he requires no teacher. The mystical method is to lead him to the point where he cannot do without the teacher.

500

The teacher who demands blind obedience from his pupil belongs to a vanishing age. The teacher who strives to make his pupil's own mind understand each step of the way he travels belongs to the coming age. The first often ends by enslaving his followers, whereas the second ends by liberating them. The first is a dictator, the second a companion. The first creates nonentities, the second, men.

501

A wise teacher will not lecture to his students, will not try the superficial way of telling them every detail of truth. But by discussion questioning and encouragement he will help them to elicit it for themselves and thus enable them to make it deeply and lastingly their own.

502

The right way to teach men is to propose truth, not impose it.

503

A philosophic teacher often prefers to let the student make his own discoveries on the basis of clues provided rather than lead him into rigid imprisoning dogmas.

504

The true teacher should stimulate thought and not stereotype it. If an aspirant is fortunate enough to get direct and personal guidance of this kind, he is fortunate indeed.

505

The master gives a candidate the seeds and teaches him how to cultivate them: how to water, nourish, and tend the plants which sprout up from them.

506

The highest type of teacher does not want and will not encourage a blind unquestioning acceptance of his own views.

507

The true teacher interprets the divine will for his disciple but does not impose it on him. Such a guide may proffer advice and tender suggestions but he will never issue orders and dictate decisions. Instead of trying to deprive the student of his capacity to intuit truths for himself, the disinterested teacher will try to create it.

508

A genuine teacher will not seek to dominate the soul of a student, will not strive to impose his own will upon him. For the teacher desires to see a natural and not a forced artificial growth, to free men and not to enslave them. The real master spiritualizes his disciple but does not debilitate him.

509

The guru who does not want to enslave disciples, will guide them to do what they themselves ought to be doing, but are weakly and foolishly expecting him to do for them.

510

A prudent master prefers not to help people but to help them to help themselves.

511

It is merely mockery to admonish a weakling to become strong if you do not put into his hands the knowledge and equipment wherewith he can acquire strength.

512

It is the teacher's duty to foster his disciple's creativeness, not his imitativeness—to encourage the disciple to develop his own inspiration.

513

The average teacher takes from his own personal experience what helped him most or what his own teacher led him to, and passes it on to the student as being "*the* Path," the *only* way to God, the sole method of arriving at truth—whether this particular way or method suits the individual type or his degree of development or not. He almost forces it on the student, even if it is contrary to the latter's entire temperament or need. The poor student finds himself imprisoned and locked up in his teacher's personal opinions and practices, as if nothing good existed outside them.

514

The wisest master lets the disciple develop in his own way, according to his own individuality.

515

Such a teacher will be the student's motivating influence while, paradoxically, encouraging him to preserve his independence.

516

What the wise teacher does is to wait for the right situations to develop in which his own efforts can be most fruitful.

517

He has waited for years, reserving the full expression of his powers until the crucial hour when the aspirant is ready to receive him. Until then, he must conceal his identity.

518

His wisdom in refusing to influence the students' decisions will not be apparent at first. Indeed it will be regarded as unwisdom—and his attitude will be felt as unsympathetic.

519

It is not the business of a master to save the disciple from suffering so much as to save him from the faults in himself which create suffering. He may suggest and advise but never impose his will upon yours. He turns a lamp upon your problems but leaves you free to work them out for yourself.

520

A master's work is not to issue commands which must be obeyed by enslaved disciples, but to formulate principles which must be understood by enlightened ones. It is not to create belief but to strengthen knowledge.

521

The philosophic teacher leaves to the individual pupil how he shall apply these principles to his own life, and does not try to chalk out the precise details of such practice for him.

522

His unwillingness to give specific advice on practical personal matters should not be construed as unwillingness to help, or as lack of interest in them. It is only that he wants the solution to come straight out of the student's own being, so that the growth will be the student's too.

523

Only the inexperienced over-enthused novice will want to share the whole of his knowledge with others, will want to let them into all its secrets without delay. The prudent expert guide is much more restrained. He carefully refrains from giving more than the others are ready for, holding the rest back for a later time. It is not only prudence which warns him against yielding all his secrets at once: Nature, in her own operations, likewise lets the mind of her animals grow by degrees through a graduated process of development.

524

It is the mark of a well-qualified teacher that he adapts his advice to fit each disciple individually. If everyone is recommended to practise the same method irrespective of his competence, his personal history and temperament, his grade of development and capacity, his character-traits and tendencies, in a number of cases it will be largely ineffectual.

525

His long-range work is to lift the disciples to his own level, but his short-range work is necessarily concerned with their levels.

526

His refusal to give everything out to everyone must be judged by this light, this recognition of the fact that there exist various levels of under-standing, and hence of readiness to learn these things.

527

A teacher of spiritual culture, ideals, principles, and practices must think of the intellectual level of those he seeks to instruct, and address his message to that.

528

Because there are different levels of aspirants, different levels of teaching are necessary.

529

He takes the view that these multiple teachings are successive steps leading in time to the highest truth and that it would be harmful or unwise to present this truth at too early a stage.

530

There are three methods of approach used by the teachers, depending on the level of the people they have to deal with. They are: first, terrorizing the lowest type by fears; second, coaxing the better evolved ones by baits and lures; third, giving a fair, balanced statement of the truth for those people who are mentally and morally on the highest level.

531

A competent teacher puts himself behind his pupil's eyes, inside his pupil's mind, and starts his instruction from what he finds there.

532

The prudent teacher will reveal what will best help people, not necessarily what they like to hear or all that he knows. He must give people what is best for them, must first evaluate how much truth they can take in. It is utterly impracticable and imprudent to give all people all the spiritual truth at all times.

533

The prudent teacher will give out only slightly more than the seeking enquirer is able to receive.

534

To explain such subtle teachings in all their fullness to anyone who will not be able to understand them or to feel as interested as the student does, would be foolish. Nevertheless, he is not the proprietor of them so he cannot keep them solely for his own use; nor is he so separate from others that their inner fate is not his concern. If someone comes who asks questions sincerely or needs comfort spiritually or seeks guidance in bewilderment, the student must give what he can. But he must give it prudently, not pouring out one drop more of his knowledge or power than is needed for the particular person at this particular stage in evolution. There is no necessity to keep truth jealously guarded, as in medieval times, nor to rush to the opposite extreme and give everything to everyone.

535

The message will reach him only when it can re-educate his understanding.

536

All spiritual progress is individual. Each man grows by himself, not as part of a group. Therefore, if instruction is really to be effective, it should be individual instruction.

537

The outer teacher's prime duty is to lead the aspirant to his own inner teacher. But if he leads the aspirant towards ever-increasing attachment, dependence, and submission to himself—that is, outwards and away from the inner teacher—then he only exploits him rather than directs him, and there is only false progress.

538

Real progress will be the fruit of their own endeavours, not of the goodwill of others. It is one of the obligations of a true spiritual guide to make aspirants feel that they have the power to achieve it and to encourage them to take their spiritual destiny into their own hands.

539

He formulates precisely and expresses definitely an idea which a number of minds are moving toward but have not yet produced. They recognize it when he gives it to them, and thus become the willing receivers of it.

540

The teacher passes some of his own consciousness and force into the disciple, thus enabling him to realize the truth of what might otherwise be but theory. Moreover he provides "truth-words" for the disciple who, by constantly ruminating over these, attains intuitive knowledge.

541

The question of helping students more individually is a question of practical functioning. The teacher wishes to keep his own freedom and at the same time leave them free too.

542

The aim of a teacher is not to create a philosophical elite for its own sake but for the larger sake of mankind.

543

The starting of a cult to gain a personal following would be abhorrent to the spirit of any truly selfless spiritual guide, but the creation of a school for spiritual development and philosophical learning he might consider helpful to many earnest but bewildered students of life.

544

The true master is to work for the few. There are several agencies who will spread their activities thinly on a wide surface but his will penetrate to a deeper level. Theirs will be more showy but his more effective.

545

Adepts not only seek the few who seek them but they also seek the fewer still who are qualified for them.

546

The teacher does not lift the veil of Isis for everyone he meets in the street but he will always lift it for those who ask aright.

547

He cannot help all the millions of mankind. He can help only the seekers among mankind. Nor can he help all the seekers. He can help only those who come into sympathetic and receptive contact with him or with his work.

Master-disciple relationship

548

To be someone's disciple is to go farther in relationship than to be his student.

549

If men call themselves disciples sharing his views, two paths become open to them. The first is to become lay disciples, who limit themselves to intellectual sharing only. The second is to become full disciples, who go all the way with him into the philosophical discipline and life.

550

One great advantage of the path of personal discipleship is that it requires no intellectual capacity, no special gifts of any kind, to get its profits and make progress along its course. What could be simpler than remembering the master's name and face? What could be easier than mentally turning to him every day in faith, reverence, humility, and devotion?

551

The advantage of having a *living* master is immense. Man is so sense-bound that it is easier for him to follow an embodied ideal than a disembodied one, easier to understand truth in action than truth in the abstract. Should anyone have the good fortune to be taken under the wing of a sage, his progress will go forward at a far quicker rate than would otherwise be possible. It is not a little thing that he has someone to turn him in the right direction or that his movement in this direction is guided by an experienced pioneer.

552

Although the master cannot do the disciple's work for him, he can put the disciple in command of the special knowledge derived from long experience which can help him do the work more efficiently and more successfully.

553
The master will teach with love what the student must learn with reverence.

554
As the Master brings the disciple to clarify his own thinking and knowledge and awareness, the latter turns his attention to what it is that he really does believe.

555
The zeal of the Master will by slow degrees permeate the heart of the disciple.

556
Under the sunshine of this encouragement, inspiration, and stimulation, the inner life expands.

557
Only those who have themselves felt it can understand how he is able to exert such drawing power and arouse such fervid devotion in disciples.

558
There is intimacy in the fellowship between teacher and disciple which is unique. There is an impersonality in this most personal of human relationships which is equally unique.

559
No other relationship, whether familial or friendly, can compare with this relationship in depth or beauty or value.

560
There is no tie so strong, no attraction so deep as that between Master and pupil. Consequently it persists through incarnation after incarnation.

561
It is a special kind of relationship, one which is less dependent on physical conditions than any other human relationship. If they never meet again, never see each other again, it remains unchangeably the same to the end.

562
The average aspirant does not find the true teachers because he would not behave himself correctly with them if he did. Sooner or later he would abuse the lofty character of the relation of discipleship and seek to force it to become a half-worldly one. It is probably true to say that even imperfect teachers, who are all that the public is likely to know, often receive from their followers frantic appeals for this or that personal intervention or

frenzied outpourings concerning this or that personal material problem for which immediate help is demanded. But even when the aspirant has linked himself up with an embodied master or invisible adept, a scriptural personage or his own higher self, he may start to assume that the higher power or person is henceforth going to settle all his personal troubles without his own exertions being called for. This is a piece of wishful thinking. The very purpose of evolution would be defeated if he were to be deprived of the opportunity of tackling his problems and troubles for himself: it is only so that his capacities can stretch out and his understanding enlarge itself. We may sympathize with the need of troubled disciples, but a wrong notion of what constitutes the teacher-disciple relation will not help them. It will lead to false hopes and the anguish of subsequent disappointment. For what is it that they are really trying to do? They are not merely using the teacher as a spiritual guide, which is quite correct, but also as a material guide, leaning-post, and father-mother, which is quite wrong. They want to shunt their own responsibilities and shift their personal burdens onto the back of a master or at least to share them with him. Such a conception of discipleship is a wrong one. Also it is an unfair one. Instead of using the master as a source of principles and inspirations to be applied by themselves in practical life, they try to exploit him, to avoid the responsibility for making their own decisions by saddling it upon his shoulders. The master cannot solve all their personal problems or carry all their burdens. This task rests with the disciples themselves. To seek to shift their responsibility for it onto the master's shoulders is to demand the impossible, the unfair, and the unwise. If successful, it would defeat the very purpose of their incarnation. It would rob them of the benefit of the experience to which they have been led by their own Overself. Such excessive reliance on the guide makes them more and more incapable of independent thought and judgement. But it should be the object of a competent guide to help them develop these very things and grow in spiritual strength, as it should be the aim of a sincere one not dictatorially to rule their conduct but suggestively to elevate it. If they are to advance to higher levels, disciples must learn to rely on their own endeavours. No master can relieve them of this responsibility. It is not the work of a philosophic teacher to save students from having to make decisions for themselves. It is, on the contrary, his duty to encourage them to face up to rather than to flee from the responsibility and profit of working out their own solutions. The prudent master will leave them to work out for themselves how to apply philosophy to their personal situations. For him to manage their lives, settle their problems, and negotiate their difficulties might please their egos but would weaken their characters. Hence, he does not wish to interfere in their lives nor assume responsibility for forming decisions on those personal, domestic, family, employment, and business problems which they ought to arrive at for themselves. At best he can point out the general direction for travel, not supply a definite map; he can lay down the general principles of action and it is for them to find out the best way of applying these principles. The agony of coming to a right judgement is part of the educative process in developing right intuitions. Each experience looked at in this way brings out their independent creative faculty, that is, makes them truly self-reliant. The principles of such solutions are partially in their hands; practical horse-sense must be harnessed to shrewd reason and guided by ethical ideals and intuitions.

563

It is not right for the would-be disciple to take the new relationship as an excuse for releasing himself from all personal responsibilities, all personal decisions. He should not expect the teacher to take entire charge of his entire life for him. Nor is it right for a teacher to accept such a position, to play a role consisting of father and mother and God combined into a single person toward an individual who has reached adult life. It will not help a disciple to let him evade his responsibilities and shirk his decisions. If the atmosphere between them is surcharged with emotion alone without the restraining balances of reason and common sense, this is the kind of situation which is likely to be brought about. A wise teacher will try to meet disciples upon the proper ground between accepting such helpless dependence and rebuffing it brusquely altogether. Any other meeting would be unhealthy emotionally and unsound intellectually.

564

Emerson: "Why insist on rash personal relations with your friend? Why go to his house, or know his mother and brothers and sisters? Why be visited by him at your own? Are these things material to our covenant? Leave this touching and clawing. Let him be to me a spirit. A message, a thought, a sincerity, a glance from him I want, but not news nor pottage. I can get politics and chat, neighbourly conveniences from cheaper companions. Should not the society of my friend be to me poetic, pure, universal and as great as nature itself?"—These words are just as applicable to the disciple.

565

Whoever entrusts himself to a master or his mind to a teaching, cannot escape his own personal responsibility for what he does. This is not to absolve either the guru or the author of the teaching from their own responsibility, which they also have, but it is to make clear that the followers share it too.

566

The disciple's reverence for the Master can still hold room for sight of the latter's failings and imperfections. If he gets enough inspiration from the Master to help his spiritual life, it would be a foolish decision to leave him because of those failings and imperfections.

567

In primitive tribal times it was the custom in most places to measure knowledge by the length of the beard. Today it is found that many of our cleverest atomic energy scientists are comparatively young and certainly beardless! It is as sensible to follow the primitive custom nowadays as it is to measure virtue by the beauty of the face. Yet it is not an uncommon attitude for self-styled truth-seekers to follow one spiritual teacher because his facial appearance pleases them and to reject another teacher because his physical figure displeases them! Says Sören Kierkegaard in *Concluding Unscientific Postscript.* "He (Socrates) was very ugly, had clumsy feet, and, above all, a number of growths on the forehead and elsewhere, which would suffice to persuade anyone that he was a demoralized subject. This was what Socrates understood by his favourable appearance in which he was so thoroughly happy that he would have considered it a chicane of the divinity to prevent him from becoming a teacher of morals, had he been given an attractive appearance like an effeminate cithara player, a melting glance like a shepherd lad, small feet like a dancing master in the Friendly Society and *in toto* as favourable an appearance as could have been desired by any applicant for a job through the newspapers, or any theologue who has pinned his hope on a private call. Why was this old teacher so happy over his unfavourable appearance, unless it was because he understood that it must help to keep the learner at a distance, so that the latter might not stick fast in a direct relationship to the teacher, perhaps admire him, perhaps have his clothes cut in the same manner? Through the repellent effect exerted by the contrast, which on a higher plane was also the role played by his irony, the learner would be compelled to understand that he had essentially to do with himself, and that the inwardness of the truth is not the comradely inwardness with which two bosom friends walk arm in arm, but the separation with which each for himself exists in the truth."

568

If you as the student choose him as your guide, and if he as the teacher accepts you, what will follow? You should not have mistaken or exaggerated notions about this relation, should not imagine, for instance, as so many have imagined, that within a week of acceptance you will have supernormal experiences, magically attain the transcendent insight, or receive hour-by-hour watchful care from him. The path is a lifetime one; it may well run into several lifetimes. For the first and second things to happen is to run contrary to the laws of nature. His own work is so widespread and so surprisingly varied, his correspondence so large, his writing labours so important, that it is physically impossible for a teacher continuously to pay personal attention to the several hundred individuals seeking his help. What help then may you legitimately expect from him? You may expect help in the three branches of this path: the development of philosophical intelligence, the practice of mystical meditation, and the living of a wise and virtuous existence. Concerning the first item, your intellectual difficulties questions and problems will be cleared up through advanced disciples or through the post or, less frequently, at personal interviews. Concerning the second item, you will be given a practical initiation at a personal meditation with him, which may even be repeated a number of times if possible. In addition you may be given the same privilege with his advanced disciples. But beyond this you must travel your own path. You must faithfully study the needful books, carry on the regular meditations, and try to adjust your actions to your ideals for yourself and by yourself. You cannot omit any part of this work and then rightfully expect the teacher to carry you forward to successful achievement of the goal. He may be there to direct, inspire, and encourage your work, but that does not absolve you from doing the work itself. When Buddha was asked by critics if all his disciples acted according to his teaching, he frankly answered: "Some do and some do not." The critics exclaimed, "How is it that even your own disciples do not follow you?" So Buddha explained, "My task is merely to show the path. Some tread it and others do not."

569

The master must have the continued co-operation of the disciple, if he is to do his best.

570

The expectations of disciples, their high estimate of his character and notion of his outlook, may help to make him what he is.

571

The disciple who does not follow the path pointed out to him, who obeys only when it is easy or convenient to obey, commits fraud and does insult to his master.

572

The student's delight in learning must be matched by the master's delight in giving.

573

The student's faith must meet the teacher's patience and the teacher's knowledge and integrity must be such as to inspire confidence in the student.

574

It is better in every way that the teacher should belong to the same sex as the disciple.

575

The attitude of the student towards his teacher is of great importance to the student, because it lays an unseen cable from him to the teacher, and along that cable pass to and fro the messages and help which the teacher has to give. The teacher can never lose contact with the student by going to another part of the world. That unseen cable is elastic and it will stretch for thousands of miles, because the World-Mind consciousness will travel almost instantly and anywhere. Contact is not broken by increasing physical distance. It is broken by the change of heart, the alteration of mental attitude by the student towards the teacher. If the attitude is wrong, then the cable is first weakened and finally snapped. Nothing can then pass through and the student is really alone.

576

Trust lays the cable and trust keeps it in place. Doubt severs the cable and mistrust destroys it altogether. Therefore it is prudent and proper for a would-be disciple to clear his doubts and answer his questions *before* choosing the teaching which he is to approach as his faith, and not after the choice has been made.

577

It is essential for aspirants to realize that in such a relationship it is the mental attitude, especially the faith and devotion—rather than outward association and physical contact—that is of true importance.

578

It is not only needful to link up with the guide in a general way by a right attitude of faith and devotion towards him but also to link up in a special way by a daily meditation which seeks to put the disciple's mind in rapport with the guide's.

579

Osmosis, the principle of absorption as a result of being with or near a thing or a person, is active here as elsewhere.

580

His silent influence can lift up the other man's inner being much more easily if the disciple sits relaxed in body and emptied in mind.

581

A master may give out his teachings, methods, and instructions. Sooner or later some among his followers—if not his opponents—will twist them, reinterpret them, modify them, or even deform them. This process even starts during his lifetime, but becomes considerable and important only after that—when he's no longer present to attend to needed corrections. This shows that not all who hear him understand what they hear, and that there are different levels of capacity among the followers.

582

The spiritual counsellor who takes personal advantage of the dependence placed upon him or of the trust shown in him, thereby renders himself unfit for such a high position. Therefore in his dealings with disciples it is best for him to maintain an independence in practical affairs and worldly relationship as well as a cool detachment in social contact and personal intercourse. It is inevitable that the disciples should feel hurt at such impersonality and such objectivity, but therein lies a protection both for themselves and for the teacher until such time as they are more developed, better balanced, more controlled, and farther seeing. Then and then only is it possible for the teacher to revise the relationship and make it not only a warmer one but even a more personal one, with safety to both sides. Disciples who are not well-balanced and are somewhat neurotic often try to get the teacher personally involved in their lives. For they want to be set free from the need of developing themselves, the duty of improving their characters, the burden of accepting their responsibilities, and the painfulness of working out emotional problems which are merely the result of their own egoism. If the teacher succumbs to their appeals, then they remain unevolved and the relationship itself remains unpracticable. But if he firmly resists them he may, by such resistance, force a change in their attitude and consequently an increase in their wisdom. In doing so however he courts misunderstanding on the part of his disciples, who may first become bewildered and later resentful. Affection may turn to anger for a time, and the disciple may even withdraw altogether. If they are so foolish as to do this their development will not only be stopped but also, what is worse, set back for months or years.

583

Possessive love is natural. We want to have and keep what we love. But when its object is another human being, there is an inevitable desire for the return of our love, for the restriction of their affection to us alone, so that what we give is not given in purity but in extended selfishness. Hence when others love you they want to deprive you of your freedom. But when the disciple loves you, he must give you your freedom.

584

It is also an error to believe that one disciple must necessarily associate with the other disciples of the same teacher. Only where there is real temperamental harmony and personal affinity should disciples associate together. Where these are lacking, it is much wiser and safer not to do so. For then the evil forces take advantage of the chance to develop disharmony, quarrels, ill-feeling, and even worse. This spoils the progress of both.

585

The real business of any disciple is with the teacher, not with the other disciples. Such a situation cannot be helped and must be accepted. Human beings are all born with different characters and dispositions. Only the sage can harmonize with all; others must recognize limitations.

586

If one cannot be happy with certain students, he must wish them well and then go his own way. He must never allow himself to be drawn into quarrels for then the evil forces become active.

587

The relationship between them is a beautiful but free one. If the disciple takes a possessive attitude and tries to annex the teacher, if he betrays jealousy of other disciples or demands as much attention as they get, he substitutes an egoistic for an impersonal relationship, fails to understand its distinctively and uniquely free nature, and thus spoils it.

588

He must insist on getting the same freedom from his disciples that he allows to them.

589

Whether physically together or physically apart, that is a true relationship between master and disciple, husband and wife, friend and friend, which refusing to be tightly possessive or personally demanding, is satisfied by the silent fact that the other exists at all.

590

No guru can lead anyone to enlightenment if he himself is attached to the role of guru, nor can any disciple ever receive enlightenment if he wants to play the role of disciple forever. Both are suffering from attachments which prevent enlightenment. This is why the whole thing becomes a stage play, whether serious or comical, in which the actors are performing their personal parts. Even if they babble about the necessity of not getting attached to the world, they are still attached to what they are supposed to be, that is, questing. A truly enlightened man has no such attachment and unless he is invested by the Higher Power with a special apostleship, or with a special mission, he would not consider himself a guru, nor anyone else as a disciple.

591

The way of leaning upon a guide, or being carried by one, is a way which of itself can never lead to the goal. It can only lead in the end to the superior way of struggling to one's own knees again and again until one is strong enough to walk to the goal. The master must not stand in the way, must not direct attention to himself unduly and at the expense of seekers' own attraction to his central inner self. Sören Kierkegaard writes in *Concluding Unscientific Postscript*, "A direct relationship between one spiritual being and another, with respect to the essential truth, is unthinkable. If such a relationship is assumed, it means that one of the parties has ceased to be spirit. This is something that many a genius omits to consider, both when he helps people into the truth *en masse*, and when he is complaisant enough to think that acclamation, willingness to listen, the affixing of signatures, and so forth, is identical with the acceptance of the truth. Precisely as important as the truth, and if one of the two is to be emphasized, still more important, is the manner in which the truth is accepted. It would help very little if one persuaded millions of men to accept the truth, if precisely by the method of their acceptance they were transferred into error. Hence it is that all complaisance, all persuasiveness, all bargaining, all direct attraction by means of one's own person, reference to one's suffering for the cause, one's weeping over humanity, one's enthusiasm—all this is sheer misunderstanding, a false note in relation to the truth, by which, in proportion to one's ability, one may help a job-lot of human beings to get an illusion of truth. Socrates was an ethical teacher, but he took cognizance of the non-existence of any direct relationship between teacher and pupil, because the truth is inwardness, and because this inwardness in each is precisely the road which leads them away from one another. It was presumably because he understood this, that he was so happy about his unfavourable outward appearance."

592

The relation between a pupil and his teacher can be based upon complete submission and dependence on authority, or it can be based on a reasonable freedom and moderate self-reliance.

593

The belief common in India and the Near East that a guru must take over your mind and your life is welcomed by the weak or misinformed here too. But it forms no part of philosophical teaching, practice, and training.

594

The rule of absolute submission to a master may be as unsafe to follow as the rule of absolute independence from a master.

595

The problem is one of reconciling the giving of complete faith to the teacher and the keeping alive of one's inner freedom to think for oneself and to receive intuition from oneself.

596

No master has the right to ask any candidate for discipleship to surrender himself absolutely, to place himself unreservedly in the master's hands and to obey unquestioningly the master's orders. The trust demanded should arise of its own accord by progressive degrees as the relationship proceeds and develops, and as the master proves by his conduct and effectiveness to be fully worthy of it.

597

Because he gives the master devotion he does not also have to give him idolatry.

598

His disciples are taught how to unite independent thinking with loyal feeling in their attitude toward him. This satisfies them both.

599

There are those who think that he neglects to answer his mail. Because he leaves their letters so long unanswered, they conclude that he means to drop them out of his life. Nothing could be farther from the truth. It is true that his mail accumulates for long periods of time. But it is equally true that he lacks the staff needed to handle it, that the pressure of work like writing and meditation and research notes leaves him little remaining time. However, those who have met him personally and call themselves his disciples often cannot understand his behaviour so he gives this published explanation. Once inner contact is established by a single physical meeting it is not necessary to have further ones with the guide although they may be helpful. Sri Aurobindo granted only a single minute to each individual at his first or later meeting with a disciple or a candidate for discipleship. Thus it is evident that he does not consider more than sixty seconds really necessary to establish it. Not only are further physical meetings not necessary but even further personal action on his part, such as writing letters to the disciples are also unnecessary even though they may be helpful. Thus a spiritual guide does not need to do anything physically or write anything personally to keep up the internal contact, it being kept up by the student's remembrance, devotion, faith, and meditation.

No disciple can be effectively trained by the long distance method of an occasional exchange of letters. He needs personal supervision, personal contact, and personal discussion of his special problems. No conscientious teacher will ever undertake to give instructions by mail and declare it sufficient. It gives too meagre a basis for accurate understanding on the disciple's part or for an adequate communication on the teacher's part.

Then again he cannot accept the position of personal counsellor under the guise of being spiritual teacher. That is not his work. Most students who keep on failing to recognize this fact against all previous and present warnings and who send letter after letter with every fluctuation of their personal moods and fortunes, in an attempt to wrest advice or intervention from him, may force him to break the external contact with him until such time as they do realize what the true situation is. If he were to adopt a counselling position and to agree to show students how to apply the philosophical teaching to every change of their own personal life, he would soon have no time to give out those teachings at all. Consequently he must refuse to respond to all these attempts often openly but sometimes hidden, often naïve but sometimes cunning, to get him personally involved in the life of the seeker or to mix both their personal problems together. So many of his correspondents try to force him into this highly personal guru-student relationship, and thus to impose their own responsibilities upon his shoulders, that he has to fall into lengthy periods of silence to protect himself. Moreover, if he were to respond to the emotional or worldly problems in the way such response is desired, it would only mean the downfall of both of them and the breakdown of their pure relationship. To maintain this purity, to safeguard the relationship itself, and to protect the master as well as the seeker, the proper teaching must be given from the start and that is: the teacher must be regarded as a symbol, not as a person. He is to be considered merely as an agent for that which he represents, not as just another human being entering into a human relation with the disciple. Often the beginner, finding that the teacher does not fully respond to his emotional craving for continuous personal attention, soon becomes disappointed. This feeling may develop until it reaches a critical stage where one of two things may happen. Either he will fail to pass the test, for so it becomes, and will withdraw altogether from the relationship—perhaps even maligning the guide—or he will continue his trust, gain a new point of view, and make the needed change to a higher attitude in the end. If, however, he allows his egoism or emotion to lead him into disobedience of this rule, he will only endanger the relationship. If he persists in this disobedience, he will even find it brought to an end for a time. So few understand what is really involved in this relationship, so many misunderstand it and are therefore disappointed by it in the beginning or along the way, that the teacher prefers with rare exceptions of well-advanced cases, not to enter into it outwardly at all but instead to offer a little friendly help without obligation.

600

No real master is ever afraid that he might lose any particular disciple. He takes possession of no one and leaves everyone as free as he found them. He understands quite well that the man's need or search and his own higher self's gracious response brought the master into the picture as an indirect medium through which the response could operate. He understands, too, that all the instruction and advice, the uplift and help which he gives the disciple originate ultimately and really within the man himself, as the latter will one day discover when he has developed his own direct access to them, and therefore refuses to regard the relationship between them egotistically.

Qualifications, duties of a disciple

601

There are inexorable laws, not of his making, which govern the opening of a spiritual relation between a master and a would-be disciple, however much his devotion and loyalty are appreciated. The chance remains open to him on a probation only, which is necessarily of a limited number of years. If during that period they are able to make personal contact, it will be helpful for the disciple's progress in understanding the teaching, and he can then profit by it to clear up misconceptions and weed out faults.

602

He may be generous enough to accept them as they are, with their weaknesses and mistakes, but the law of karma is above all human emotions, whether they be generous or ingenerous. It demands full payment and distributes to them the consequences of their actions.

603

The master did not formulate these laws governing the quest and, however urgent the plea of his disciple, he cannot do away with them.

604

No aspirant has the right to seek personal discipleship with a genuine teacher before he has sufficiently developed himself for it, any more than a child who has not learned to read and write has the right to seek entrance into a college.

605

The immediate presence of a teacher acts as a catalyst upon the student. His defects, no less than his virtues, cannot then be hidden for long, and circumstances will usually so arrange themselves that these qualities will glaringly reveal themselves in time. Hence this is necessarily a probationary period. Tests will come not through any arbitrary act on the part of the teacher but through the ordinary events of everyday life and also through persons met. They are not alone tests of a ethical kind—after all, we are all sinners until we realize truth—as of his devotion to truth rather than its counterfeits. The student will be tested first to observe how far he can remain personally loyal to the teacher—because the latter stands in symbolic relation to truth—despite the efforts of critics and enemies to put a plausible face on their opposition. The most elementary condition of spiritual instruction is complete confidence between the teacher and pupil. All sorts of blind critics and malicious enemies will appear from time to time to attempt to disturb that confidence. They are unconsciously or consciously the instruments of the adverse elements in nature. He will be tested, too, by surface shocks to his prejudices, preconceived notions, and expectations. He will be tested to reveal how far he is willing to go in the unselfish service of humanity when such service comes into conflict with his personal interests. It does not follow that if he does not know when and where he is being tested the test is unfair. It is for him to use his intelligence at such times as at others, and to consult his pledge whenever doubts arise and difficulties occur. These tests will sometimes be plainly evident and therefore comparatively easy to pass through, but there are others which are more subtle or disguised and therefore more difficult to pass through. However, all tests have one object alone—to detach him from the path towards truth. If he keeps this clearly in his mind, it will help him to understand them, and those who emerge with unwavering confidence despite all the oppositions encountered will receive their reward. If after the probationary period is over—and its length cannot be fixed for it will vary with each individual—those whose feet still follow the teacher unhesitatingly and completely will naturally find the interval of time between probation and acceptance is much shorter than will those in whom doubts still linger and hesitation still arises.

606

From the time when he begins to take instruction from his teacher, the disciple also begins a period of probation in his inner career and of separation from his inner weaknesses. The probation will enable him gradually to show forth all the different aspects of his personality and will indicate how receptive he really is to the teacher's influence. During this process, qualities which are lying latent beneath the surface will arise above it; situations will arrange themselves in such a way as to force him to express them. In short, what is hidden will become open. Thus he will be given the chance to look to his moral foundations before he advances to the intensive mystical training which places hidden power and hidden knowledge in his hands. Without first getting such a foundation, he who gets possession of these powers may soon fall into overpowering temptations, with disastrous results to himself and others. The inner conflict which results from the probation will force him to face himself, to look at the weaknesses which are present within him and to try to conquer them. If there is no other way to get him to do so, then he will have to take the way of suffering their consequences so as to have them brought home to him. Such a phase of the disciple's career will naturally be filled with strains for himself and with misunderstandings about himself. The term of probation is a period of severe trials and strong temptations. However, the principle of probation is a sound one. Out of the vortex of its tests and stresses and upheavals, he has the chance to emerge a stronger and wiser man.

607

His probationary period is concerned with the general purification of character from egoism and animality as well as with its sensitization to intuition and instruction. Without such a basis to work upon, it would be dangerous for him to venture into mystical work or public service. Nor would the teacher permit him to do so, as there are inexorable laws, not of his making, which govern the matter. He must be on guard and not mistake psychism for spirituality, pseudo-intuition for the real thing, mix personal motives with altruistic service, nor lose himself in dreams and fantasies instead of finding himself in inspired action. These faults are common to most mystical aspirants. The Quest is deadly serious and demands so much. It is far easier to go astray from it than to keep on it.

608

An aspirant who approached a Zen Master in Japan was refused personal instruction. Nevertheless, he waited around in the vicinity for half a year. Then, tiring of the lack of success, he abandoned further solicitation, resolved to depend on his own efforts, and arranged to depart. But on the very eve of departure the master sent for him and agreed to teach him.

609

It is not the custom of a true master to accept personal students externally and formally from among those who apply for the first time, but only from those who have been in touch with him for some years at least and hence have had sufficient time to make sure that this is really the teacher they want. Such a teacher would not desire and ought not to accept those pupils who do not belong to his orbit by inward affinity. He would be foolish to accept a candidate whose true call is with some other teacher, unwise to permit a passing enthusiasm to waste his own time and disappoint the enthusiast's hopes. It is easy in transient moods of enthusiasm to make a mistake in this matter and to find that he is not, after all, the kind of man they originally believed him to be or the kind of teacher that best suits them. So for their sake no less than his, it is better to look elsewhere unless they have the patience to wait a few years before making such a firm and final decision. For every teacher will naturally possess his own notion of the qualifications for discipleship which he values most and seeks most. He always places more stress upon deep loyalty than upon any other virtue. He would not even mind so much that his students should drink alcoholic liquor to excess as that they would fail him in this regard. Fidelity is the finest of virtues in his eyes. Disciples who lack this will soon be dropped. But if he asks for loyalty he does not ask for slavishness. He will be perfectly satisfied to be taken for an ordinary mortal without being turned into a perfect, unerring god. He is the last man to wish to be set up for what he is not. Nor will he demand from anyone that blind servility which does duty with most aspirants in place of the genuine loyalty that ought to be offered. Externally and formally, however, there is nothing to stop anyone meanwhile from appointing himself, if he so wishes, a student—mentally, secretly, and internally. For discipleship is self-created by the mental attitude of devotion which by reaction spontaneously brings him interior help. He will not then really need the external signs of acceptance.

610

He will be handicapped to some extent by a consciousness of the difficulty of securing adequate loyalty to a teacher who refuses to surround himself with all the paraphernalia of ashrams and all the trappings of guru-worship—both of which are repugnant to him. There are excellent reasons in the student's own interest—and perhaps to some degree in the teacher's, too—why in this case such personal loyalty must be emphatically insisted on. The pupil's allegiance will sooner or later be subjected to the unexpected strain of severe tests. The adept possesses far too sensitive a temperament and far too strong an independence to endure with indifference the telepathic reflections of this strain, which are invariably produced when the relationship effectively exists with the profound obligations on both sides which it entails. He may be philosophic enough to smile at misunderstanding or desertion but he will also be human enough to be sensitive to them. For even were a student to break with him he could never break with the student. His own conception of loyalty embraces a wider stretch than the frail seekers are likely to understand. Some indeed have been so deceived by the compulsions of personal karma and the logic of mere appearances as to imagine that he is devoid of human sympathy and indifferent to human feelings.

611

The Master is well aware of the bitter and painful lessons the aspirant must learn before attaining maturity and balance, and wishes it were possible to stretch out a helping hand. During these difficult times, outer lines of communication should be kept open for they are helpful and, indeed, are necessary until the individual becomes sufficiently intuitive. The Master never closes the inner lines, but they need maintenance on both sides if they are to be effective.

612

He may wonder why he receives so little direct help and personal encouragement from his teacher during the first few years of their relationship. He has to reach a certain point in his mental development first and this cannot be until he has experienced events which are like tests.

613

For anyone to try to lose his personality in someone else's, even in a guru's, is a desertion of his own divine powers. Nevertheless, in the case of beginners it cannot be helped—where they are seeking a guru's assistance. But the sooner the guru makes them ready or instructs them to stop this practice and to lose their personality in their own higher self, the better for them. It is a question of direction. In merging in someone else's personality they are going outside of themselves; in merging in their own higher being they are going inside.

614

In Pythagoras' school at Crotona, the pupils passed through a series of three grades, and were not allowed personal contact with Pythagoras himself until they reached the highest or third grade.

615

If the Master had no patience with his disciples, he and they would soon part. If he had no belief in their eventual evolution, he and they would never join.

616

If a man has hitched the wagon of his spiritual effort to the star of a competent and worthy spiritual guide, it is nonsensical to object that he surrenders his freedom whenever he surrenders his own personal judgement to the guide's or even whenever he obeys a command from the guide. For who chose the guide? He, himself. By the exercise of what faculty did he make such a choice? By the exercise of free will. Therefore the initial act was a free choice. It was also the most important one because it was causal, all his other acts as a disciple being merely its effects, however long be the chain which extends from it. It is because he respects the larger wisdom of the guide and trusts his disinterestedness that the disciple follows him in thought and practice, not because he has become a puppet.

617

The aspirant who believes that he can come to a master for a few days or weeks and glean the teaching will glean only a sample of it. It will take him all his life not only to receive what a master knows but to be adjudged worthy of and ready for it. If he lacks this patience and humility, he will fall into self-deception.

618

Plato has pointed out in his seventh epistle that the philosophical wisdom "requires long continued communion between pupil and teacher in joint pursuit of the object they are seeking to understand, and then suddenly, just as light flashes forth when a fire is kindled, this wisdom is born in the mind and henceforth nourishes itself."

619

Two such individuals as Master and student are linked together by ancient ties. Much may remain to be done in the future as it was in the past. If, in a previous incarnation, the student attained a higher phase of development than at present, this must again be achieved before results can appear in consciousness. In such a case he should work especially hard to make progress.

620

In the earlier stages of their relation, the disciple needs to attach himself more and more closely to the Master. He is still learning what the quest is, still weak-willed, uncertain, and undeveloped. But in the later stages he should release his hold on the master, discipline his feelings, and let go of what has become so dear to him. For now he should increasingly depend on making for himself the direct contact with his higher Self. (Memo to P.B.: use this para as the key to rewriting essay on spiritual self-reliance.)

621

He should constantly look forward to the time when he will be independent enough to steer his own course. It is not meant that he should be left with nothing but his ignorance and weakness to guide him, nor that he should face all his perplexities by himself, but that he should face many or most of them as he can and that he should carry to the teacher only those which seem too hard to understand or bear. The teacher may occasionally intervene to help on his own initiative but only if and when he deems it desirable and necessary to do so. In this way the object will be fulfilled of leading the disciple to increasingly correct thinking and more careful behaviour.

622

It is naturally strongly repugnant to a developed mind to allow another to have such great power over his own, whereas it is strongly attractive to an undeveloped one.

623

Excessive guru-worship provokes a reaction, a critical, sometimes sceptical attitude from which there must also be a recoil. Only after that can an honourable, honest, and true relationship be established. He should rather object to anyone's making a cult out of him. Why not respect his wish and let him remain what he is—a researcher?

624

Faith in the master is the first step, obedience to his injunctions is the next one, devotion toward him is the third step, and remembrance of his presence, name, or image is the fourth. Such following of the master and practice of his teachings will bring his graces.

625

Those whose temperament is innately submissive and dependent make better disciples than the others. But they are less likely to advance farther than the others.

626

But if the teacher must have the capacity to point out the right way, the student, in his turn, must have the capacity to travel every step of it in thought with him.

627

There are some tremendously difficult problems involved in the highest Quest. The key to these problems must be placed in his hands by the teacher. The wisest plan for him, therefore, is to work out in detail and patiently the few hints given by the teacher, to study the books suggested and to plod on the path doggedly, thinking of it as a period of patient preparation for the karmic time when he will assuredly receive what he is seeking. This he will get if he has the right mental equipment, if he has expressed the desire for guidance in the right quarters, and also if he recognizes the necessity of serving humanity.

628

If a teacher must put into finite phrases every communication from his inner being to a pupil, if he must use material means for every transmission of his own thought, then the man is not yet ready to be a disciple.

629

The disciple who has to depend on constantly receiving letters from his teacher is ready only for inferior teachers. The disciple who imagines that, because the teacher has not written him for two or three years, he is no longer interested in helping the disciple or has forgotten him or is disappointed in him is utterly mistaken.

630

If he becomes so dependent that every problem as it arises is at once put before the teacher for solution, the consequence will eventually be an utter helplessness before all problems. The capacities for independent judgement, for taking the initiative, for showing creativeness and forming decisions, will decay and even disappear.

631

Becoming a satellite and revolving around a guru may be beneficial to a man. But the harm begins when this revolution becomes a permanent one, so that he is never again able to move into a fresh orbit and fulfil the evolutionary intention secreted within his own being.

632

It is absolutely indispensable for the disciples to learn how to live their own lives.

633

The guide must not only be competent to do what he proposes to do, but the disciple also must be qualified to take advantage of it.

634

"Rare is the true disciple," says an old Asiatic text.

635

It is better to have a few earnest students who willingly work hard for their self-improvement than a mass of students who do nothing more than read books and talk among themselves.

636

The kind of student he likes to see, but unfortunately rarely does see, blends a fine moral character with good intelligence and sound practicality, all topped by profound mystical intuition and a proper sense of reverence. Such a one is thoroughly dependable and reliable, his words are not the mere froth of emotion to be quickly forgotten.

637

When a seeker's determination to follow the quest becomes tough enough not to be deviated by adversity or by luxury, he is ready for a teacher.

638

This eagerness to become a disciple and learn truth is the first necessary qualification. Without it nothing can be done; with it everything will come naturally in automatic response from the Overself.

639

It is not enough that the would-be pupil is ripe. He must also be able easily to enter completely into sympathetic relationship with the particular teacher to whom he applies.

640

Reverence for the master is based on the belief that the Overself is working through him. Any lack of this quality deprives the disciple of available help.

641

He must first feel humble before the master's high achievement.

642

The would-be disciple must supply faith and loyalty, obedience and practice, along with the aspiration which brings him to the teacher.

643

If a hearer receives the master's words with joy, that is one indication that he is ready.

644

When he entrusts himself to a teacher's care he should cultivate patience and not seek immediate results. It is a serious matter to break away from a teacher and it should not be done in haste or it may bring bad results.

645

It is not necessary to display frenzied fervour in order to be a devoted disciple.

646

If the disciple feels personally humiliated or becomes hysterically tearful at the teacher's well-meant fair and constructive criticisms, he is not only suffering needlessly but also rejecting the expert help for which he came to the teacher, even though the form it takes is unexpected and disagreeable. Good advice is still good even when unpalatable.

647

Nobody need remain long puzzled if he will come humbly and converse frankly with his teacher in any difficulty, instead of proposing to regard himself as fit and qualified to sit in judgement upon his teacher. His humility will always be met by kindness and his frankness by an equal frankness. The teacher is ever ready to help him clear up these difficulties, but he is not ready to assist any to the slightest degree who come with a mind already prejudiced to distrust, or who do not come at all but assume their fitness to understand the teacher or his doctrine prior to initiation and acceptance.

648

A genuine teacher who is sincere, competent, kindly, and illumined will know this truth—that groups of the same grade reincarnate together—and, knowing it, will himself expect and accept only his "own." For if, through sentimental soft-heartedness, he yields to the importunities of those who are not in inner harmony with him, then either the flow of events or the disharmony of the student will break the relation and separate them. Similarly, an earnest aspirant who feels that his inner life belongs to a particular teacher will, if he is wise, desist from making experiments or from wandering to other hearths, and remain loyal to this teacher. For if, through emotional enthusiasms or through misunderstandings arising from his own limitations, he strays elsewhere, then the ultimate sense of inner dissatisfaction or the unexpected pressure of outer disillusionment will turn his feet homeward again.

649

The seeker who has found the path proper to him and the teacher in affinity with him should waste no more time in the experimental investigations of other paths, other teachings, and other teachers. If he is to get the full benefit of his association he must remain absolutely loyal to his guide. If he is to make the quickest progress in the shortest time, he must cease wandering about and remain on the chosen path until he arrives at its goal.

650

If in the beginning he is to cast his net so widely as to search for truth in every corner, in the middle of his course he is to narrow his world until he has no ear for anyone else except his teacher. Only so can concentration be achieved. In the beginning, width; in the middle, depth.

651

The belief of ignorant seekers that by visiting a number of teachers they will accumulate a stock of knowledge and help, is sheer self-deception: on the contrary, they will end in confusion. A disciple may study the teachings and follow the practices of masters other than his own without harm provided first, that they are not discordant with the latter's and second, that his sense of personal loyalty is not weakened.

652

It is permissible to have various teachers for lesser subjects, including Yoga, but is impermissible to follow more than one Master in the Quest of Higher Truth.

653

If it be true that a man cannot desert this Quest without being forced back onto it by life itself sooner or later, it is also true that he cannot desert the Master of the Quest without having to return to him sooner or later. For just as pursuance of the Quest will become inseparable from the happiness that he seeks, so devotion to the Master will become inseparable from the salvation upon which that happiness depends. Why this should be so is one of the mysterious workings of Destiny which can only be illuminated when and if it be possible to illuminate the earth lives of his far past.

654

The Master says to a straying one: "I take you into my heart. You are now my accepted pupil. But profit by the lessons of the past mistakes made by you and remain resolutely with me. Whether you return only in heart or also in body, is not of material consequence to me, but it will be to you."

655

Although guidance and teaching from other sources should be gladly welcomed as enrichment or supplement, as completion or rounding-out, the inner affinity is so personal, so intimate, so deeply felt, that no one else is really able to take the place of the karmically destined guru.

656

The aspirant must not seek counsel from anyone other than the teacher, or he may be unwittingly led to a path which, while permissible for others, would be inadvisable for him.

657

Many aspirants are volatile in their loyalty and mercurial in their beliefs. They change gurus as they change clothes and denude themselves of earlier teachings when new ones appear. However there may be some good in this as well as bad. If they change from an inferior to a more advanced guru, or from an imposter to a knowledgeable person, or from a commonplace platitudinous belief to a superior and original one, obviously the change is for the better. In this way they may in the end and during many years study several facets of the truth. Others simply move from one phantasy to another.

658

Where a teacher genuinely derives his authority from the higher self, reverence and obedience, love and respect should surely be his deserts.

659

Of all the many forms of work which a man can find to do, of all the several ways in which his active functions can express themselves, there is none higher than this, that he guide men out of illusion into reality. It is not wrong therefore to give his office great reverence and himself great devotion.

660

Our debt to these spiritual teachers is unpayable. This is because that which directs the body is more important in the end than the body itself.

661

We ought to be grateful and respectful to *all* those great lights of the race who brought it truth, whether they be dead or alive, Occidental or Oriental. Yet at the same time we ought to be specially grateful and specially respectful to the particular one who brought us to see the truth more than any other did.

662

The Very Reverend W.R. Inge has rightly pointed out that Christ chose his twelve apostles not only because they were naturally and extremely religious men but also because they were loyal enough and brave enough to live and die for their Master.

663

Few are ready to pay the entrance fee of lifelong loyalty and steadfast service which are demanded, for this payment must be made in actual practice and not in lip movements alone.

664

The disciple should trust and walk unwaveringly at the Master's side even when understanding cannot keep pace, and his fine loyalty should shine out like Sirius in the sky.

665

The quality which will endear him most to the teacher, and which will carry him farthest on the Quest, is loyalty. Yet this same good quality will be the biggest obstacle in the way of the seeker who is so gullible, so superficial, and so poor in judgement as to attach himself to an unworthy or incompetent teacher.

666

To find many candidates for discipleship is easy but to find a few disciples is hard. There is much enthusiasm over a newly gained master, but little sustained loyalty to an old one.

667

Unthinking mystics still praise this quality of servile obedience which primitive gurus demanded from their followers. Thoughtful mystics no longer do so.

668

A guide who can understand his disciple's character and stimulate his intelligence, who can open to him the gates of higher worlds and newer views, does not need to hold him by the bonds of blind obedience.

669

Without a passive and humble attitude of the mind, a devotional and reverent feeling of the heart, the profits of meeting a man who has come close to the soul are largely missed. Criticism erects a barrier.

670

To listen properly to a guru, is not to bring in the ego with its interpretations. To read correctly from an inspired guru's book is to keep out the common tendency to put in one's own personal meanings. In short, let the mind Be Still and know the Truth!

671

It would be useless to place oneself under the guidance of a teacher if one were not prepared to obey him.

672

"You are full of your own opinions," said a modern Japanese master to an inquiring intellectual. "How can I show you Zen? First empty your cup."

673

If the master's exposure of his weaknesses is offensive to him, then he unfits himself for further discipleship and will receive no further advice.

674

When a man who is still in his pupilage deems himself to be wiser than his master, he is being led astray by the cunning flattery of his ego.

675

If this stimulation by contact with a master makes him assert his little ego, because he thinks he has become more "spiritual" than others, then the good done him and the inspiration given him are endangered by the conceit bred in him.

676

If a man is strongly egoistic and arrogantly self-opinionated, if he lacks humility even when he approaches a Master, then not only can he not follow the path but he must circle around looking for its gate. Such a man, uneducable and unteachable, is unfit for the path of discipleship. Life is the only teacher he is ready for. It is intelligent enough to bring him exactly the kind of experiences he needs—crushing disappointments, frustrations, humiliations, and disasters.

677

If the disciple does not obey the regime laid down by the teacher but follows his own ideas as to what he ought to do, then he is not truly surrendering his ego, but is thereby showing his attachment to the ego. Consequently he will not get the hoped-for results. When disappointment follows he should not blame the ineffectiveness of his teacher for this but rather his own obstinate egotism.

678

The teacher has an immense task when he is asked by the ordinary seeker to accept him as a personal pupil. For the latter unconsciously seeks confirmation of what he already believes and therefore has come to teach the teacher! Consequently the master is compelled to refuse him. For the seeker comes to him filled with his own ideas of what constitutes truth and in what direction the path leads, what the teacher ought to say and how behave. All these modes of thought are mere encumbrances from the teacher's standpoint, and all these prejudices are heavy shackles. To ask the seeker to abandon these obsessions with the past immediately will meet with failure in almost every case—only in the rarest type of seeker is there likely to be an immediate obedience. With others there is not even the desire for release from these intellectual and emotional patterns which imprison the man, these habit-mechanisms in which he has allowed himself to be caught.

679

While waiting to find a trustworthy spiritual guide, the best thing to do in the meantime is to constantly discipline his character and endeavour to gain inner tranquillity so as to provide improved conditions for the reception of Grace. Let him search out the defects of character and exert himself to get rid of them. Let him examine his life every day and see where he has done well and where he has failed in this matter.

680

Too many aspirants waste their time in trying to follow the path of discipleship when they possess too little qualification even to permit their entry. They are unprepared. It would be more profitable for them to bestow upon the improvement of their own psyche the thought they bestow upon the quest of a master.

681

If a man insists on asking for the attentions of a personal teacher before he is sufficiently prepared to benefit by them, then his rash importunity will be punished. For he will find a false teacher, a guide to untruth and darkness rather than to reality and light. Enough work should have been done on himself and by himself in mental and emotional discipline, in moral striving, in intellectual preparation, and in meditational practice to justify his request for instruction. Otherwise he may be really actuated by egoistic ambitions which are secretly hiding beneath his spiritual aspirations, or he may be too unbalanced emotionally to accept in his heart the serene impersonal wisdom even when it is proffered him.

682

Even if there are no adepts who could give the necessary inner assistance to quicker progress on the Path, this need not deter him from continuing efforts towards spiritual realization and thus making himself ready for a guide when Destiny permits him to have one. The inner work which he alone can perform consists in the unremitting efforts to develop a high moral character, together with religious aspiration and mystical contemplation. The ideal of altruistic service should also be held in mind, combined with intelligent judgement and practicality.

683

Despite the absence of a teacher, it is still possible to intensify his efforts. His surroundings offer part of the material for study; his personal history can be explored for a greater awareness of the meanings of his past and present experiences; and every situation offers an opportunity for a more objective observation of himself.

684

Continuous and honest effort in self-study and self-observation, an objective analysis of past and present experiences when subjected to the light of higher understanding, daily practice in meditation, and an ever-present attitude of faith and devotion certainly will improve the student's possibilities for the opportunity of meeting with the Master.

685

Instead of searching vainly for a teacher or waiting idly for one, he should take the teaching he already has, follow the injunctions already laid down, use the knowledge already available.

686

Students who fail to do the work on themselves yet look for a master, waste their time.

687

Work on oneself is most important. When one has purified his character, cultivated discrimination, achieved some measure of balance, finally understood the lessons of past experience, acquired a certain degree of self-control—mental, moral, and physical—and developed the necessary aspiration to lead a truly spiritual life, then, and then only, will he be in a position to benefit from instruction from a Master.

688

It would be well if young aspirants would take a sufficiently long time in a general survey course in comparative religion and metaphysics before they settle down to some kind of a choice. They should first come to such a clearness.

689

The badly balanced, the wildly hysterical, the unadjusted and unintegrated personality, the neurotically self-centered, should not trouble a teacher for higher development when they have yet to attend to, and finish, their ordinary development as human beings. They have not the right to claim entry on a path which demands so much character and capacity from its very beginning.

690

Most of the aspirants who want to associate themselves with a master do so prematurely. Consequently they fail to find him or else find only pseudo-masters. What they really need is to associate themselves with a psychological counsellor or with a broad-minded wise clergyman, with someone who has effected a good solution of his own personal, emotional, and relational problems and is competent to help them solve theirs. Only after his work is done, only after he has cleared the way for a higher activity, only after he has prepared them to respond readily to the guidance of a master, should they seek such a one.

691

It is needful at times to remind a man that he—and not those to whom he has entrusted his soul and spiritual destiny—is responsible for it. The belief that he has passed on its care is illusory.

692

It is not the teacher who can sever the disciple's attachment to worldly life, for a man's heart is his own most intimate, most private possession. The disciple must do it for himself. It is *he* who must realize the necessity of renunciation and it is he alone who must change his feelings accordingly. Such a change requires constant thinking about values and incessant disciplining of tendencies. Who else but the disciple is to think these thoughts and exercise this will if the result is to be shown in his character? The teacher cannot really help him in any vicarious sense, cannot save him from the stern task of working upon himself.

693

The reason why the master cannot remake another man miraculously is because no man can think for another one. Each can do it for himself alone.

694

We must gain our advancement through our own personal efforts and by our own merits. No master can do our walking for us nor hide our weaknesses from the inexorable laws which govern the quest. Flattery helps little. It is the duty of the guide clearly to perceive and frankly to expose to the disciple the evil parts of his character and the weak places of his consciousness.

695

He may give the correct technique but he cannot give its ineffable result. That, you must earn for and by yourself. He cannot even promise you a successful outcome of your own endeavours. That is bestowed only by the grace of God.

696

"No one can purify another," asserted the Buddha.

697

No master can or will do for a man what he is quite unwilling to do for himself.

698

No master can take away from a disciple his failings and weaknesses.

699

No man can really be responsible for another man: each makes, and must accept, his own karma.

700

Even in the ancient Egyptian mysteries, the disciple who attended the college temple after having successfully passed the initial test which gave him entry had to learn this same lesson of self-reliance. Edouard Schure, the French writer on this subject, says: "He was left much to himself, so that he might *become* rather than merely know, and so he was often surprised at his teacher's coldness and indifference. To his anxious queries came the reply: 'Wait and work.' Doubts came to him at times, frightful suspicions of his teachers, but they would pass."

701

It is impossible for any proclaimed master to give lasting illumination to any disciple, however fervent, since it is impossible for the latter to establish completeness of development and the balance which follows it automatically, except by his own inner activity.

702

Despite all delusions to the contrary, no master can pick up a disciple and transfer him at a jump to the goal—permanently.

703

In the presence of an illumined man, we have the chance to become different for a while, to reflect some of his light into ourselves. But the reflected light, being borrowed, will fade away. We cannot find exemption from the labours necessary to generate our own merely because we have found association with someone whose own labours are finished.

704

No one can teach you how to realize your own true being, that is, no one except yourself, for the realization has to be yours. The revelation leading to it will have to be yours, too, and the understanding which will lead up to the revelation comes from your own effort. This is why I often say that it is an exaggeration on the part of the Indians to say that salvation is impossible without a master. He may help us to correct our thinking, encourage and inspire us, but the work has to be done by ourselves. No master can give the full realization to another person—impossible.

705

Spiritual awareness is not like a landed estate which can be handed down as an heirloom to another. Those who want it must create it for themselves.

706

This consciousness cannot be got from another man by transfer (although its presence in him may be felt by sensitivity) but only by one's own hard toil.

707

The right action done in the wrong way becomes wrong in itself. Although it is right to look towards a teacher for guidance and inspiration throughout the course of his quest, it is wrong to become over-dependent on that teacher.

708

People approach the saint-type primarily to get what is called in India a *darshan*. This may be variously translated as a glimpse, a spoken blessing, a sight, a view, an initiation, or a silent benediction. He is a phenomenon and they stand at a distance to gaze at him, to admire him, or to be overwhelmed with awe by him. The few minutes or days or weeks or months or years taken up—the duration is immaterial for extension in time does not change the nature of the happening—leave the devotee with the same character, the same consciousness that he had before the meeting. Its service is to portray the goal, not to bring him nearer to perfection in any way. The delusion that the longer they stay with him the farther they travel on the road to perfection remains a delusion still. The *darshan* leaves them with their weaknesses and faults, their egoism and animality un-touched. The work of getting rid of these things is *theirs* to undertake and no *darshan*-magic can be a substitute for it.

709

The belief that a guru will do for him once and for all what in the end he has to do for himself belongs to the untutored masses and the sectarian mystic circles.

710

Only the self-deceived or the charlatanic will offer to save you. All others will offer only to guide you. "You must labour for yourselves," warned the Buddha. "The Buddhas are only teachers."

711

It is the common way to demand entry into enlightenment through someone else. This renders it needful to make clear that nobody, not even the best of gurus, can bestow final and lasting realization—a glimpse is the most he can possibly pass on and there are not many with that capacity. Even in such cases, his disciples must work diligently and win it them-selves.

712

The services of a spiritual director in correcting errors, providing in-struction, stimulating aspiration, and fostering intuition are immense; but they are only a prelude to the services a student must render to himself.

713

Those who leave their spiritual future totally in the hands of their guide, lose the years which could be spent in developing themselves.

714

It is not enough to receive a teaching from someone else. The truth of the teaching must be tested by personal experience, the worth of it should be measured by personal knowledge.

715

It is the guide's duty to hold up a lamp on a dark path but the disciple must decide for himself the speed and distance of the journey along that path. No command is laid upon him, for it is he who must estimate the strength within him and the opportunity without. He is given full freedom in making his decision. It is unfortunately the case that many emotionally unstable persons are attracted to mysticism, with the result that they spend years with their dreams of mystical achievements but do nothing to convert those dreams into realities, or else flit from one dream to another.

716

If the student responds sufficiently to the hints given him or the counsel bestowed on him, the teacher will be encouraged to go farther.

717

The teacher can only help one to help himself. *Ultimately* it will be by his own efforts alone that the student uncovers the wisdom and beauty he is seeking—and which are even now within him. Such efforts, in order to be successful, must be courageous and continuous: repeated failures should serve only to stimulate deeper determination.

718

In the end each seeker has to become his own teacher by putting all his experience, his beliefs, his ideas, to the test.

719

It is possible to bring this truth within the mind's sight but not within the will's reach; in this matter each man must do his own work. Whoever offers him a free redemption plays God.

720

The disciple will learn in the end, by experience, that he must look to himself alone for salvation. The last words of the dying Buddha, addressed though they were to his own disciples, have been a useful guide to me: "Look not for refuge to anyone besides yourselves."

721

Do not be satisfied with being a disciple. Try to become like the master.

722

If you wish, call it self-making—this process of using one's own mental powers, one's own emotional energies, to actualize the new being that is his best self. It does not seek like a mendicant for free transformation by another person, a guru. It makes use of the highest kind of imagination, a deeply relaxed suggestive visualization. Whatever is called for to bring on enlightenment exists within himself already, but it is latent and undeveloped. By study, exercise, and practice the aspirant can be his own teacher. Sooner or later he will have to take this work into his own hands. The notion that someone else can or will do it all for him is delusory, the belief that a guru can absolve his duty is adolescent wishful thinking. If the result is to have any lasting value, it must be self-wrought or in the end the aspirant will have to start again, use this approach, and throw away the negative thought that he is helpless without someone else who must be sought and found. The kind of teacher who is really useful will put no emphasis upon himself but upon the aspirant's own work, and then see him at intervals only. Once the materials needed are pointed out, the student should teach himself; and this he can do only through self-practice.

723

You must play the teacher to yourself. He cannot tread the path for you: you must walk and work by your own effort. The mother cannot grow up on behalf of the child, no matter how greatly she loves it. The adept cannot do your growing-up for you. Nature's laws must prevail. He has shown you the way: use your will to follow it. But devote a little time each day to keeping open the channel of communication with him and thus receive his impetus, his inspiration to help you. So although you must strive by your own use of free will, do not imagine that you need strive unaided.

724

Working along the line that the teacher found suitable for himself, slavishly and artificially trying to produce a copy of him, will in the end not even produce that but a caricature instead. For only the teacher's bodily acts will be imitated; his Spirit is invisible and therefore cannot be imitated.

725

Why should anyone copy another's artwork? Why should Whistler paint pictures in the same way that Gainsborough did? Whistler remained loyal to his own conceptions. Why then, going further, copy another's lifestyle? We may honour a master's inspiration but yet express our own in our individual way.

726

It is true that followers have no right to burden the teacher with their personal problems, that they should learn manfully to shoulder their difficulties and not pass them on to him. Yet human nature is weak, the teacher kindly. What they may do without taxing his strength is to place the problem before him in a prayer, thought, or meditation silently, and not in letter or interview. If they will keep their distresses, troubles, or indecisions to themselves in *this* way, such reticence will not be to their loss. It is indeed a sign of neuroticism when an aspirant plagues a teacher too frequently or on too trivial matters. Such conduct is quite suited to children but not to adults. It reveals too egocentric a person, one who is unwilling to bring the stage of novice to an end because the dependence on another person is more comforting and much easier than endeavouring to settle his own little problems.

727

Too many disciples commit the fault of being too demanding and too possessive in their attitude towards the teacher. In the end they become a burden, a liability, or even a nuisance to him. They ought to give him devotion, yes; they ought to think often of him for inspiration and guidance; but they ought not to turn themselves into emotional parasites who are unable to live on their own vitality at all.

728

The eagerness to surrender every responsibility, every decision, every care to a spiritual guide—which is so prominent in India—is only praiseworthy in some cases. In others, it is neurotic and infantile, an attempt to secure indulgent pity, protection, and gregarious support despite the fact that childhood has been physically outgrown. To take it as a sign of advancement, and to use it as an excuse to evade pressing work of self-reform and self-discipline, is deplorable.

729

A calm trust in the man's leadership is one thing, but a hysterical clinging devotion to his personality is another.

730

He who turns himself into a burden to his teacher by shirking his own responsibilities and throwing them on his teacher, is being selfish as well as weak.

731

Whoever does not understand that the guide must lead him to where he will seek his own way, will go on endlessly looking for teachers, one after the other, or else become a spiritual hypochondriac, a semi-invalid needing the guru-doctor to dance constantly in attendance on his ego-centered symptoms.

732

It may be that the effort to imitate his master will enable the disciple to excel himself.

733

If you are willing to accept the gift of Grace, which a true teacher is forever bearing, through your prior willingness to give him your faith and devotion, and to give it not because he wants it or anything else for himself but because he is a purified channel for your own Overself's power, then you may expect to see the past wiped out as sins are forgiven and the future made brighter as new energies are born in you.

Cultivating the inner link

734

The way of discipleship means that there is to be constant endeavour to live in the master's mental atmosphere. Of course this can be done very feebly and only occasionally at first. Success depends not only on the pressure of perseverance but also on the sensitivity to thought-trans-ference.

735

The aspirant who comes into the presence of someone who functions on a high moral and mystical or philosophical level—and feels the attraction, charm, spell, influence, or force of his personality—can, after a sufficient time or association, be stimulated in development quite markedly. It is the case not only of benefiting by the other man's words and copying his example, but also of directly experiencing the telepathic working of mind upon mind.

736

If they believe in the genuineness and reality of telepathy—as they must if they believe in philosophy at all—then they must accept our declaration that inner communion renders unnecessary the outer communion, that the sense of inner presence of the guide renders unnecessary his letters, visits, and other external signs.

737

We know that the mind can both project and receive thoughts. Telepathy becomes more and more a scientifically recognized fact. Where affinity harmony and preparation exist, the spiritual guide can project calming, uplifting, and spiritualizing mental waves to the spiritual aspirant.

738

The silent wordless and unprepared hypnosis of a subject is a factual pointer to the understanding of the silent wordless and telepathic influ-ence of a disciple by his guide. As the power of suggestion becomes dynamic in the hypnotist, so its higher octave, the power of grace, be-comes dynamic in the spiritual guide.

739

That mental waves can be transmitted from master to disciple, that spiritual peace can be reflected from the mind of one to the mind of the other, is not merely a new theory but really an old practice. It has been known and done in the Orient for thousands of years.

740

The master's work is carried on by word-of-mouth, by written statement, and by personal example. But it cannot end with these methods, for they are all external ones. So it is continued by telepathic impulses, by inspirational impact, and by mental osmosis. These are internal ones.

741

Such communication between the teacher and student might be called "Telementation."

742

The Master may add his spiritual vitality or inspiration temporarily to the disciple's by merely wishing him well. If this is done during the Master's prayer or meditation, the disciple's subconscious will spontaneously pick up the telepathically projected flow and sooner or later bring it into consciousness. If, however, something more precise and more positive is required, he may consciously will and focus it to the disciple while both are in a state of meditation at the same time.

743

The projected ideas and concentrated thoughts of a man who has made a permanent connection with his Overself are powerful enough to affect beneficently the inner life of other men. But even here nature requires the latter to establish their own inner connection with him in turn. And this can be done only by the right mental attitude of trust and devotion.

744

The conscious personal mind of the teacher may know nothing of the help that is radiating from him to one who silently calls on him from a long distance, yet the reality of that help remains.

745

This internal quickening and intense telepathy between the master and the disciple can only occur if the requisite conditions exist.

746

Even at the beginning of probation the seeker will often be given a hint of what awaits him later through mystical experience resulting out of the contact with the teacher. But whether he gets it or not, from the moment of acceptance there will come to every student a sense of peace, and above all, an inner stability and certitude which will become one of the greatest assets in his life.

747
Again and again the novice falls into mistakes about the telepathic communications which he feels he is receiving from the master. He regards them as such when they are nothing of the sort, or he interprets them in too material or too egoistic a manner. The master sends a thought-current to him which is intended to lift him up to a diviner, hence more impersonal level. He, however, drags it down to a lower, more egocentric level.

748
The telepathic impulses which he sends out to others during these times of prayer or meditation are most often received quite subconsciously. Only later is their effect felt or their origin suspected. His disciples may not be aware of any new reception of truth or beatitude at the time. But increasing clarification or growing liberation may slowly change their course.

749
It is also possible to take any revered person as a master and, in one's own mind, make him the teacher. Even though no meeting on the physical level may occur, one's attitude of attention and devotion in meditation will draw from him a reaction which will telepathically give whatever guidance is needed at the time.

750
Just as the glance, the touch, or the spoken word may carry the ardour of mutual desire from man to woman so may it also carry the initiatory blessing or the spiritual gift from master to disciple.

751
Like the message of the Overself to a meditating mystic, the help which comes from such a teacher is above thinking but it translates itself into terms of thinking. In this process of translation, it is seized on by the ego and interfered with.

752
The guide may send his blessing telepathically only once but if it is powerful enough it may work itself out through a hundred different experiences extending over several years. Because he identifies himself with the timeless spaceless soul, his blessing may express itself anywhere in space and anywhen in time. Moreover he may formulate it in a general way but it may take precise shapes unconsciously fashioned by and suited to the recipient's own mentality and degree of development.

753
Some critics reject the idea of Grace and declare its impossibility in a world governed by strict cause and effect. The meaning of the word suggests something or anything of an immaterial moral or material nature

that is given to man. Why should not the Master who has attained a higher strength wisdom and moral character than that which is common to the human race, give aid freely out of his beneficent compassion for others struggling to climb the peak he has surmounted? He certainly cannot transmit his own inner life to another person in its fullness. But he can certainly impart something of its quality and flavour to one who is receptive, sensitive, and in inward affinity with him. If this too is denied then let the objector explain why both the feeling of and the sense of the Master's presence pervade the disciple's existence for many years after his initiation, if not for the rest of his life.

754

The master, by a process of telepathic transfer, enables the disciple to get a glimpse of what the realization of his own spiritual possibilities can lead to.

755

The pupil who has been allowed to sit in meditation with a master should be able to carry on with this impetus, even though it happened only once. It is really an initiation.

756

During this initiation meditation, the disciple may actually feel a stream of power flowing out to him from the master, but it is not essential that he do so.

757

What the master reflects and radiates into the disciple's deeper mind at this sitting, will necessarily incubate for a period of time which may be measurable in minutes, days, months, or even years. No one can predict how long it will be, for not only are the disciple's readiness, capacity, and affinity determining factors but also his destiny. Nor can anyone predict whether the result will appear slowly, gently, little by little, or suddenly, with violent jolting force.

758

The master is forever after present in the disciple's heart, whether the disciple sees him again or not.

759

From the hour of this initiation the master will be much in his thoughts and the sense of affinity will be often in his heart.

760

The experience which the candidate has at the initiatory meditation with the master is often (but not always) a herald and token of his possibilities of later attainment under this particular master.

761

He must work harder than ever on his character and, by crushing his ego, sensitize his mind for the reception of the spiritual Grace that is to come during initiation.

762

It seems as if the Master has come into his consciousness and thereby changed its quality and area. If the change is necessarily for a brief while only, it is still a memorable one.

763

The number of meetings needed with the initiator into meditation will naturally differ in different cases.

764

When he tells the candidate of some great truth, looking straight into his face, something may happen over and behind the mere words.

765

A look from Jesus was enough to make some men renounce their worldly lives and follow him. Such is initiation through the glance.

766

The power which lies in a pen is only intellectual, thought carried from one mind to another. But the power which shone out of his eyes was spiritual, beyond thought. Gaze met gaze throughout that period; mine blinking and flickering often, the rishee's never once faltering. There are some lines of an American Seer which I would like to wind around this evening of which I am writing. They occur in the essay on "Behavior" by the inspired American optimist. Emerson's words run: "The eyes indicate the antiquity of the soul. What inundation of life and thought is discharged from one soul into another, through them. The glance is natural magic. The mysterious communication established across a house between two entire strangers, moves all the springs of wonder. . . . The eyes will not lie but make faithful confession what inhabitant is there." I verified the truth of these sage words to the full. And since mine was a feeble and stunted growth, it gave way and was overpowered by that of the other man.

767

The aspirant who wishes to become the student of a particular teacher must remember that, should he be accepted, he will receive no formal *outward* acknowledgment of the fact. This is because the way to find a Master is invariably an *inner* process. When the student has developed the necessary moral qualifications and mental receptivity, the Master's presence will be inwardly felt and recognized. Once this has been experienced, he will find that simple devotion and adherence to the path the Master points out—and to himself as a symbol of that path—is all that is needed to ensure progress. Thus, the student finally realizes that all outer teachers, all paths and initiations are mere theatrics compared with this.

768

The true master does not call disciples to reside in any ashram but to unite with himself. And he is, in his own sight, a mental and not a physical being. Hence they can find and meet him in thought anywhere. The necessity of living in an ashram with him is an illusory one. All that is requisite is a single meeting between him and the disciple. Physically such a meeting can achieve its purpose in a few minutes. Thereafter both may remain permanently apart physically and yet the inner work can continue to develop all the same. For the relation between them is primarily a mental, not a physical one. Even in ordinary life we see that true friendship and true love is mental affinity and not a mere neighbourhood of fleshly bodies. The disciple's intense faith in and emotional veneration for the master, however far distant they may be from each other, plus the necessary mystical ripeness, will telepathically create true association. But without them, his grace is like a spark falling on stone, not on tinder. Furthermore, by the higher powers of his mind, the adept can really help devotees at a distance even though they may never attend his ashram. Those who live in an ashram can get from him only what they can absorb in their inner being. But precisely the same can be done by those who do not live in one. His thought-presence will be found by them to be just as effectual as his bodily presence.

769

As the disciple is slowly led onwards along this difficult path, confidence in the teacher is replaced by consciousness of the teacher, that is, he finds as an inner presence the mental atmosphere of the teacher and thus comes to know him much better.

770

The tie with such a master sustains him in many a dark experience.

771

A wise teacher imposes no dogmas upon his pupils; the latter may believe or doubt as they wish, so long as they follow the path he has pointed out. Discipleship is really spiritual union. It is not academic remembrance of words. It is a placing of oneself in such a receptive attitude that the spirit of the master may enter in. No speech is necessary to effect this and in silence it is more readily achieved; anything else is only giving instruction, which is not the same as proffering discipleship.

772

In the end, the only way the earnest seeker can find a teacher is to find himself. The deeper he penetrates into the mysterious recesses of his own spiritual being, the closer he comes to the ever-present master within—the higher self. The longer he looks, the more powerful will be its attraction, the more magnetic its spell over him. This is true for all students generally, but it is especially true for those students who have had the good fortune of coming into personal contact with a living teacher. It is not by their physically seeing him or personally speaking to him or corresponding with him that they enter into real contact with such a teacher, but rather by finding his presence within their hearts in thought, feeling, and imagination, by responding passively to the intuition of such a presence, and by accepting the guidance of its prompting to a more spiritual existence. Thus not only is man's soul within him and must be found there, but even his living embodied teacher is within him, too, and must be found there likewise. It is not by living in the same house with a teacher that discipleship becomes a fact. It is not by sitting year after year in the same ashram with him that devotion is shown or the path is followed, but by seeking him intuitively and obeying his inward leading away from the surface of the ego to the deep centre of the soul. When this is realized, it will be realized that a distance of seven or seven thousand miles will not be long enough to separate a pupil from his master. An absence of seven years will not be enough to weaken the sense of his presence and of inner contact with him. The sooner the aspirant recognizes this truth, the quicker will he make progress.

773

Once both the meeting, however brief, with the master and the parting from him have taken place, the candidate's next and hardest task will be set him. And this is to learn to accept the *Idea* of the master as being not less real than the body of the master. The disciple must learn to dwell mentally in the sacred presence as satisfyingly as if he were dwelling physically in it.

774

To take these great masters into one's life merely to worship them outwardly and not to worship them deep in one's heart as the Ideal to be faithfully imitated, is to fail in becoming their disciple.

775

It is not merely that knowledge is passed on or instruction is memorized. The student is required to do something more. He has to introvert his attention earnestly and keep himself passive to the subtler feelings which now tend to form themselves within him, to submit resignedly to their sway and to merge into union with them.

776

The Master is always there, behind the disciple, always ready to give him stability, guidance, inspiration, peace, and strength. If the disciple does not find these things coming to him from the Master, the fault is in himself, the blockage is self-created, is somewhere between the two, and only he alone can remove it.

777

If the disciple becomes responsive enough, if his mind is harmonized with the master's, there will be a feeling of his presence even though a continent's width separates them. The master's nearness will sometimes seem quite uncanny.

778

Yet the deeper we travel, the less need have we of thoughts and words, for all multiplicity collapses in this marvelous unity. We can neither think nor talk of this sublime state with any accuracy. Hence the only medium whereby we can properly represent it is—silence!

779

Hence the competent teacher gives his best teaching not through lectures, talks, or books but through this magical, mysterious, yet effective silence wherein the higher initiations are wrapped.

780

To sit with such a teacher in the right receptive attitude for a single hour of meditation may bring more than ten years of previous self-effort could bring. For he can telepathically carry the other's power of attention to a depth in the stillness which is habitual with him but which is rare or unknown to most. Thereafter one of the veils is torn aside and one can more easily penetrate to the same depth alone.

781

He should ask himself whether he is attracted by the teacher's mind or body, whether he is devoted to the teacher's thought or flesh. If he can answer correctly he should grant that real discipleship exists only when the sense of the teacher's physical form is absent and his spiritual being is present. And this indeed is the case. The outer relation is only a beginning, a slight foretaste of the richness possible in this inner relation, this union of heart and soul. Then the disciple finds that the teacher's nearness to or distance from him is not to be measured in miles, is not an affair of what can be seen sensorily, but of what can be felt mentally.

782

Sat-sang, or inner affiliation with the master, is regarded as more important than outer association with him.

783

Just as the proximity of an electrified wire coil can induce a current of magnetism in a bar of soft iron, so the proximity of such a man can induce some of his own inner stillness to appear in a disciple.

784

There are two ways whereby help is given by a master to his disciples. The first is a conscious one whereas the second is not. And it is the second, the apparently less important way, which is really the commonest one. Just as the sun does not need to be aware of every individual plant upon which it sheds its beneficent life-giving growth-stimulating rays, so the master does not need to be aware of every individual disciple who uses him as a focus for his meditations or as a symbol for his worship. Yet each disciple will soon realize that he is receiving from such activities a vital inward stimulus, a real guidance and definite assistance. This result will develop the power unconsciously drawn from the disciple's own higher self, which in turn will utilize the mental image of the master as a channel through which to shed its grace.

785

What the master gives by way of personal example and verbal precept is only the beginning and not the end of what he can give. The silent inward transmission is even more important.

786

To the extent that a teacher helps in the growth of a disciple's inner life, he shares in it.

787

Teacher and student share each other's world.

788

When the impact of his physical presence is absent, the power of his spiritual presence may become plainly evident.

789

The gracious image of the master will reappear constantly before his eyes. And he would rather have its magical presence, together with the rebuke that may come with it, than not have it at all.

790

He feels vividly at some moments, but only faintly at other moments, that the master is in the background of his life.

791

He will not only feel the master's personality as if it were somewhere near or close together with him, but will also absorb inspiration from it and add some of its peace to his own.

792

He draws into his very being these noble influences emanating from the master.

793

Wherever he may be, the intelligent disciple can create inner contact with his master by finding the latter's mental image within himself as a deep vivid and actual presence.

794

Mystic Union of Master and Pupil: The best way to follow a teacher is to possess yourself of his spirit. The rest will take care of itself. When the disciple's maturity meets the teacher's grace, the path to spiritual attainment is really opened up.

795

The disciple is bound to the guide with a tie of inner attraction which, without the consent of destiny or the guide himself, he cannot break!

Master as symbol

796

The soul will lead him by stages to itself. Hence it may lead him to reverence for some scriptural personage or to devotion toward some living master and then, when these have fulfilled their purpose, away and beyond them. For the quest is from the world of things and men to the world of Mind's void; from thoughts and forms to the thought-free formless Divine.

797

The attraction to a teacher, which often happens involuntarily, is due in part to the fact that the seeker does not know God and has never seen God. But he can know and see this human being, the teacher who does know God.

798

To the groping aspirant, a true Master must ever be both the symbol of the divine existence and the channel of its power.

799

The notion of pure spirit or even of the higher self is too vague for most aspirants, and hence too difficult as a theme for concentration. The mental image of an inspired man gives their thoughts something concrete to fasten on and their aspirations something immediately recognizable to turn towards. Here, then, is a prime value of having a human ideal.

800

The Infinite Power seems too inaccessible and too exalted to be mindful of human needs, whereas the Messenger or Prophet or Master, being human himself, seems much nearer and more approachable, more likely and more willing to take an interest in those needs.

801

The master is a visible and manifested presence and therefore one that he can more easily recognize, more quickly get help from, than the invisible and unmanifested higher self within him.

802

Here arises the need of a Symbol, to which his heart can yield loving devotion and on which his mind can practise intense concentration.

803

Because so few can even detect their true self, or hear its voice in conscience, or sense its presence in intuition, the infinite wisdom of God personifies it in the body of another man for their convenience, inspiration, and aid.

804

The master is the symbol of the Higher Power for everyone who feels affinity with him.

805

The vivid actuality, the personal freshness of a living and once-met Symbol can never be equalled, for most people, by the historic actuality of a dead one or the mental freshness of a distant but never seen one.

806

The Master embodies the disciple's conscience.

807

Jesus described himself as the Door; the Bab of Persia referred to himself as the Gate. What did these prophets mean? The average seeker needs a symbol, a form through which he can pass to the formless. Such a form then becomes a door or gate for him. The mental image of the prophet who most attracts him provides him with it.

808

Although there is no need to follow the herd into fanatical guru-adulation there is a need to regard him properly for what he is—a channel for higher forces, an instrument for the higher power—and so deserving homage and reverence.

809

To see what such a man is in bearing and conduct is itself a silent form of instruction.

810

The fact that the spiritual guide has a human form gives something for the disciple's imagination to take hold of and keep firmly concentrated on. A properly controlled, wisely directed imagination can be a powerful aid in mystical exercises.

811

Another value of a master is that in his person we can verify under everyday conditions the fact of a superior state of his and the practical importance of the philosophic ideal.

812

If he has such faith in and devotion to his teacher, he should make use of this attitude not to rest until he himself is all that his teacher is. The latter can be used as an example of what can be done by the human being who is determined to live as he is meant to live, and to be as he is meant to be.

813

He is to keep the Ideal ever before his eyes, and to recognize that it over-limns the personality of his master.

814

The picture of the Ideal is held in his subconscious mind all the time and becomes the pattern to be imitated, the invisible Master to be followed with faith and with love.

815

It is affiliation to the master's mind, not propinquity to his body, that will bring these benefits. But where both are possible, the result will be better.

816

It will not be until a late stage that he will wake up to the realization that the real giver of Grace, the real helper along this path, the real master is not the incarnated master outside but the Overself inside his own heart. What the living master does for him is only to arouse his sleeping intuition and awaken his latent aspiration, to give him the initial impetus and starting guidance on the new quest, to point out the obstructions to advancement in his individual character and to help him deal with them.

817

What he feels about the Master's power may be true but it is a sign of his elementary state that he places it outside himself.

818

The true meaning of a master to the disciple's understanding should be as the presence and force, the revelation and voice of his own inmost spiritual being.

819

Let us be more concerned with the quest of right principles rather than impressive persons, for this will put our attitudes to all events on the right plane. Because this simple truism was forgotten most of the religious and mystical movements have gone astray.

820

The proper attitude is to regard the Master as a symbol of the higher power, so that the veneration and devotion proffered are directed towards that power. To look upon him as an intermediary, between the disciple and God, is to fall into the error of looking outside his own self for that which, when he finds it, will be within him and nowhere else.

821

Think more deeply than the conventional mass of guru-followers dare to do and you will come to perceive that in the end there is only one Teacher for each man, his own Overself; that all other and outer gurus are merely channels which IT uses. "It is He who lives inside and speaks through the outer guru's voice," declares a Tibetan text. Why not go direct to the source?

822

The higher self is the ultimate spiritual guide whom he is to revere and the real spiritual helper on whom he is to rely.

823

When disciples follow a teacher, what is it that they really follow? Suppose the master advocated cruelty and preached selfishness—would the disciples still continue to follow him? Obviously, they would not. This is because their *own* inward feeling would reject the teaching. It shows that they are really following the teacher within themselves, the voice of their own Higher Self. It is this Higher Self within them which makes them seek out and respond to a true teacher, for he is really an outward embodiment of this Self.

824

The outer objectified master is not the real one but only a shadow cast by the sun inside. His disciples too often make the mistake of relating themselves to his body, and placing overmuch emphasis on that visible relationship, when what really matters is relating their mind to his mind. This can be done only within themselves. Only in their own higher self can they meet and know their master.

825

Those who interest themselves in personalities take the wrong path. A master's ideas are the best part of him. Let students take *them* and not trouble themselves about his appearance, career, traits, and habits.

826

We must make a distinction between a doctrinal principle and the human personality who serves as the vehicle for such a principle. The principle will live when the personality is dead. Our absolute loyalty, therefore, must be bestowed on what is immortal, not on what is mortal. The human disseminator of the principle should receive only a conditional allegiance. The pure Idea may incarnate itself in the man but he may sully, betray, or pollute it with his human error, prejudice, or selfishness.

827

The embodied master, being human, will have some or other of the human imperfections. Sooner or later the disciple will note and become critical of them or disturbed by them. But the inner Light is perfect and will rouse only admiration, devotion, and satisfaction.

828

I have never said that the disciple should not feel love for the teacher, for that inevitably arises of itself and is indeed the basic force that draws the one to the other. Without it there could be no discipleship. But it is necessary to understand that the love is really felt for the divine presence which is using the teacher. It is not felt for the guru (teacher) as a person. That is the correct condition. If, however, it is diverted to the guru's person, then it is spoilt, rendered impure, and the true relationship is broken. In fact, idolatry sets in. The emotions of attraction and reverence which are felt need not be given up, but they should be directed to the true source, the higher power which is using the teacher, and not towards his personality at all.

829

The human symbol under which the devotee receives his inspirations and illuminations in vision or feeling is, after all, personal to him. It is not a universal one, not for all mankind at all times and in all places. Consequently his onward progress will one day demand of him that he transcend it. However useful and even indispensable it has been, it will best fulfil itself when he is able to forget it.

830

It is rarely and reluctantly that a true master will give personal interviews. He finds that so many enquirers come either with an idealized preconceived picture of what he looks like (or ought to look like) or with certain prejudices which are activated when they see him, that in many cases the good work done by his writings may be nullified by the disappointment consequent on the meeting. This is because few persons are sufficiently nonmaterialistic to look behind physical appearances for the mental reality of the man interviewed. Most come carrying a preconceived picture of some perfectly wonderful, perfectly handsome, perfectly saint-like Perfect Friend. The ideal is not realized. They leave the meeting disillusioned. It is better for their sakes that he remain behind the barrier of written words and not let them meet him face to face. How many prefer pigmentation to proficiency as a standard of spiritual wisdom, as shown by the numbers who cannot accept a dark-skinned Indian for teacher! How many are held prisoners by their preconceptions! How many reject both a teacher and his truth merely because they dislike the shape of his nose! What hope could a bandy-legged master have to find any disciples? Of course, the seeker who confounds him with his body is really still unfit for philosophy and ought not be given any interview until life and reflection have prepared him to take proper advantage of it. It is unfortunate that this human weakness is so common. This is one of the lesser reasons why the philosophic discipline has to be imposed on candidates for philosophy as a preliminary to be undergone before its threshold can be crossed. The real teacher is hard to behold. For he can be seen partly with the heart, partly with the mind, but rarely with the eye of flesh. He is the invisible man, whom they can recognize only by sensing, not by seeing him.

831

The duty is laid upon a master to show the value of his virtue by his conduct and to attract men towards it by his example. It is not the man that we are to reverence but his noble attributes and his inspired mind.

832

In the final reckoning we are not the disciple of this or that man but rather the disciple of the Overself.

833

Gautama saw much evidence among the Hindus of their traditions of guru-worship and their cults of personal adulation. To prevent this arising among those who accepted his teaching, he commanded that his own person was to remain unpictured in art, ungraven in image. But this was too much to ask of sentimental, devotional, and emotional humanity.

834

Jesus tried to turn the minds of his followers from the man to Spirit, from the body to Overself but, like Muhammed, Buddha, and Krishna, failed. He told them not even to call anyone Master, nor even to call him Rabbi. But history shows how greatly they disobeyed his instruction.

835

Even if the Symbol were a man devoid of spiritual power and light, its effects would still appear beneficially within his life. This is because he has *imagined* it to be powerful and enlightening and the creative power of his own thought produces some benefit. If however the Symbol were an evil and living man, then the effects would be more or less harmful. This is because a subconscious telepathic working exists between the two minds through the intense devotion and passive submission of one to the other. But if the Symbol were a genuine living mystic, then the devotee's thought could *draw* from him—and without his conscious will or knowledge—benefits greater than in the first case. It is possible to get still greater benefits if the seeker attaches himself to and becomes the disciple of a living genuine sage. For to the above-mentioned effects will be added the latter's deliberately given help and blessing.

836

Despite popular superstition and wishful thinking it is true that no master can bestow his own enlightenment on others as a permanent gift. But does this make his attainment valueless to them? No, for it proves to them both that the Overself *is* and that man may commune with it. The few who are more sensitive or more perceptive gain more from personal contact with him—either inspiration for their quest or, if more fortunate, a momentary glimpse of the far-off goal.

837

The Master as Symbol: All this talk of master and disciple is vain and futile. You yourself, when attracted to a certain man in whom you have faith, set him up as a master in your own mind, keep him there for a number of years, and eventually drop him when you no longer feel the need of a human symbol of the Infinite. All this time it is your own higher self which is guiding you, even when it is using the mental image of the guide you may have selected for the purpose. All this time you were moving in the direction of the discovery of your Overself inwardly even when you seemed to be moving towards an external master. If you find ABC a helpful symbol, use him as your master, but do not ask him to confirm this usage for the choice was *yours*. No confirmation from him is called for. Why doubt the guidance of your Overself? If you accept the master in full faith, by that very act you are showing faith in the leading given you by the Overself. Your obedience to it is enough. It has accepted you or it would not be drawing you inwards, as it is. ABC is one with it. Therefore how could the master refuse you? But do not lose sight of the inwardness of the whole process by going to him for an outward sign. Do not materialize it. Make use of him if you wish to, and if he is what you believe him to be, your faith will not be wasted. Your act of mental creation will not lead to hallucination so long as you know that the true ABC is not his body but his mind.

838

The humble appeal of the seeking soul direct to God (or one's own Overself) will in time bring direct help without the intermediary of any human being. If anyone believes that he has entered into realization solely through the blessing of a master, then there will surely be a disillusionment one day. The real duty of a master is to point out the correct path at each different stage of the aspirant's life, to keep up his faith until he knows the truth for himself and not through somebody else's words, to inspire him by his own example and encouragement never to desert the quest and to show that its benefits are worthwhile, to give his grace in the sense of taking a personal interest in the student's progress and telepathically to keep the student within his own consciousness.

839

If discovery of Truth is the discovery of the answer to "Who Am I?" then what better Master can there be than the "I" itself—the unknown Knower rather than the familiar, known ego? Yet so few seekers have taken it on trust: nearly all venture it in dependence on some other man. And what can that Master do *in the end* better than teach his disciple to see his *own divine* face?

840

"A visible Murshid (Master) is a gateway unto the Unseen Master and a portal unto God, the Unknown. But yet, in the end, neither God, Master, nor Murshid appear in the 'I Am'"—Mayat Khan

841

The argument as to whether a living master alone can "save" men or whether a dead one can also do so, is a fallacious one. No man is saved by another man. His own soul is his real saviour. When he believes that a master, living or dead, is saving him, his own soul is actually at work within him at the time but is using the mental image of the master to serve as a focus-point for his side—that is, the self-effort side—of the process. Thousands who never knew the living Jesus have felt the real presence and dynamic power of Jesus enough to convert them from sinful to Godly lives. It was the *idea* of Jesus which they really knew, not the man himself, as it was grace of their Overselves which was the true presence and power they admittedly felt. They concentrated their faith on the idea but the reality behind it was the unknown Overself. They needed the idea—any idea—as a point in their own form-time-and-space personal consciousness where the formless, timeless, placeless, impersonal soul could manifest itself to them.

842

There are hands in every country, among every people, outstretched to God for inward help. The responsibility to answer these prayers rests therefore primarily with God. Any man who apparently gives the needed help is only an intermediary. Neither the power nor the wisdom which he manifests is his own. If he perceives that fact, he will be humbled by it.

843

The true teacher acts by proxy, as it were, for the aspirant's Overself until such time as the aspirant himself is strong enough to find his own way. Until that moment the teacher is a shining lamp, but after it he will withdraw because he does not want to stand between the seeker and the latter's own self-light which gradually leads the disciple to dispense with him!

844

With the thought of the higher power, an image will spontaneously spring up in his mind. It will be the image of that man who manifests or represents it to him.

845

The philosophically correct attitude is to cherish the deepest reverence for him, to remember and commune often with his kindling interior presence, and to control the lower self by the ideal pattern he affords.

846

If he rejects praise it is because he wants it bestowed where it really belongs, and not upon himself to the denial of that source. It belongs to his master or to the Overself; the power behind all his praised activities is not the ego's. For by such properly placed credit, the world may come to know, or believe, there is that higher power.

847

"He who sees the Teaching, sees me."—Buddha

848

Much emotion-born fallacious writing and consequent belief prevails in Western and Oriental mystical circles. The question must be asked: if a dead master is just as good or, as one South Indian ashram now claims, even better than a living one, why do any masters trouble to reincarnate at all if they can exert their influence or give their training just as effectively by staying where they are? And this question applies not only to the minor lesser-known teachers of small groups but with equal force to the major prophets like Buddha and Jesus.

Here is the point at which part of the confusion and much of the fallacy arise. People generally have been led by society, including their parents, to adopt and follow one of these major Prophets. This is done partly in the belief that he is still in touch with them from a heaven-world, partly out of unquestioning acceptance of his revelation, and partly because of the social necessity of belonging to the membership of some organized church. The revelation and the church continue to survive the prophet's death and thus continue to be available for the help of followers born in later centuries. But the vehicle through which he himself was able to communicate directly, the intellect and body—that is, the ego—have ceased to exist. There is no further possibility of such communication. Where it seems to occur, the mental image of the prophet has been assumed by the Higher Self of the devotee to satisfy his demand and need. The usefulness of a living teacher to those who have no such experience or to those who are uncommitted to a deceased one, is obvious.

849

When the master dies, the disciple will find that there is no one to take his place. Such an affinity cannot be duplicated. But what he gave the disciple will live on inside him. How can he be like the unthinking hordes who yield to their passions without compunction?

850

When a master is no longer living in flesh and blood, what will be the effect upon his relations with others? Those who are willing to use their reason rather than their sentimentality upon the matter can fall upon the fact itself. For those who are still in the elementary stages—which usually means the mass of his followers—he is no longer operative.

851

Some persons, deprived of their guru by a sudden change of circum-stance, or by death, have found themselves bewildered, at a loss, or even have collapsed with a nervous breakdown.

852

What he leaves behind is not himself but the revelations he received, the instructions he gave, and the techniques he favoured.

853

If the life of Jesus be viewed symbolically—as the lives of such divine men often are in part—the same necessity, at a certain time, of physical separation from disciples to bring them into mental nearness, appears. Jesus told them: "I tell you the truth, it is expedient for you that I go away; for if I go not away, the Comforter will not come unto you. When He, the Spirit of Truth, is come, He will guide you into all truth."

854

If there is a genuine inner relationship between them, then he will feel that a part of the master has never left him, even though the master is himself long dead.

855

If he is still alive, the personal help of a master is certainly valuable. If he is not, his spirit is too remote from the physical world to be helpful to the ordinary aspirant in any other than a general impersonal way. His influence is then carried by writings left behind, by the thought-forms he left during his lifetime in the mental atmosphere here, and by the few disciples closest to him in the inner sense. Otherwise, only an advanced yogi, able to raise his consciousness by meditation to the same plane as the master's, could get any contact at all. It is as necessary to his disciples that he leave them deprived of his guidance as well as of the consolation of his presence as it was earlier necessary for them to have them while he was still on earth. After all, it is their own Overself that they are seeking. They must begin to seek it just where it is—within themselves and not in someone else. The time has then come when, if they are to grow at all, they must cease drawing on his light and strength and begin drawing on their own. The very hour of his departure from them is appointed in their destiny by the infinite intelligence, which has sufficient reasons for making it then, and not earlier or later. If they must henceforth strive for direct touch with the Infinite and no longer lean on the encouragement of an intermediary, this is because they are at the stage to make better progress that way, whatever their personal emotions may argue to the contrary.

856

Whether it is really those who publicly and loudly proclaim how close they were to the Master who were so, or those who silently and secretly practised what he taught, the world is often in no position to judge.

Graduation

857

The question whether a rejection of the guru is a necessary stage in order to find the Truth for oneself can be immediately answered. It is not at all necessary for anyone to reject the guru at any stage. But—at a certain stage it may be advisable to withdraw *physically* from him. That is a matter for guru or disciple to decide, and also the length of time for such an absence.

858

"In time when the relationship is sufficiently established between master and pupil the pupil has to continue on his own," wrote the Sufi Master Insar-I-Kamil. *This is important but insufficiently known.*

859

The teacher is a support needed by the disciple to help him progress through successive stages of the quest, as they are stages of thinning illusion. When he stands on the threshold of reality, then the last and thinnest illusion of all must be left behind, the support of any being outside himself, apart from himself, for within him is the infinite life-power.

860

It is written in the Hindu texts that by living in the company of a guru, saint, or sage one acquires a measure of his enlightenment, holiness, or wisdom. How widely different this measure can be, how ever little and how very large, only exceptional personal experience or a long, comparative study of the records can tell. Side by side with this text, to amplify or correct it, ought to be put, and well mused over, a little incident I once observed in South India, in which the principal character was a very earnest young monk, Swami Dandapani. He had lived for five years, on and off, as an office assistant in the ashram and as a devoted follower of Ramana Maharshi. One day he was expelled forthwith and ordered to leave within twenty-four hours. At night, when everyone had retired to sleep, he went to his guru to inform him of the expulsion and to take farewell. At the end of this occasion he wept. The Maharishee restrained him: "Don't be a fool! You should know that this physical *Sat-sang* [personal company in an ashram] is only for beginners. When one advances to a certain stage it is better to go away if further and real advancement is to be made. For then one is compelled to seek, and find, the inner guru, within the mind and heart. Even the little birds have to get away from their parents' nest when they have grown wings: they cannot stay always in it. So too the disciples have to practise away from the ashram what they have learnt here, and find there the peace they found here." I followed the Swami's further history as he was a good friend. Years later he became a guru in his own turn, acquired a number of disciples, and settled in his own native village in his own ashram. My own observation, farther afield, is that some seem to acquire nothing at all, whereas others acquire a great deal, from *Sat-sang*. Whether this acquisition comes about by a kind of osmosis, or by instruction and discussion, or, more likely, by a resultant arising from all three, the necessity of looking within oneself, working with oneself, and depending on oneself cannot be evaded.

861

Sri Ramakrishna told seeking newcomers: "Keep on visiting this place." But he also told them: "It is necessary *in the beginning* to come here off and on." I once heard Sri Ramana Maharshi tell a young Indian disciple who wept at being forced to leave him: "Living in ashrams is only for beginners. The more advanced have to go away and develop from there. You have been here five years. If you want to progress you can now do so best by going away from here."

862

The animal which at a certain age deserts its offspring to force them into self-reliance is like the rare guru who tells the overstayed learner it is time to leave.

863

But the law of life is growth. Is he to remain a passive receiver of someone else's teaching in perpetuity? Can he stand still under another man's shadow or is he to emerge out of pupilage into the light?

864

The true teacher so develops his disciples that they can come closer and closer to the time when they can find their way without him. All his service is intended to lead them toward graduation, when he himself will no longer be needed.

865

No disciple does his master adequate honour until he himself is able to stand and walk alone.

866

The man in whom intuition is well-developed or who is able to practise meditation sufficiently to hear the Interior Word, can manage without a master.

867

If he has found the correct path and has travelled with a teacher as far as this stage, thenceforth he may travel by himself. He is now free for he is now able to guide himself.

868

In the end he must free himself inwardly from all things and, finally, both from whatever teacher he has and from the quest itself. Then only can he stand alone within and one with God.

869

Whether or not it is historically true that there was the battle mentioned in the *Bhagavad Gita* is unimportant to us of the twentieth century. But the psychological interpretation of it as meaning that Arjuna was ordered to fight not his parents and relatives but his *attachment* to them, is important. It is the same teaching as that of Jesus' hard saying about the necessity of taking up the cross and denying father and mother. All this we can understand even where we cannot follow it into practice. But it is bewildering to be told that a time comes in the disciple's development when attachment to the teacher must also be broken. He must free himself from the very man who has shown him the path to liberation from every other form of attachment. His liberation is to become total and absolute.

870

In the last verse spoken by Arjuna in the *Gita*, he declares that all his doubts are gone and that he has gained recognition of the true Self. Hence all his questions cease. His enquiry into Truth has come to an end. Nothing more is said either by him or his teacher. Both enter into a state of silence and this silence is revealed as the highest, because the spirit is beyond both the agitations of intellect and the babble of speech. It is best felt and known, understood and communicated, through such inner stillness.

871

Do not stray into waters that are too deep for you. Do not try to grasp the mystery of your master. You cannot do it and you will never do it, for if ever you came to the very edge of succeeding in doing it both you and he would disappear from your ken. Do not seek to touch the untouchable. It is better to accept him for what he is and let it go at that than to indulge in useless speculations and erroneous fancies. It is not that your are to repress the faculty of enquiry, but that you are to exercise it in the right place and at the right time. Your task now is to understand yourself and to understand the world. When you have come near the close of completing those two tasks, you will then be faced with the further task of comprehending the true character of your master but not till then. For then only will you be able to comprehend him correctly; before then you will only get a wrong notion, which is far worse than no notion at all. The last lesson of these words is: trust him where you cannot understand; believe in him where you cannot follow, and no regret on this point need ever be yours.

INDEX

Index

Entries are listed by chapter number followed by "para" number. 3.229, for example, means chapter 3, para 229, and 6.290, 309, 397, etc., means chapter 6, paras 290, 309, 397, etc. Chapter listings are separated by a semicolon.

C

cable, between student and
teacher 6.175, 575, 576
calmness 5.377; 6.407, 418, 729, 737
Carlyle, Thomas 3.87
celibacy, definition of 3.229
character 3.16
development 1.31; 2.220, 272, 402;
3.18, 198, 236, 271; 4.38, 62;
5.46, 103, 302, 382, 389, 437;
6.166, 708
and karma 5.85
moral 3.246
Christ 3.221; 6.333, 665; *see also*
Jesus
Christ-consciousness 5.61, 156, 285
Christianity 3.18; 4.76, 78; 5.86, 187,
234
Christian Science 5.187
churches 3.99, 138, 142, 144, 161,
247, 264
Coleridge, Samuel Taylor 3.87
compassion 2.91; 6.78, 396, 418, 753
conformity 3.18, 24, 25, 27, 28, 30,
48, 57, 66, 68, 70, 193, 324
Confucius 6.333
Consciousness 1.2, 20, 62, 81, 118,
128, 191; 2.13; 3.94, 95, 102;
5.76, 175, 297, 405
Cosmic Vision 5.285
crime 2.148, 468
Cromwell, Oliver 5.242
cults 1.192; 2.78; 3.75, 76, 130-177;
6.346, 435, 543, 833
culture 3.117, 324

D

dangers 1.121; 2.2, 126, 425, 430,
433; 3.185; 5.427, 431, 438, 441;
6.290, 469, 607
darshan 6.708
death 1.152; 2.452; 5.416

desires 2.140, 175, 244, 277, 286,
290, 399, 406
destiny 2.426, 427, 503; 3.41; 6.170,
653, 691
detachment 3.242, 296
devotion 1.161; 3.262; 5.182, 225;
6.550, 557, 577, 619
Dillip Roy 6.149
discipleship 2.143, 480; 3.69, 120,
122, 263, 280, 295, 297; 4.38;
6.206, 276, 562, 599, 734, 771; *see
also* Chapter 6
probationary period of 6.601, 605,
606, 607, 751
discipline 3.184, 236, 237, 241, 259
philosophic 3.209, 255; 5.38, 330;
6.475, 549, 593, 830
discrimination 3.91, 180, 189; 6.100,
154, 155, 238, 260
disillusionment 1.151; 2.170, 196,
205, 246, 297, 299, 306; 6.830,
838
dogma 4.87
duty (of man) 1.6, 117, 118, 120,
133

E

Eastern Christian Church 6.386
Eddington, Sir Authur S. 5.335
ego 1.142; 2.253, 401, 423; 4.19;
5.25; 6.26, 135, 237, 329, 839,
846, 848
need to relinquish 1.27; 2.93, 105,
170, 283, 284; 3.304, 306, 314;
3.364; 5.89, 322; 6.14
perfection of 3.217; 5.12
tactics of 1.39; 3.102, 4.60; 6.5,
487, 488, 599, 670, 675, 676, 677,
731, 746
of teacher 6.331, 334, 342, 363,
366, 373, 378, 411, 415, 416, 465,
468, 473, 493

egocentrism 3.207; 4.108
egoism 5.89; 6.413, 475, 477, 480,
582, 587, 674
efforts to cure 5.78; 6.607
Egyptian mysteries 6.700
Emerson, Ralph Waldo 2.108, 156,
235; 3.86, 87, 168, 328; 4.119;
5.36; 6.119, 373, 564, 766
enlightenment 3.219, 220; 5.126,
172, 175, 182, 209, 300; 6.370,
407, 590, 701, 707, 722
sudden 5.314
evil 5.455
evolution 3.133, 278; 5.76
human 2.215; 3.183, 234; 5.76,
195, 336
of universe 1.125; 5.11

F

Fachi-yao Sung, Ching 1.101
failure 2.282, 431, 503; 5.44
faith 1.112; 2.99; 3.244, 274, 278;
6.347, 453, 550, 576, 577, 599,
619, 768, 812, 814, 837, 841
family life, *see* householder
fourfold path 5.84
Fox, George 3.86
Franck, Sebastian 5.286
freedom 1.106; 3.9, 12, 14, 54, 57,
127, 138, 152, 159, 165, 169, 183,
189, 196, 198, 208; 6.398, 592; *see
also* independence
intellectual 3.11, 12, 64, 168, 295
friendship with other Questers 4.49

G

Gainsborough, Thomas 6.725
Gandhi, Mahatma 2.176
glimpse 2.312; 3.85, 87; 4.33; 5.106,
109, 300, 320, 330, 332, 337, 440;
6.3, 72, 405, 707, 754, 836
gnana 1.62

God 2.462; 3.51, 97, 130, 259, 314,
325; 4.86, 113; 6.174, 838, 842
relation to 1.15, 89, 109; 5.313, 326
within 3.220, 306; 5.210
grace 3.221, 264; 4.80, 113; 5.127,
419; 6.435, 679, 753
expressions of 2.2, 266; 3.115;
6.784
and self-effort 3.252, 314; 5.77, 86,
89; 6.761
and teacher 3.274; 6.2, 6, 14, 58,
695, 738, 753, 768, 794, 816, 838
unpredictability of 5.127, 419
groups, *see* Chapter 4; 3.130-177, 211,
315, 320
and philosophers 3.45, 136; 4.98,
101; 6.543
and philosophy 3.139, 141; 4.78,
99, 105
guidance 3.74, 120, 244, 265, 268,
274, 275; 6.119, 160, 281, 332
guide, *see also* guru; master; prophet;
and teacher; 6.178, 186, 200, 270,
307, 353, 384, 385, 427, 458, 474,
484, 486, 489, 497, 538, 543, 562,
599, 712, 810, 822
as channel 3.115, 314; 6.52, 334,
658, 738, 784, 798, 808, 821
dangers of 3.279, 310, 311; 6.248,
331, 413, 469, 485, 582, 662, 675
finding 3.87; 6.140, 141, 175, 193,
562, 679, 682
need for 3.102, 251, 269, 274, 275,
294, 298, 301; 6.20, 22, 30, 48,
79, 148
proper relation to 3.120, 251, 256,
257, 259, 260, 262, 265, 267, 283,
295, 307; 4.43; 6.11, 132, 177,
254, 261, 360, 380, 395, 474, 562,
582, 601, 605, 616, 728, 820
and self-reliance 3.297; 4.99
and telepathy 6.737, 738

mental presence of 6.734, 768
osmosis and 6.578, 740, 860
philosophic 6.28, 177, 475, 490,
495, 498, 499, 503, 521, 562, 593,
599
recognition of 6.1, 9, 47, 121, 142,
189, 190, 191, 196, 210, 216, 223,
225, 227, 229, 299, 308, 801, 830
reverence for 6.550, 553, 640, 658
spiritual 6.247, 285, 292, 333, 381,
434, 451, 527, 532, 567, 599, 660
telepathy 6.175, 176, 208, 382, 610,
734-742, 745, 747-749, 752, 754,
768, 780, 838
Tennyson, Alfred Lord 2.1
tests 6.146, 290, 599, 605, 606, 610,
612, 700, 718; *see also* dangers;
discipleship, probationary period of
of teacher 2.3; 6.88, 153, 156, 290,
384, 406, 407, 717
for teacher 6.270
Theosophic teaching 6.319
Thoreau, Henry David 2.341
threefold path 5.414, 421
Touch of the Untouchable 5.172
Toynbee, Arnold 5.213
"transference" 6.270
Truth 5.106, 175, 359, 360
capacity to receive 1.99; 2.79, 148,
379, 398; 3.179, 194; 4.104; 5.74
discovered by and for self 2.159,
187; 3.2, 4, 5, 40, 50, 289; 4.42,
48
eclectic 1.189; 3.106, 107, 112, 113,
119, 120, 126, 129, 138, 239
and groups 3.145, 152, 154; 4.23,
39
requirements of search 2.59, 123,
149; 3.132, 157, 189, 210, 329,
374; 4.42, 70
as reward 2.316; 3.234; 5.354, 357,
360

thirst for 1.120; 2.52, 61, 111, 113,
207, 256, 258, 297, 299; 3.2; 5.54,
58, 68, 359; *see also* aspiration
and unity 5.111, 234
value of 3.40, 54; 5.129, 146, 250
truth-words 6.540

U
Upanishads 3.234

V
Vedanta 3.135
Vedas 6.76
virtue 5.375; 6.33, 192, 360, 568,
605, 609, 831
Vivekananda, Swami 5.92
Void, The 5.115, 337

W
war 2.230; 5.396
What Am I? 1.15; 2.209; 3.1
Whistler, James Abbott McNeill 6.725
Who Am I? 6.839
Wilde, Oscar 4.114
wisdom 2.39; 3.191; 5.75, 411;
6.618
witness, experience of 5.337
Wordsworth, William 3.87

Y
Yoga Vasistha 1.62

The 28 Categories from the Notebooks

This outline of categories in *The Notebooks* is the most recent one Paul Brunton developed for sorting, ordering, and filing his written work. The listings he put after each title were not meant to be all-inclusive. They merely suggest something of the range of topics included in each category.

1 THE QUEST

*Its choice —Independent path —Organized groups —
Self-development —Student/teacher*

2 PRACTICES FOR THE QUEST

Ant's long path —Work on oneself

3 RELAX AND RETREAT

*Intermittent pauses —Tension and pressures —Relax body,
breath, and mind —Retreat centres —Solitude —
Nature appreciation —Sunset contemplation*

4 ELEMENTARY MEDITATION

*Place and conditions —Wandering thoughts —Practise
concentrated attention —Meditative thinking —
Visualized images —Mantrams —Symbols
—Affirmations and suggestions*

5 THE BODY

*Hygiene and cleansings —Food —Exercises and postures
—Breathings —Sex: importance, influence, effects*

6 EMOTIONS AND ETHICS

*Uplift character —Re-educate feelings —Discipline emotions —
Purify passions —Refinement and courtesy —Avoid fanaticism*

7 THE INTELLECT

*Nature —Services —Development —Semantic training —
Science —Metaphysics —Abstract thinking*

8 THE EGO

What am I? —The I-thought —The psyche